Conversations with Jim Harrison

Literary Conversations Series
Peggy Whitman Prenshaw
General Editor

Photo credit: Patrick Smith, 1997

Conversations with Jim Harrison

Edited by
Robert DeMott

University Press of Mississippi
Jackson

www.upress.state.ms.us

Copyright © 2002 by University Press of Mississippi
All rights reserved
Manufactured in the United States of America

10 09 08 07 06 05 04 03 02   4 3 2 1
∞
Library of Congress Cataloging-in-Publication Data

Harrison, Jim, 1937–
    Conversations with Jim Harrison / edited by Robert DeMott.
      p. cm.—(Literary conversations series)
    "Books by Jim Harrison": p.
    Includes index.
    ISBN 1-57806-455-4 (alk. paper)—ISBN 1-57806-456-2 (pbk. : alk. paper)
      1. Harrison, Jim, 1937– —Interviews. 2. Authors, American—20th century—Interviews. I. DeMott, Robert J., 1943– II. Title. III. Series.
PS3558.A67 Z49 2002
818'.5409—dc21
[B]   2001046917

British Library Cataloging-in-Publication Data available

Books by Jim Harrison

Plain Song. New York: W. W. Norton, 1965.
Walking. Cambridge, MA: Pym Randall Press, 1967.
Locations. New York: W. W. Norton, 1968.
Stony Brook Holographs. Stony Brook, NY: Stony Brook Poetics Foundation, 1968. (With Robert Duncan, Denise Levertov, Jerome Rothenberg, Louis Simpson, Jonathan Wieners, Charles Simic.)
Five Blind Men. Fremont, MI: Sumac Press, 1969. (With Dan Gerber, George Quasha, J. D. Reed, Charles Simic.)
Outlyer and Ghazals. New York: Simon and Schuster, 1971.
Wolf: A False Memoir. New York: Simon and Schuster, 1971.
A Good Day to Die. New York: Simon and Schuster, 1973.
Letters to Yesenin. Fremont, MI: Sumac Press, 1973.
Farmer. New York: Viking Press, 1976.
Returning to Earth. Berkeley, CA: Ithaca House, 1977.
Letters to Yesenin and Returning to Earth. Los Angeles: Center Publications, 1979.
Legends of the Fall. New York: Delta/Seymour Lawrence, 1979.
Warlock. New York: Delta/Seymour Lawrence, 1981.
Natural World: A Bestiary. Berrytown, NY: Open Book, 1981.
Selected and New Poems, 1961–1981. New York: Delacorte/Seymour Lawrence, 1981.
Sundog. New York: E. P. Dutton/Seymour Lawrence, 1984.
The Theory and Practice of Rivers. Seattle: Winn Books, 1986.
Dalva. New York: E. P. Dutton/Seymour Lawrence, 1988.
The Theory and Practice of Rivers and New Poems. Livingston, MT: Clark City Press, 1989.
The Woman Lit by Fireflies. New York: Houghton Mifflin, 1990.
Book for Sensei. Pacifica, CA: Big Bridge Press, 1990.
Just Before Dark: Collected Nonfiction. Livingston, MT: Clark City Press, 1991.
The Raw and the Cooked. New York: Dim Gray Bar Press, 1992.
Julip. New York: Houghton Mifflin/Seymour Lawrence, 1994.
After Ikkyu and Other Poems. Boston: Shambhala, 1996.
The Sumac Reader. Ed. Joseph Bednarik. East Lansing: Michigan State University Press, 1997.
The Road Home. New York: Atlantic Monthly Press, 1998.
The Shape of the Journey: New and Collected Poems. Port Townsend, WA: Copper Canyon Press, 1998.
The Beast God Forgot to Invent. New York: Atlantic Monthly Press, 2000.
The Boy Who Ran to the Woods. New York: Atlantic Monthly Press, 2000.
The Raw and the Cooked: Adventures of a Roving Gourmand. New York: Atlantic Monthly Press, 2001.
A Conversation. West Chester, PA: Aralia Press, 2001. (With Ted Kooser.)

Contents

Introduction   ix

Chronology   xxi

A Chat with a Novelist   *Jim Harrison and Thomas McGuane*   3

A Good Day for Talking: An Interview with the Author of *Wolf* and *Farmer*   *Ira Elliott and Marty Somerness*   9

Contemporary Authors Interview   *Jean W. Ross*   23

An Interview with Jim Harrison   *Kay Bonetti*   29

The Man Whose Soul Is Not for Sale: Jim Harrison   *Hank Nuwer*   45

The Art of Fiction: Jim Harrison   *Jim Fergus*   63

Publishers Weekly Interviews: Jim Harrison   *Wendy Smith*   93

The *Diddy Wah Diddy* Interview: Jim Harrison   *Aloysius Sisyphus*   98

A Man Lit by Passion: Jim Harrison   *Tom Auer*   105

Siren Song: Will Success Lure Poet/Novelist Jim Harrison Out of His Midwestern Lair?   *Robert Cross*   112

An Interview with Jim Harrison   *Thierry Jousse and Vincent Ostria*   123

A Conversation with Jim Harrison   *Joseph Bednarik*   133

Season of the Wolf   *Anthony Brandt*   144

Jim Harrison: "What I'm Thinking About for Two Hours"   *Casey Walker*   151

Lord Jim: A Sense of Place   *Terry W. Phipps*   164

An Interview with Jim Harrison   *Eleanor Wachtel*   175

Creating Habitat for the Soul: An Interview with Jim Harrison   *Robert DeMott and Patrick Smith*   193

Interview with Jim Harrison   *Carrie Preston and Anthony Michel*   221

Index   241

Introduction

Jim Harrison has a reputation for being a fiercely independent, private, and even reclusive writer, who chooses to live in areas of the United States which are at least several hours' drive from major airports. He is a sophisticated citizen of the world who knows the cultures of Hollywood, Key West, Manhattan, and Paris first hand. Yet by his own admission he is also an "outlyer," strongly attached to rural locales in northern Michigan, southern Arizona, north-central Nebraska, and Montana. Beside providing the landscape, flora and fauna, dramatic weather, and protagonists for much of Harrison's fiction from *Wolf* (1971) to *The Road Home* (1998), these flyover regions, far removed from America's "dream coasts," harbor numerous personal "thickets," which enable his writing by framing reality, promoting ritual, creating anonymity, providing solace, or furnishing restorative habitats. He told Patrick Smith and me, "Your only alternative as an artist is to create your own habitat for your soul. I figured out that my main obsession is freedom, and if I didn't have the freedom of close access to the natural world, I wasn't going to survive."

The upshot of Harrison's elusiveness is that he is not a person one can always simply drop in on; arranging to see him requires luck, good timing, patience, preparation, facilitation, and a reasonable amount of travel. (The sign in front of Harrison's Lake Leelanau home reads, "Do Not Enter This Driveway Unless You Have Called First! This Means You.") Harrison prefers to keep his distance and, further, is reputed to discourage interviews because they focus on the banal aspects of ego rather than on art. In "A Chat with a Novelist" Harrison trumped future interviewers by satirizing the genre's pretensions and poking fun at its preoccupation with otherwise meaningless aspects of writers' private lives. Nevertheless, Jim Harrison has been exceedingly generous with his time and energy, quite liberal and forthcoming with his opinions about his work, and increasingly—even disarmingly—cooperative about himself. In 1998, his busiest year (on a multiple city book tour to promote *The Road Home* and *The Shape of the Journey*), Harrison sat for at least seventeen sessions with media representatives.[1] The title of an early interview here—"A Good Day for Talking"—rings a signature chord.

Indeed, in Harrison's life and art there is such an extreme predilection for talk that occasionally the voice in his art and the voice of his interviews collapse into one. Statements in his fiction, poetry, and essays turn up verbatim in his interviews. The dialogue in Harrison's fiction and the talk in his life merge in a border area, where the narrative of voices and the voices of narrative mingle. "With me it's all about presence," he told me on 2 September 2000.

Yet for such an animated and brilliant conversationalist Harrison can be guarded about personal revelations. "A Chat with a Novelist" is a cautionary text for future conversations involving Jim Harrison himself, because something is always being kept back. Talking becomes a form of self-protection, a hide-and-seek strategy that allows him to satisfy convention while also keeping his innermost material intact for his art. Harrison's renown as a cantankerous bad boy of American letters often precedes him and clashes with interviewers' perceptions, and his exotic reputation and cult status have made him the subject of distorted myths. (He has spent a portion of nearly every interview refuting or dismissing charges of his "macho" image.) Expecting a brawler, a boor, or a primitive wild man, interviewers are surprised to find him disarmingly thoughtful, sensitive, and erudite. It is a situation which sometimes causes confusion, resentment, and misrepresentation. And because Harrison has an entertaining and colorful story for nearly everything that has happened in his uncloistered life, determining who the real Jim Harrison is can be complicated. Harrison's French translator says: "J. H. lets himself be nicknamed Big Jim by his friends, but he often talks about himself as Poor Little Jimmy. Which image should we choose? The one about the giant or the one about vulnerability? Which nickname is the right one? Is there even one? How can we see clearly through all these smokescreens?"[2]

The answer lies elsewhere. Publication of twenty-two acclaimed volumes of poetry, fiction, and nonfiction prose (he also wrote approximately fifteen to twenty screenplays) in the thirty-six years from 1965 to 2001 indicates that, if Harrison has been unashamedly "quadra-schizoid" in his choice of multiple genres, he has also been unstinting, even old-fashioned, in his devotion to and possession by art as a single cause.

From the time sixteen-year-old Harrison transferred his religious fervor from born-again evangelism to writing poetry, until now, his consistently productive later years, that possession is a central reason for being. His desire to be a writer was a combination of patently romantic convictions about the appeals of an unbridled, hedonistic artist's life and a profound boredom with the middle-class way of life. A precocious teen from a hard-working, rural Michigan family, Harrison had grown up with a tradition of physical outdoor pursuits (farming, hunting, fishing, camping), and yet he also had a markedly philosophical and aesthetic side. Encouraged by his parents and at least one memorable high-school teacher and librarian, Bernice Smith, Harrison read widely in all kinds of literature, from the typical boy's adventure fare (by Zane Grey, Ernest Seton Thompson) to the most sophisticated modernist texts (by Rimbaud, Rilke, Joyce, Faulkner). He also traveled to New York, Boston, and California during those generative years and began to form strong opinions about the relationship of art to life and the need for writers to be outsiders.

In July 1956 the eighteen-year-old Harrison wrote a letter to John Ciardi, poetry editor of *Saturday Review,* in which he complained harshly about the contemporary poet following a "vogue instead of the nature of his emotions." He also submitted to Ciardi a handwritten poem, the first he had ever sent out to be considered for publication. "The Existentialist" was, Harrison admitted, "influenced" by Sartre and Kierkegaard. The free-verse poem contains some brooding night thoughts typical of an angst-filled teenager, but in identifying the locus of "a little life," not in "inspired rhymes of cinder stars / but the remnants of snow in April . . . ," it also points the way to his awareness of nature as a register of value and to the commonplace as a ground of being for art. A decade later these aspects marked Harrison's first book of poems, *Plain Song,* but they also reverberate through the whole of his career. Although "The Existentialist" was never published, it is important as a window into Harrison's formative imagination and the dimensions of his future passion. The poem also adds resonance to this statement forty years later to Casey Walker: "Writing isn't something for people who don't want to spend their entire lives in it, and most people figure out that commitment early, by age eighteen. You see you don't get to be a lot of things, that writing will take a full commitment."

In an otherwise restless existence, commitment is all. "The way you eat," Harrison told Jim Fergus, "bespeaks your entire attitude toward life." From the outset Harrison has shown "that appetite for life so ravenous" (as fellow Michigander Theodore Roethke puts it in his poem "The Pure Fury"). In an interview with Sedge Thompsen on National Public Radio's syndicated program, *Fresh Air,* 23 August 1990, Harrison spoke of the "erotics of writing," which he defined as "an intoxication with the ordinary in life. I think writers get lost by being very brilliant about perimeters and being very brilliant about edges, and then they forget the core. Food and sex are at the core." Harrison's newest collection of nonfiction is prefaced by a parable entitled "The Man Who Ate Books." Harrison's take on the world is characterized by his self-confessedly "fatal" appetite for language and experience, his hunger to devour life in as many of its varied guises and forms as possible. Eating, devouring, ingesting, tasting become the central bodily metaphors that link all his most compelling pursuits, including, cooking, hunting, fishing, reading, and writing. "Even the occasional glories of our sexual lives can be drawn into this picture. . . . All of our sensualities and passions merge because we are one person and it's best not to neglect any of those passions if we wish to fully live our lives."[3]

Whether considered as justification or rationalization, Harrison's catchy gastronomical motto—"Eat or Die"—transcends his food journalism and bespeaks an orientation toward the world's body that has resulted in an unbroken arc of attention and inclusiveness, not only for himself but for his characters as well (many of whom transparently share their author's specific interests, habits, obsessions). From Swanson, the bewildered narrator of *Wolf: A False Memoir,* through the brooding, globetrotting Tristan in his epic novella, "Legends of the Fall," to the incomparable Dalva Northridge, who takes all of the male world's prerogatives as her own in *Dalva* and *The Road Home,* Harrison's signature creations, in pursuit of their place in the world, exhibit a single-minded energy and hunger that reflects Harrison's own mandate. However, his conception of fictional characters has widened and ramified over the years. As Harrison has increasingly abnegated his own ego (the result of long-standing Zen practice and psychoanalysis), he has entered more fully into Dogen's world of ten thousand things. This is not a matter of mechanical "discipline" (a word Harrison abhors), but of soulful empathy and openness, and a willingness to listen to the demands of his own dream life.

Harrison's receptivity has allowed him, as a writer, to make significant breakthroughs. For instance, in the late 1960s he appropriated the ancient Persian ghazal form in his poetry, and in the late 1970s he developed his own brand of the densely packed novella form. (Four collections later he is credited with helping kindle the current boom in the short novel.) And in the late 1980s he entered the voice and/or consciousness of women—first Dalva, then Clare in the novella "The Woman Lit by Fireflies," then Julip Durham in the novella "Julip." Explaining the background of his masterpiece, *Dalva,* he offered this striking image to Tom Bevier: "I wanted to write something new.

Introduction

To cross the Rockies. On foot. At night."[4] If one of the hallmarks of an important writer is the ability to continually surprise and challenge us with daring transformations, then Harrison fits the bill.

Harrison lives through his books, and they have changed—grown deeper, more reflective—as he has matured toward a larger vision of empathy. "I tend to think of art as essentially androgynous and that gender is a biological rather than a philosophical system," he claimed in a *New York Times Magazine* piece, "First Person Female" (16 May 1999). Those changes are reflected in his interviews, which in recent times, especially since the late 1980s, have become less brittle, restrictive, and strident than they once were. "So don't tell me you can't change your fiction," he announced to Jim Fergus. "Habit is what destroys art." Indeed, he has gone so far as to argue persuasively for portraying the entire range of human emotion in his fiction, even if it means risking sentimentality, one of the cardinal sins of literary criticism. "The novelist who refuses sentiment refuses the full spectrum of human behavior.... I would rather give full vent to all human loves and disappointments, and take a chance on being corny, than die a smartass," he confessed to Wendy Smith. If understanding just who Jim Harrison is gets complicated in the following pages, it will help to keep this clear-cut admission in mind.

Although the following compilation is merely suggestive of the larger record of Jim Harrison's oral, print, and electronic media interviews, it should prove useful in creating a historical context for many of his published works. While Harrison does not slavishly interpret his texts directly, he does situate them among their participatory and ambient circumstances. His comments provide a parallel conversation to the one carried on in his prose and poetry and reveal a highly literate and intellectual writer whose work and talent is best measured against a vast intertextual tradition. An omnivorous reader and compulsive researcher, Harrison has never been reticent about quoting or praising influential writers; consequently, these discussions provide ample evidence of his affinity with a wide range of precursors from Wang Wei to James Hillman.

More importantly, it is hoped these talks will supply a loosely related narrative of his progress as a major contemporary American writer who is equally and consistently at home in poetry, fiction, and nonfiction. This collection should also aid in signifying the depth and range of Harrison's considerable intellectual and political preoccupations, his fierce social and ecological conscience (especially America's deplorable "soul history" regarding Native Americans), his aesthetic beliefs, and his authorial obsessions, as well as his pet peeves, candor, humility, sense of humor, and patience, even when posed with the same questions over and over or when prompted to recount again and again his litany of key formative life experiences.

Harrison is an innovative, powerful, and savvy writer whose true subject, as with Melville, Faulkner, and Morrison, is the capacious and tragic dimension of individual consciousness. When Casey Walker asked him to describe "the core, the spirit" of his work, Harrison replied: "This consciousness, I would say. Otherness. Otherness to remind ourselves of the bedrock of life, and death, and love, and suffering." And yet despite the prevalence of this multifaceted theme and a challenging, even daunting, level of intertextuality in his work, Harrison has not yet reached the critical academic audience in America he deserves (though this has not been a noticeable cause of disappointment to him). This neglect is partly his own doing. After a brief stint as an administrative assistant and teacher at SUNY Stony Brook, Harrison left the university environment for good. "I wanted to be a writer in the old sense of staying on the outside," he told Wendy Smith. "I can live for about a year on the proceeds from the first draft of a screenplay, which sometimes takes only six weeks, and I think that's more fun than hanging around some fucking college town for ten months waiting for summer vacation." Except for occasional readings, public appearances, award conferrals, and the like, Harrison has not returned to academia, though he has satirized it unmercifully in characters such as Michael in *Dalva* and Shelley in his novellas, "Brown Dog" and "The Seven Ounce Man."

Straightforward, deliberately outrageous, often profane, and sometimes crude in his opinions on nearly every topic of interest to him under the sun, especially the liabilities of university creative writing programs and the deleterious effect of political correctness (dramatized in a recent novella, "The Beige Dolorosa"), Harrison, is, nevertheless, considered a "writer's writer," whose independence, technical abilities, serious attention to craft, and creative priorities are cherished. If the number of dust jacket encomia Harrison has penned in the last thirty years is any indication, then many of our most respected and accomplished contemporary writers, including Rick Bass, Richard Ford, Dan Gerber, Sam Hamill, Barry Hannah, Linda Hogan, Ted Kooser, Peter Matthiessen, Tom McGuane, Simon Ortiz, Jack Turner, James Welch, Terry Tempest Williams, and Gerald Vizenor, have looked to him for advice, encouragement, approval. What Gertrude Stein once said of Paris applies to Harrison—it isn't what he gives you, so much as what he doesn't take away.

To sense that liberatory gift is to begin to understand how and why Harrison has created a strongly committed—one wants to say fanatical—international following among many professional reviewers, media critics, independent booksellers, and general readers in almost two dozen different languages. Michael Walker's cameo of Harrison performing a public reading in the courtyard of Dutton's bookstore in Brentwood, California, captures what is at stake: "Here, then, is the flip side of Harrison's all-expenses paid screenwriter's life: the artist, his thin blue blazer flapping in the wind, amid the faithful who stand in the cold and dark to watch him, flanked by a nervous bookstore employee who shines a flashlight over his shoulder, as he reads the writing that they love."[5] And though no one is more acutely aware than Harrison of being "just another novelist" in a "town where writers earn more for a two-page treatment than for a book but are treated as interchangeable cogs in an oily machine," he is one of those rare writers who reaches a wide and diverse audience that cuts across national, racial, gender, regional, and cultural lines.

In the long run, contemporary theorists tell us talk and art, speech and writing, are different. In assembling this collection I have favored traditional literary question-and-answer interviews, because they allow Harrison to develop his responses more elaborately than in many of the numerous but briefer newspaper and popular magazine profiles where his comments are reduced to snappy one-liners. In doing so I have sacrificed snapshot for panorama. The preponderance of interviews with Harrison focus on his fiction, and that pattern is reflected here as well. But Thierry Jousse and Vincent Ostria's interview in *Cahiers du Cinema* was chosen because it pertains to Harrison's screenwriting career, a neglected area of concern, and also because it is representative of a host of foreign (especially French) interviews that would, if gathered, make up an additional volume in their own right. Joseph Bednarik's session with Harrison is an exception, too, because it foregrounds Harrison's poetry. However, in no way should the amount of space allotted to fiction be taken to reflect Harrison's own preference. He remains as committed to poetry as he was when he first began writing.

These selections approximate the original conversations in varying ways, some more spontaneously, some less so, some more editorially polished, some less so, than others. Inevitably, there is also much overlapping, repetition, echoing, and call and response. It is impossible to ignore (and not be delighted by) Harrison's discursive style and digressive manner when he is talking across a table from you. Michael Walker says that a "conversation with Harrison is inevitably punctuated by his wheezing, cackling laughter, especially when that subject takes a particularly absurd turn. . . ." Of course, some transcripts do those aspects more justice than others.

Readers accustomed to the complex rhetorical structure and lapidary quality of his fiction will, however, glimpse some of those same acrobatic patterns among several of the following pieces. Harrison often talks around a subject first, going this way, then that, before he finds the route he wants to follow. He habitually contextualizes his answers by providing a kind of intellectual or emotional surround. In short, Harrison often feels his way haltingly toward his answer (a process some interviewers have been more desirous of replicating than others). Asked by Eleanor Wachtel whether he has found a balance in his life, Harrison replied:

> Well, I better have because I'm sixty now. But I don't know if that's true. I think balances are temporary and any time you think you could fix yourself in one place, that's absurd. Properly, life lived properly, is a river. Or that Yeatsian concept that life is best viewed as a dance. You know, an interminable dance. So, if I thought that I had reached some point, I would hit myself over the head because the path is the way. You have to keep reaching the point on the continuum, you know. It never stops, even for a moment. I would say there is a bit more consolation now, because what I had thought as a young writer was that I would never whine if my books stayed in print and so they have. So that's the only thing you hope for.

The river, the dance, the path: though Harrison isn't so naive as to be unmindful that end results and tangible products issue from entitled self-interest and determined agency, these three metaphors emphasize process as a kind of reward in itself and summarize his fluid mythic way of being in the world.

The interviews are arranged in the order of when they were conducted, rather than the order of their publication. Interviews that were conducted over an extended period of time, or interviews that are composites of two or more sessions with Harrison (Wachtel; DeMott and Smith) are appropriately noted. In two instances I have compared the original audio version with the subsequent printed version and have noted that there are differences (Bonetti) or incorporated with permission original interview material deleted from the published account (Wachtel).

Obvious typographical and factual errors by interviewers and/or editors

Introduction

have been silently corrected. I have not, however, corrected Harrison's occasional fibs, memory glitches, or misprisions. Harrison's memoir (tentatively titled *Off to the Side*), constellated around his life's obsessions, is now in the works and will no doubt provide a master version of his autobiography, which is already to be found piecemeal in nearly everything else he has written since the mid-1960s. Harrison is a complex, multifaceted person. Like most of us, he has been complicit in forwarding a certain view of his life, and like most of us, he is a bundle of contradictions and inconsistencies, so a healthy dose of Keats's negative capability is necessary for smooth sailing in these pages. The vagaries of time and the imperfections of memory being what they are, no attempt has been made to reconcile conflicting versions of Harrison's responses in these interviews. The chronology supplies correct dates for previously disputed events mentioned in the following interviews, such as Harrison's marriage to Linda King (1959), his Michigan State University degrees (BA, 1960; MA, 1966), and his departure from SUNY, Stony Brook (1968), and publication of his many books.

If Jim Harrison is occasionally a cavalier authority on the specific dates and factual minutiae in his life, he is an unimpeachable source of other pleasures. I first encountered him when I read "A Sporting Life," an article that appeared in—of all places—*Playboy* in 1976 (reprinted in *Just Before Dark*). I was born and raised in New England, and like Harrison, had more or less misspent my youth by excessive trout fishing and grouse hunting—willful personal indulgences which always made me feel slightly guilty and socially marginal. Harrison's candid essay is as sharp now as it was twenty-five years ago for its refusal to traffic in stereotypes or to endorse misguided notions of sporting life. However its real lesson had less to do with woods and waters than with the necessity for an "opposite field," a physical identity, an arena of activity separate from the routine of spoken or written words. What's good for a writer seemed to be good for a teacher as well, I told him when I approached him for the first time in January, 1996, at the Fourteenth Annual Key West Literary Seminar, devoted to American Writers and the Natural World. He seemed less interested in the fact that I was assigning his fiction in graduate seminars than that I had recently started training a young English setter, and on that basis I established a fortuitous contact that led to a couple of lengthy interviews Patrick Smith and I conducted in 1997 and 1998, and eventually to the idea for this book.

Indeed, this book would not have been possible without the sustained encouragement, generosity, and hospitality provided by Jim and Linda Harrison at their homes in Lake Leelanau, Michigan, and Patagonia, Arizona; the kindness of John Harrison and Nick and Mary Dumsch; and the exemplary efforts of Patrick Smith, whose Ohio University doctoral dissertation on Harrison (forthcoming in revised form from Michigan State University Press) I supervised, and who has since been a cherished co-participant in Harrisonian pursuits, and a major instigator in establishing a Jim Harrison Society in the American Literature Association (the inaugural meeting took place in Cambridge last month). I am pleased to acknowledge three Harrison afficionados and charter members of the society: Beef Torrey of Crete, Nebraska; the originators of the Jim Harrison website (www.jimharrison.org), Joseph Bednarik of Copper Canyon Press, Port Townsend, Washington, and Keith Comer of Idaho State University, Pocatello. They, too, have furnished their parts toward this book.

I also thank Ohio University's Department of English for funding two doctoral research assistants—Rae Greiner (fall quarter 1998), and Thom Conroy (spring quarter 2000); and especially Dean Joe Berman of Ohio University's Honors Tutorial College for funding Anne Langendorfer's research apprenticeship in 1999–2000—her editorial skills, resourcefulness, and enthusiasm made the whole project smoother than it might otherwise have been. My attention to Harrison's writings was substantially sharpened by discerning graduate students Mike McCollister and Chris Walker, whose MA theses on Harrison I directed. In addition, Christian and Dominique Bourgois, Harrison's Paris-based French publishers, provided an extensive archive of French interviews, many of which were translated by my OU colleague Dominique Duvert. The staff of the interlibrary loan department at Alden Library tracked down a number of fugitive items. I am also grateful to Peter Berg, Director of Special Collections at Michigan State University's Libraries for permission to quote Harrison's unpublished poem and correspondence to John Ciardi and Tom McGuane, and George Plimpton for allowing me to reprint Jim Fergus's interview.

I'd be remiss if I forgot Nick Reens, who provided good cheer up in Michigan, Amy Hundley of Grove/Atlantic for her repeated help, and Jim McClintock of Michigan State University, Ron Primeau of Central Michigan University, as well as Nancy Bunge, Carrie Preston, and Lilli Ross, for various kindnesses as well as serious interest in Jim Harrison's work and career. At University Press of Mississippi Director Seetha Srinivasan believed in the project from the beginning, and Anne Stascavage was especially patient in bringing the manuscript to its present status. Background conversations, letters, and faxes with, from, and by Harrison cronies Guy de la Valdene, Dan Gerber, Doug Peacock, Louis Owens, Jim Fergus, Ted Kooser, and Richard Ford were much appreciated and highly valued.

Finally, this book is dedicated to Joyce Harrington Bahle, who opened doors and kept them open; and to my wife, Andrea Berger DeMott, who aided, abetted, and facilitated in more ways than I could ever count or repay.

RD
June 2001

Notes

1. Consult "An Annotated Chronology of Jim Harrison Interviews, 1971–2000," <www.jimharrison.org>.
2. Brice Matthieussent, "La Strategie du Furet" ("The Strategy of the Ferret"), *Jim Harrison, de A áa W* (Paris: Christian Bourgois Editions, 1995), 11 (translated by Dominique Duvert).
3. Jim Harrison, *The Raw and the Cooked: Adventures of a Roving Gourmand* (New York: Atlantic Monthly Press, 2001), 2–3.
4. Tom Bevier, "The Softer Side of Macho Man," *Michigan: The Magazine of the Detroit News*, 6 March 1988, 19.
5. Michael Walker, "When the Wolf Howls," *Los Angeles Times Calendar*, 12 June 1994, 34.

Chronology

1937   James Thomas Harrison born 11 December in northern Michigan town of Grayling, the second of five children of Winfield Sprague Harrison (government agriculture agent) and Norma Olivia (Wahlgren) Harrison. Both parents avid readers.

1940   Harrison family moves to Reed City, Michigan.

1945   Harrison accidentally blinded in his left eye by playmate with broken glass laboratory beaker.

1951   Though raised Congregationalist, Harrison experiences religious conversion at Baptist revival and becomes preacher at fundamentalist youth fellowships and president of Bible Club.

1952–56   Family moves to Haslett so Harrison children can be within commuting distance of Michigan State University. Father works for United States Soil Conservation Service. Harrison attends Haslett Rural High School where he plays offensive left guard and defensive middle linebacker on football team. English teacher and librarian, Bernice Smith, encourages Harrison's sophisticated reading interests with *Nation* and *Saturday Review*. In 1953 after a summer working as busboy at Stanley Hotel in Estes Park, Colorado, religious urge fades and he transfers his fervor to literary pursuits. During sophomore year, announces intention to become a writer; receives first typewriter for seventeenth birthday. In 1954, in the summer before his junior year, Harrison and a friend drive to Greenwich Village in New York for a few days to investigate bohemian life. Elected president of graduating class and of student council but resigns from latter. In September 1956, enrolls at Michigan State University in East Lansing.

1957–59   A period of restlessness, occasional travel, and temporary residence in New York City, San Francisco, and Boston. Drops out of Michigan State toward the end of his freshman year and hitchhikes to New York's Greenwich Village (at different times lives on McDougal Street and Grove Street). Returns to Michigan State in the fall of 1958, but drops out. Goes to Boston, then hitchhikes to California. Works at various odd jobs, including as crop picker. In 1959 returns to Michigan State. At Michigan State part-time jobs include working at library and horticulture farm. Marries Linda May King on 10 October 1959.

1960 Earns B.A. degree, Michigan State University. Daughter Jamie Louise born 21 May. Fellow students at Michigan State include poet and novelist Dan Gerber, novelist and screenwriter Tom McGuane, both of whom later become lifelong friends, and Robert Datilla, who later becomes Harrison's agent.

1962 Father and younger sister Judith killed in head-on automobile accident in November. Harrison leaves graduate program at Michigan State.

1963 Moves to Cambridge, Massachusetts, and lives with brother John, a Harvard librarian, in apartment on Kirkland Street; works for two years as book salesman at Campbell and Hall, a general wholesaling firm, and is joined by wife and daughter.

1965 Moves to Kingsley, Michigan. Has odd jobs as laborer, hod carrier, brick layer, and carpenter. Publishes three poems in *Nation* on 15 February and 5 April, and five poems in *Poetry* (August). On the strength of reading ten of Harrison's poems, Denise Levertov recommends his first book, *Plain Song,* for publication by W. W. Norton. Encouraged by mentor Herbert Weisinger to complete graduate work, Harrison writes essay about his poems which becomes master's thesis, "The Natural History of Some Poems."

1966 Harrison earns MA degree in comparative literature at Michigan State University. Turns down teaching position at Northern Michigan University to follow Weisinger to State University of New York, Stony Brook, where he becomes Weisinger's assistant, then assistant professor of English.

1967 Receives first of three consecutive annual National Endowment for the Arts grants. Publishes limited edition chapbook, *Walking.* In October participates in Writers and Artists' March on the State Department, Washington DC.

1968 Publishes book of poems, *Locations.* With Weisinger and Louis Simpson organizes world poetry conference at Stony Brook 21–23 June. Contributes "Dreams" to *Stony Brook Holographs* (Stony Brook, NY: Stony Brook Poetics Foundation), a collection

	of handwritten poems. Though listed in the 1968–69 Stony Brook catalogue as assistant professor, in June resigns and returns to Michigan. Purchases Lake Leelanau, Michigan, farm. First issue of *Sumac* (poetry magazine) appears in the fall, edited by Harrison and Dan Gerber. Begins visiting Florida Keys for winter fishing.
1969	Awarded Guggenheim fellowship. As part of Poets-in-the-Schools program, gives poetry readings and residencies in the Southwest. Publishes *5 Blind Men,* poetry collection with Dan Gerber, J. D. Reed, George Quasha, and Charles Simic. Begins to work sporadically on a novel, "Cities of the North." Meets painter and writer Russell Chatham in Key West and they become lifelong friends. (Beginning in 1979 all Harrison's books are published with cover art by Chatham.) In October suffers severe back injury when he falls from bluff during grouse hunting trip along Manistee River and spends a month in traction at Munson Hospital in Traverse City.
1970	While recovering from back injury (complicated by penicillin poisoning) is urged by McGuane to complete a novel.
1971	Daughter Anna Severin born 6 April. Publishes novel *Wolf: A False Memoir* and poems *Outlyers and Ghazals*. *Sumac* ceases publication after nine issues, but Sumac Press continues to publish individual books. Publishes essay, "Plaster Trout in Worm Heaven," in *Sports Illustrated,* beginning association with *SI* that lasts until 1975. In October makes literary pilgrimage to Moscow and Leningrad with Dan Gerber.
1973	Publishes novel *A Good Day to Die* and poems *Letters to Yesenin,* which he considers an "anti-suicide note." In February travels to Africa with Dan Gerber.
1974	With McGuane and Richard Brautigan contributes to and acts in *Tarpon,* documentary movie on saltwater fly fishing filmed in Key West, Florida, directed by Christian Odasso and Guy de la Valdene.
1975	Publishes novel *Farmer.* Writes screenplay of *A Good Day to Die* for documentary filmmaker Frederick Weisman, but film is never made. Meets actor Jack Nicholson on the Montana film set of *Missouri Breaks.*
1977	Publishes poems *Returning to Earth.*

1978 Visits Nicholson on Durango, Mexico, set of *Going South;* Nicholson loans Harrison money ($30,000) to pay off debts and finance writing for a year. Meets Seymour "Sam" Lawrence, who becomes his publisher at Delacorte, Dutton, and Houghton Mifflin. In winter visits Jolli Lodge in Lake Leelanau, where he writes novella, "The Man Who Gave Up His Name," and in concentrated nine-day burst "Legends of the Fall," a novella based in part on journals kept by William Ludlow, his wife's great-grandfather, an immigrant Cornish mining engineer who accompanied General Custer on Black Hills expeditions.

1979 Publishes combined reprint volume, *Letters to Yesenin* and *Returning to Earth* and breakthrough novella collection *Legends of the Fall,* which includes "Legends of the Fall," "Revenge," and "The Man Who Gave Up His Name." Begins writing screenplays in Hollywood for Warner Brothers. Work as contract screenwriter lasts until 1997. Employs Joyce Harrington as administrative assistant. Purchases cabin on Sucker River in Michigan's Upper Peninsula.

1981 Publishes novel *Warlock* and poetry collection *Selected and New Poems, 1961–1981.* Publishes first of four food columns in *Smoke Signals,* a small press, limited circulation literary journal in Brooklyn, NY. Publishes limited edition chapbook of poems, *Natural World: A Bestiary.*

1982 *Selected and New Poems, 1961–1981* appears in paperback.

1984 Publishes novel *Sundog.*

1986 Publishes signed limited edition of poems, *The Theory and Practice of Rivers and Other Poems.*

1988 Publishes novel *Dalva.* Beginning with premiere issue, Harrison becomes contributing food editor of *Smart,* mass circulation magazine.

1989 Publishes *The Theory & Practice of Rivers and New Poems.* Film, *Cold Feet,* co-written earlier with Tom McGuane, released. In the January/February issue of *Smart,* publishes the first of ten "Sporting Food" columns which continue through October/November 1990.

1990 Publishes novella collection *The Woman Lit by Fireflies,* which includes "Brown Dog," "Sunset Limited," and "The Woman Lit by Fireflies." *Revenge,* feature film based on novella of same name, is released. Harrison receives screenwriting credit with Jeff Fiskin. Publishes preface to *Russell Chatham: One Hundred Paintings* (Livingston, MT: Clark City Press). Receives Mark Twain Award from the Center for the Study of Midwestern Literature and Culture for distinguished contributions to Midwestern literature. Begins regular winter residence in Patagonia, Arizona.

1991   Publishes *Just Before Dark: Collected Nonfiction.* Publishes introduction ("The Chippewa-Ottawa") to George Weeks, *Mem-kaweh: Dawning of the Grand Traverse Band of Ottawa and Chippewa Indians* (Grand Traverse, MI: Grand Traverse Band Tribal Council, 1991). In March publishes in *Esquire* the first of twenty-five monthly food columns, "The Raw and the Cooked," which continues through December 1993.

1992   Publishes *The Raw and the Cooked,* a chapbook of three *Esquire* food columns. Works on filmscript, "The Last Posse," a western, for producer Douglas Wick and Harrison Ford, and a filmscript about photographer Edward S. Curtis for Columbia Pictures. Neither is produced.

1993   Subject of documentary film by George Luneau and Brice Matthieusent, *Jim Harrison: Entre Chien et Loup* (English version: *Jim Harrison: Half Dog & Half Wolf*). Honored by Institute Lumière in Lyon, France.

1994   Publishes novella collection *Julip,* which includes "Julip," "The Seven-Ounce Man," and "The Beige Dolorosa." *Wolf* (film) released (not based on *Wolf: A False Memoir*). Harrison is associate producer and shares screenwriting credit with Wesley Strick. Publisher and friend Seymour Lawrence dies.

1995   *Legends of the Fall* (film) released. Publishes introduction ("Hunting with a Friend") to Guy de la Valdene, *For a Handful of Feathers* (New York: Atlantic Monthly Press, 1995). Begins researching "Earth Diver," another novel about Dalva Northridge.

1996   In January is a featured participant in fourteenth Key West Literary Seminar, "American Writers and the Natural World." Publishes *After Ikkyu and Other Poems* (Boston: Shambhala). *Carried Away,* feature film version of *Farmer* is released.

1997   Publishes introduction to *The Sumac Reader,* edited by Joseph Bednarik (East Lansing, MI: Michigan State University Press). In May is featured participant at eighth annual Astonishing Travelers "Festival International du Livre" in Saint-Malo, France. Ends Hollywood screenwriting career. Publishes foreword ("High on the Hog") to Roger Welsch, *Diggin' In and Piggin' Out: The Truth about Food and Men* (New York: HarperCollins, 1997).

1998   Publishes novel *The Road Home* in French in July, then in English in October. Publishes *The Shape of the Journey: New and Collected Poems.* Becomes contributing editor to *Men's Journal,* mass circulation magazine, and consultant to Orvis sporting goods company.

1999   In April is awarded Evil Companions Literary Award (given annually by *Colorado Review* to writer living in or writing about the American West). Wins Michigan State University College of Arts and Letters Distinguished Alumni Award. In May is honored at tenth annual Astonishing Travelers "Festival International du Livre" in Saint-Malo, France. *The Shape of the Journey* is finalist for *Los Angeles Times* Book Prize.

2000   Novella collection *The Beast God Forgot to Invent* (includes "The Beast God Forgot to Invent," "Westward Ho," and "I forgot to Go to Spain") published in French in April, then in English in October. Publishes autobiographical children's recovery story *The Boy Who Ran to the Woods,* illustrated by Tom Pohrt. Awarded Spirit of the West literary achievement award by Mountains and Plains Booksellers Association. In October is awarded Michigan State University's Distinguished Alumni Award.

2001   Begins writing book-length memoir. Serves as featured speaker at ceremony on 4 May marking Carnegie Mellon University's annual Pauline Adamson Awards for Excellence in Writing. In November publishes *The Raw and the Cooked,* collection of food columns, then *A Conversation,* limited edition letter press book of poems with Ted Kooser.

Conversations with Jim Harrison

A Chat with a Novelist
Jim Harrison and Thomas McGuane / 1971

From *Sumac,* 4 (Fall 1971), 121–29. Reprinted in *Just Before Dark: Collected Nonfiction* (Livingston, MT: Clark City Press, 1991), 225–34. Reprinted with permission of Jim Harrison.

When I turned up Deep Creek Road the sheep bordered the cattle guard and their "ba ba ba bahhs" seemed to reflect the question: why would anyone live here? But I drove on through the Engleman spruce and withered sedge for a few miles then turned when I saw BUSHWACK PALACE branded into a rail fence with McGuane, Prop., below it. I drove another mile through a pasture of sudan grass noticing the flattened rattlers with their clouds of flies on the road, a few conical piles of bear doodoo with even more flies and prairie falcons hovering in abstract gyres above the trail. Why not live here? I queried myself. When I drew up to the ranch which closely resembled the movie set from *Shane* Mr. McGuane's huge dog jumped bristling onto the car hood but her master's voice called and we walked through the darkened house to a yet darker study. I noticed Mr. McGuane looked a trifle old for his age which hasn't been determined though I would guess between the mid-twenties and mid-thirties. Like the redoubtable Pynchon he makes an unfortunate fetish out of privacy. *Pourquoi?* Who knows. Perhaps no one cares but that's not what we're talking about, is it? There was a two gallon swiveled decanter of cheapish gin and some ice on his bare desk. Mrs. McGuane, nee Portia Crockett, brought in a pewter platter of braised leeks and sweetbreads which we nibbled at with a chilled off-year Chateau Margaux. Mr. McGuane glowered as if this intrusion for the sake of contemporary letters was unwelcome. He put on a Linda Rondstadt and a Dollie Parton album and sang along rather loudly with them, not well I might add. My questions punctuated this noise with some difficulty.

Interviewer: Is it true what you said about Bob?
McGuane: Nope.

Int: You seem to key off the midwest in your work. You were born and raised there but you commute between Montana and Key West without a nod to Michigan and its rich literary milieu. Why?

McGuane: I have a genetic horror of the midwest, a dark image of the past where Mortimer Snerd screwed three thousand times a day to build that heartland race.

Int: Oh.

McGuane: Yet I miss those piney woods, those beaver ponds and rivers, the feebs and dolts who run the bait shops and gas stations, the arc welders in the legislature, the ham with chicken gravy that poisoned me in Germfask when I fished the Driggs.

Int: You're not denying your roots?
McGuane: Cut that shit out.

Int: A.O.K. What do you think of the Drug Generation?
McGuane: The Driggs is a fine river for brook trout.

Int: Must I always be a wanderer between post and pillar, the virgin and the garrison, the noose and the cocktail lounge?
McGuane: That's your bizness.

Int: Who do you think is really good right now?
McGuane: Grass. Hawkes. Landolfi. Cela.

Int: Do you care to elaborate?
McGuane: Nope.

Int: Were it possible, how would you derive the novels you would like to write?
McGuane: Cervantes, De Rojas, Rabelais, Swift, Fielding, Machado de Assis, Melville, Gogol, Joyce, Flann O'Brien, Ilf and Petrov, Peacock, Dickens, Kafka, Chesterton, Byron of the letters.

Int: Do you think Nabokov excessively conumdramatic?
McGuane: Is that like hydramatic?

Int: You jest, mega-fop!

(A two day interruption was made here to attend a Crow Indian Pow Wow. The interviewer became very ill from semi-poisonous tequila which he mistook for white table wine. The Custer Battlefield of Thomas Berger fame was visited. How life imitates art!)

Int: Officially Montana is your residence, is it not?
McGuane: Yes, the bleak cordillera of the Absaroka consoles me.

Int: Why don't you live on one of America's marvel coasts?

McGuane: I'm glad you asked. I've been to those places. And the Left there to which I belong was developing an attitude toward the people of the interior and the unfashionably pigmented poor that is best described as racist. For example the Left implicitly considers any white born in the south to be congenitally evil.

Int: What about the whole "novel scene" now?

McGuane: Only that the serial preoccupations of fiction could be replaced by the looped, the circuited and the Johnny Carson Show. Even something so ductile as an eclaire has an inner dynamism not inferior to a hard-on or a terrified Norway rat.

Int: I think most of our readers are unfamiliar with your interest in pastry.

McGuane: It ends with eclaires and their analogue reality (or not).

Int: I wonder how many of our readers realize that your aunt was the celebrated Irish novelist Flann O'Brien?

McGuane: Very few.

Int: What other things come to mind that our readers probably don't realize.

McGuane: What is the name of your magazine?

Int: *Sumac,* which unfortunately some think is french for stomach.

McGuane: Well one of the things that *Stomach* readers doubtless fail to realize is that D. H. Lawrence was Norman Douglas' wife. It was the first society function hazarded by the widely resented "surfboard aristocracy" of Tasmania, also I might add their first transvestite wedding.

Int: Oh. One critic describes your fictions as being "laced with canals of meaning and symbolism."

McGuane: Yes, yes . . .

Int: Is that true?

McGuane: O yes, yes yes . . . Why gee yes.

Int: What do you think of, I think it was either Granville Hicks' or George Steiner's contention, that fiction should be spelled "fickshun?"

McGuane: No.

Int: What of your fabled love of animals?

McGuane: I would handily commit 3300 acts of artistic capitulation to keep my dog in Purina.

Int: Why have you never mentioned the Budweiser Clydesdales in your work?

McGuane: O god, hasn't that been done to death?

Int: May I ask for the first sentence of your new novel?
McGuane: Of course. "Upstairs, Mona bayed for dong."

Int: MMMMmmm. How ironical. Yesterday in the local tackle shop I was told you had invented a new fly for trout.

McGuane: Yes, I call it the Republican Indispensible. You tie it up out of pig bristles and carp feathers.

Int: Have you ever caught Gila trout in New Mexico?
McGuane: No.

Int: Arizona?
McGuane: O, not at all.

Int: Are you offended by calling a large trout "Larry Lunker" as do many of our sporting writers?

McGuane: Au contraire. The term frequently hangs on my lower lip like a figment of dawn.

Int: Are you stoned?
McGuane: No, Intermittently never.

Int: What constitutes a horses ass in our literature?
McGuane: A difficult question! I'd say 1. parsimony 2. sure fire Babbitry 3. snorkeling 4. New York 5. San Francisco 6. Irving Berlin 7. this is your life not theirs 8. pick up sticks 9. Mary Jane and Sniffles 10. U.S.A. Meatland Parcels 11. a million baby kisses 12. a bad cold 13. corasable bond.

(Mr. McGuane ran out in the rain to install a new starter solenoid in his Porsche 911T. We then left immediately for the Black Foot Reservation in Browning, Montana to see the birthplace of James Welch. We were there for three days. Mr. McGuane unfortunately mistook tequila for a widely known ginger ale, hence spent much time yodeling in the thundermug as the Irish would put it.)

Int: I'm interested in what you think of Barton Midwood's contention that the modern novelist has lost his audience. They've all gone to the beach.
McGuane: Hopelessly true. We're lucky if they've gone no farther than

the beach. If they were at the beach a year ago when Midwood made the statement they are surely in Tibet by now.

Int: What is the last book you didn't write?
McGuane: *The Possums of Everest.*

Int: I understand you were working on a contemporary western but have abandoned it?
McGuane: Yes, the book was centered in Big Pie Country or Big Fly Country, whatever you will. The title was *Ghost Riff-Raff in the Sky.*

Int: Why did you give up the title *Wandell's Opprobrium?*
McGuane: It would have sent everybody to Tibetan beach.

Int: Don't you think the title should have been *Walkie Talkie?*
McGuane: Not at all.

Int: Your politics, rather the lack of them, is a point of interest to some critics. Do you have a comment.
McGuane: I suppose I am a bit left of Left. America has become a dildo that has turned berserkly on its owner.

Int: Do you feel lionized?
McGuane: I feel vermiculized.

Int: Do you have any deeply felt interest in poetry?
McGuane: O, a great deal. So much in fact that I find myself overwhelmed. I would like to add this, for decades the Pruniers' restaurants have had the reputation of being the best seafood restaurants in the world.

Int: What of your college years?
McGuane: I graduated from Black Pumpkin in 1956. Since then, I might add, our Pumpkin group has dominated American letters.

Int: What about the underground?
McGuane: What about the underground?

Int: I mean what about the Underground?
McGuane: Oh. The Underground has become the Overground, in essence a parable of the Gay Cabellero.

Int: Is that in the same genre as the Spanish Cavalier?
McGuane: No. Only that every hamster is a hostage to fortune.

Int: Have we touched on organic gardening?

McGuane: We had one of those things out at the end of the lawn. A lot of work. Then a certain horse named Rex got loose in the night and ate the whole plot to ground level. Sad to say but the most organic thing in the world is pus. I read it yesterday.

Int: Are any of your friends living in domes?

McGuane: Yes. I have a close friend who has built a $100,000 home that looks precisely like a Spalding Dot.

Int: The golf ball, I presume?

McGuane: Yes. From time to time he and his family can be seen scuttling in and out one of its pores. It's a noble way of life. Also, they have a duck inside with them.

Int: Where has everyone gone?
McGuane: Bolinas.

Int: All of them?
McGuane: All of them.

Int: For the striped bass?
McGuane: For the pachouli.

Int: Why did you call your dog Biff.
McGuane: Sprat.

Int: Dink?
McGuane: Frab. . . . [snit].

The interview terminated here. An inevitable tedium seized us. Mr. McGuane attempted to sing from Jarry's *Ubu Roi* accompanying a Merle Haggard record. Then he read to me from some aerosol cans he gathered in the bathroom: "Never spray toward face or open flame, avoid inhaling. If rash develops discontinue use. Contains riboflavin." etc. . . .

A Good Day for Talking: An Interview with the Author of *Wolf* and *Farmer*
Ira Elliott and Marty Somerness / 1976

From *Chronicle*, 1 (20 October 1976), unpaginated. Reprinted with permission.

Visitors travel northwest from Traverse City to reach his sixty acre farm in Leelanau County. During the cold, crisp days of Autumn the roadway is carpeted with decaying leaves—orange, red-orange, brown, all swirling in the cold, clear winds coming off Suttons Bay. Well off the main road one can see a two-story wooden house, a weather-beaten shed, and an old, tin barn. When guests pull alongside a yellow pickup truck parked in a dirt driveway he steps out of his house wearing faded jeans, boots, and a blue flannel shirt. He shows the way into his home, one wall lined with books—from Hemingways to Dostoyevskys to Joyces—and into a small, modestly furnished living room, the sunlight slanting through a corner window. He serves up burgundy wine in giant goblets.

This is Jim Harrison in his environment, the rural northern Michigan he writes about. Born in Grayling in 1937, Harrison was one of five children born to a country agricultural agent and his wife. He spent his youth in Reed City and Haslett, then set off to college in nearby East Lansing. He was graduated from Michigan State University in 1960 with a Bachelor of Arts degree. After some years of confessed loafing and gallavanting about the country, he received his Masters degree in comparative literature from Michigan State in 1965; his thesis was a paper explaining how he got his first poetry published. He will return to his alma mater this February for a poetry reading, though he finds East Lansing "frightful."

After completing his formal education he taught for a short time in New York, a job he says he could not do again. He married in 1959 and now has two daughters, with whom he has shared his farm since 1967. Harrison says his early reputation was founded on four volumes of poetry, *Plain Song, Locations, Outlyer,* and *Letters to Yesenin*. But he now believes he is known primarily for his three novels. In addition to his books, he has written for *Sports Illustrated, Esquire,* and the *New York Times Book Review.*

His first novel, *Wolf,* concerns one man's quest for identity and freedom through the primal levels of nature and sex. *A Good Day to Die*—which still brings unkind words—is a statement about the decay of America's ecology and how a band of individuals try to turn back the tide of civilization by blowing up a dam. His most recent work, *Farmer,* published earlier this year, is the account of a middle-aged schoolteacher and his battle to choose between a nymphet student and a widowed co-worker.

Compared to Hemingway, Henry Miller, James Dickey, even Rabelais, Jim Harrison remains an eclectic soul who generally avoids the literary crowd, preferring local farmers and country people. Yet he has traveled from coast to coast, in France, South America, and Africa. The only livable American city is San Francisco, he says, and when he visits there he and fellow author Richard Brautigan enjoy bar-hopping together. But such indulgences are permitted only two months a year; the other months are devoted to working, sometimes locking himself in a shed—during the summer—or upstairs in a bare room lined with John MacDonald novels, for up to nineteen hours a day.

He prefers Wakoski over Plath, Chandler over Hammett, Hunter Thompson over James Reston. He admires the stamina of Joseph's Nez Perce Indians, and borrowed Chief Joseph's quote, "today is a good day to die" for the title for his second novel.

He here discusses his work (including his latest project, a comic novel about Traverse City), drugs, the Nobel Prize, hunting, sex, death, Michigan State, Detroit, movies, country music, literary critics, and on and on. Slowly a portrait of the man and the artist emerges. The picture starts here . . .

Chronicle: What do you think of book reviewers and critics?

Harrison: Well, I think there's a difference between book reviewers and critics. Book reviewers are largely what we call in the trade pork and beaners. It's such an ill paying job that you find that anyone with a very distinguished intelligence is not interested. I mean the only people that pay well for reviews is the *New York Times.* I reviewed a few times a year for the *Times* Book Review and it pays decently. But your average newspaper reviewer doesn't pay well at all. No, I never pay any particular attention to them. I just got a big batch of reviews from Spain where *A Good Day to Die* came out, but I don't read Spanish so I have no idea what they say.

Chronicle: How long have you been writing?

Harrison: Oh, I started when I was sixteen. But you know how you start, it's largely a joke. It was another eleven years before I published anything. That was the first book of poems. I was living in Boston and sent some to a poet I'd heard about and she'd just become a consulting editor for *Norton* and she said "Do you have some more" and I did and she took the book. Actually, when I signed my first book contract I'd never published anything in a magazine, which is sort of ass backwards. it was a stroke of luck.

Chronicle: Are you still writing poetry?

Harrison: Oh, yeah. That's the center, you know. I started out, actually, writing fiction—short stories—but I've never published a short story. I wrote about twenty but I couldn't even find them now. It's the most exacting form, to work within the short form, same thing with poetry. You start short.

Chronicle: Your work doesn't appear to be the work of an academician so why did you work to earn your masters?

Harrison: The worst thing about academic writers and people who teach writing or live within an academic atmosphere is that it shears them of a base. People think after they teach a while that academic life is a microcosm of the rest of the world, which it very clearly isn't. It's sort of . . . well, do you read Hesse at all? He wrote a book called *Magister Ludi* which is the bead game, a very closed, extraordinarily provincialized atmosphere, which maybe it should be for its purpose, for teaching. But I think that's terribly unhealthy for the writer, unless it's a writer of a particular kind. Let's say if I just continued writing poetry I would have been cornered into having to take a teaching position. Literally no one can make a living as a literary novelist. Then I started writing longish type essays for the back of *Sports Illustrated* and they pay very well. So every time I'd write one of those I'd have three months to work on my own things.

Chronicle: Do you find the atmosphere more real here than in an academic community?

Harrison: I wouldn't say it's more real. God, there's nothing more unpleasantly real than an academic community. It's good to know every sort of person. In an academic atmosphere you're not going to know, say, the farmer down the road or the country bartenders.

Chronicle: How do you physically and mentally get set for writing?

Harrison: On a novel I crank up for a long time. I haven't written a novel

I haven't thought about writing for three years. When it gets ripe enough in my brain I just sit down and write it. I write the first draft in usually about six weeks. I work every day, all day. The kind of novels I've written, so far at least, you have to get it all down before you change your mind. The alternative is not bothering to write it at all. That's something you're fighting all the time, what (Thomas) McGuane calls the loss of cabin pressure. I've started another one the other day and this one I've been cranking up along time. For the first time I've taken a lot of notes because it's more elaborately structured than any novel I've worked with before.

Chronicle: Can you tell us about this new work?

Harrison: No, or I'll lose interest. It has to be a little foggy in your head so you can have some surprises when you sit down. It'll be my first comic novel.

Chronicle: Do you know how it ends?

Harrison: Yeah, I think. But I might change my mind by the time I get there. But you've got to keep it a little bit juicy and fuzzy. It's like a woman. Sometimes if you know her too well you lose interest, but if you can keep them deliciously mysterious you can at least maintain the fantasy. So it's worth going on. I wrote a bunch of screenplays last year and it was helpful in the sense that I wrote one comedy. I'm working on an idea now for (Jack) Nicholson whom I got to know over the last year and I don't have any idea whether it will be made or not.

Chronicle: What literary form do you feel most comfortable working in?

Harrison: None more than the other. I think if you've messed around as much as I have you tend to feel fairly comfortable in all of them.

Chronicle: Is writing hard?

Harrison: Oh, God yes. It's very definitely work.

Chronicle: Do you enjoy the actual process of writing?

Harrison: Yeah, that's the big thing. That's the only real reward you ever get out of it, is the joy of making a novel, in creating it. The pleasure once you get a little older, not to sound like an old crank, but the pleasure you get out of a really good review is about a minute and seventeen seconds. Although a really bad review can cause you anguish for a couple of days. But the thing that keeps you going is the pleasure of actually doing it.

Chronicle: Do you ever look through your books after they're finished?

Harrison: No, that would be sort of unhealthy. Occasionally when I'm very drunk I'll look just to see what I said and you can get some surprises because you don't really remember writing parts of it and it does interest you if you've forgotten it.

Chronicle: In *Farmer* there is a part which says Joseph poured himself a wishkey. Was that a typographical error?

Harrison: Oh of course it was. That book is the most free of typographical errors. But publishers have proofreaders, then my wife does it, then my daughter does it, then I do it, and you still have some errors. There's a printer's superstition that there has to be one error in a book, too. That's odd.

Chronicle: Do you try to avoid what might be called literary circles?

Harrison: I think it's only dangerous if you spend too much time in them. I think there has been a certain disintegration in Vonnegut's talents since he's moved to New York City. You didn't see that in *Breakfast of Champions,* but I think you do in this new book *Slapstick.* I don't like it at all but maybe it's only a momentary lapse. But he was a late comer and he wanted his little kick of being recognized. (Saul) Bellow said something beautiful once. He said loneliness to a writer—since it's basically a lonely trade—is like a giant whale trying to survive on a single piece of plankton.

Chronicle: Do you enjoy the recognition? Do you enjoy people coming into your home?

Harrison: No, I hardly ever let anybody into my home. I'm really awful that way. I generally run for the fucking closet. I'll admit if I'm in New York or something like that in a cafe it's nice to meet a lot of influential people that have actually read your work and want to see you and everything. But not on working days. I know a lot of people up here that actually read my novels but we don't talk about it; they don't bother me. A wonderful thing about living in a place like this is the privacy.

Chronicle: What do you think about contemporary novels and novelists?

Harrison: I think of my immediate generation, those people from thirty to forty, McGuane is the best. Ed Hoagland had a good essay and . . . it hasn't been a particularly juicy time for new novelists. I don't see all that many and I read addictively. I think it happened to the generation of the twenties. You didn't have any great number of good writers but you had three or four fabulous ones, like Faulkner, Hemingway, Fitzgerald, Sherwood Anderson, Dos Passos, so on like that. Now the people a generation ahead of me say those early forties or fifties you have a great number of really good writers, but no fabulous writers. It's sort of a reverse of the twenties. You've got a lot of fascinating novelists but you can't say, no matter how much you like Norman Mailer or Phillip Roth or Updike or any of those people, Updike, Hemingway or Updike, Faulkner. He's just not in that league.

Chronicle: Would you say Bellow, Faulkner?

Harrison: Yeah, I think almost. I really felt good about Bellow getting the prize because I don't know who else they could have given it to. Really an extraordinary mind. But I read most of what Mailer writes except his boxing stuff which is sort of projected nonsense. Everytime Mailer used to get drunk he wanted to arm wrestle somebody and you know anyone in any grain elevator throughout the midwest would've knocked him silly in a second. Know what I mean? I read my friends, like Brautigan, McGuane. The best novel of the last decade was clearly (Gabriel) Marquez's *One Hundred Years of Solitude.* It takes your breath away. Or Gunter Grass's *Tin Drum.* Fabulous book. I read everything Tom Berger writes, Peter Matthiessen I love too. There's a reverse snobbism, too. Someone like Ed Doctorow was a very literary novelist and nobody ever bought his books so he wrote *Ragtime,* which I thought was a lovely book, very entertaining. Then everybody comes down on his case for writing a mass appeal book like that. When I used to go around giving poetry readings and they hear you've written some screenplays you're always getting lectured about integrity by full professors who make three times as much as you. They're on the take from the state, as it were. Oh, you've gone Hollywood, whatever that means. It's largely an assortment of pimps and coke dealers, that's what Hollywood is, you know? The pimps being the agentry. It's an amusing place once you get used to it. I really got a sense of non-arrival when I was sitting at the pool at the Sunset Marquis. I recognized the people on either side of me and I was trying to think . . . and on one side of me reading was Harry Reems of *Deep Throat* and on the other side was Kinky Freedman of Kinky Freedman and the Texas Jewboys. He's a wonderful character. Writers, I think, are sometimes productive to the extent that they remain sort of child-like about certain things. They stay operative for that reason. That's the other thing. How can you stay child-like when you're at a university?

Chronicle: Why do you write about ordinary people, outside the university community?

Harrison: Because the people in Morrill Hall bore me. A farmer who lives with an allegiance to a 200 thousand year old agricultural cycle is infinitely more interesting to talk to. They notice things, their head isn't so full that they can't see things. But that's coming down a bit too hard because I also like to talk to auto company executives on airplanes. That's really fascinating. They tend to bark when they talk. They always want to tell you how unhappy they are. You ever go into Beggar's Banquet? It's such a shock to get a good meal in this state in a restaurant. I went to Detroit once four years ago. That was unbelievable. I was supposed to do a story for *Sports Illustrated* on bar pool so I took a local hustler and bartender from here and went down to Detroit. It was unbelievable. It's like the old west, everybody's armed to the teeth and shooting at each other. Totally grotesque.

Chronicle: Is that the only time you've been to Detroit?

Harrison: Yes. Except through the airport. I don't see any reason to go there at all. I met the executive editor of the *Free Press* and he asked me if I ever wanted to write anything for them and I said yes, I want to write about Detroit as a basement city. All the grief their teams have given me since I was a little boy. Following the Tigers and the Lions, and I followed them faithfully for twenty five years. You get to be one of these old fools who sits around talking about Bobby Lane. You read Bellow?

Chronicle: Some.

Harrison: I don't know. I don't know what you're particularly interested in because I thought of the whole compulsion to write novels as one that you don't largely examine. This idea of the goose trying to watch himself lay the golden egg, he's not going to do it. I'm having fun trying to write a long comedy about Traverse City. Maybe I'll have to move away when it comes out.

Chronicle: Is there material?

Harrison: Oh, yes. It's just like every place else, all that sense of self-congratulation that small cities have. It's not any different than Babbittry in *Main Street.* Sinclair Lewis, forty years ago. Lot of extremely pleasant people, though.

Chronicle: What about Hemingway?

Harrison: I don't really think about him much. I started doing a column for *Esquire* which I ran out of patience with after five months just because I don't have anything left of my journalism boogie. So I wrote about five columns for *Esquire* under "Outdoors." They wanted me to do a column on Hemingway and, it was one of the most difficult things I ever tried because it was only six pages. It occurred to me that I never examined my feelings about him. In some senses he was just such a pompous, wretched human being, in that macho sense. On the other side he was an unquestionably brilliant writer. A lot to admire about what the man did.

Chronicle: What about the Hemingway comparisons?

Harrison: Oh, I don't like those at all. I don't see any similarities, but maybe that's unusual. You know he was a doctor's son and doctors' sons—this is another off-the-wall comment—are peculiarly arrogant for some reason. And I can like them very much. Growing up in northern Michigan in an agriculture family naturally I fished and hunted, then when you reach the age of majority and you start reading Hemingway and you write books yourself and then somebody tells you because you're fascinated with fishing and hunting you're like Hemingway. Well, that's nonsense, you know? Faulkner fished and hunted all the time but it wasn't so well publicized. But it's fun talking to people in Key West who are illiterate but used to know Hemingway. I once met an old Cuban fisherman down there and we asked him about Hemingway and all he said was he's a wonderful boxer and was like a hippie—he didn't wear shoes. And that's all he remembered about Ernest Hemingway, that he was a wonderful fighter and didn't wear shoes. I think Faulkner had it down pat when he said it doesn't matter if a good writer has a swimming pool because he's a good writer, and if a bad writer has a swimming pool doesn't matter because he's a bad writer. Something crazy like that. But that's a particularly Zen functional attitude that those people had. You know a marvelous writer like Henry Miller is a health-giving writer.

Chronicle: With whom you've also been compared.

Harrison: Yeah, I don't think about that too much. Anytime in my twenties when I got depressed, I could read someone like Henry Miller and get out of it. Such tremendous thrust from his own late liberation. He didn't print a book until he was forty three, I think it was.

Chronicle: Who, then, do you think has influenced you?

Harrison: Oh, everybody influences you. You just usually resent it when you see it in a review.

Chronicle: One review said Rabelais. How about it?

Harrison: Oh, a little bit, yeah. I always enjoyed reading him. You learn technically how to put together a novel in an interesting way. McGuane said he learned more from Raymond Chandler about putting together a novel than anybody else, and I certainly feel that way. Chandler and John MacDonald. I love to read MacDonald. I've read all fifty of them. Other people you learn nothing from but enjoy equally. Like Joyce. After Joyce there's no follow-up to *Finnegan's Wake*. He took that particular form as far as it goes. What could someone conceivably write after that?. But it was a very gradual process, taking thirty-five years of his life. Oddly enough, I like some of the late Hemingway. I loved *Islands in the Stream*. That was the first book where curiously enough he could write about his children. He'd softened to the extent that he was less concerned with his own heroics. It was sort of a twilighter, an autumnal book.

Chronicle: Have you seen Mary Hemingway's book?

Harrison: Oh, I read some reviews of it, yeah. I don't largely like that kind of book. Well, I'll read it probably but mostly it's a self-protective collection of gossip, probably. Though I guess she admits how bad he could be.

Chronicle: Would you like to talk about *Wolf?*

Harrison: If you'd like. *Wolf* is a strange book to me because what happens is you write a book and then you're all done with it and I still get kind of curious, off the wall mail from that book. I got a strange letter from a guy that parked cars in Indianapolis in these big car lots, and they have this little shed in the middle and somebody had a paperback of *Wolf* and he read it and this almost total illiterate immigrant wrote me this letter about it. You know you get that strange kind of response to some things you write. McGuane and I were fishing in Key West and he said, 'you got a Guggenheim why don't you write a novel?' What had happened was I had a terrible hunting accident. I'd fallen down a cliff and it really screwed up my back and I had to be in traction at Munson (Medical Center in Traverse City). I just sat there and said gee, why don't I write a novel. It's intensely autobiographical because I couldn't think of anything else to write about. It's probably eighty-five, ninety per cent autobiographical.

Chronicle: What's the connection in your work between hunting and nature and sex?

Harrison: I'm not sure where the nexus of that would be. I don't think I hunt acquisitively, and when I did I was never a good shot. I don't know if that could be construed as being more or less sexual or not. In hindsight I'd say *Wolf* was basically about freedom, the compulsion to be free and to work it out for one's self.

Chronicle: How did the idea for *Farmer* come to you?

Harrison: With the smell of a weed in the barnyard. I wanted to somehow pay some debt to a way of life that was almost totally vanished. That is, a small farm as a way of life. You know when you get done with a novel you're walking around in a daze, you've been so immersed in it it's just a delicious feeling to work for a long time on something that gives you a great pleasure. After you finish it, though, you tend to have a total post-natal depression. In seven, eight books now I've never found out how to avoid that. I wish I could. Most people never get totally wiped out except sexually, and that's really the only time you're freed of your ego. That's why people in the sixties loved acid as much as they did because it freed you, if only for eight hours. Then I think people got scared of it.

Chronicle: Joseph drinks quite a bit in *Farmer,* Swanson drinks and smokes marijuana in *Wolf.* What are your feelings about smoking dope and other sorts of drug using?

Harrison: I don't smoke very much dope. I don't know anything I can say very interesting about drugs that's worth quoting. Just about everybody smokes a little dope. I don't think it's mystical. But I think the only drug I've had real problems with in my life has been alcohol, which has to be considered a drug like any other drug.

Chronicle: Have you ever tripped?

Harrison: Oh yeah, yeah. Not any great deal. You know, it's a funny thing, at Michigan State in 1960, I heard from a friend that you could write away and order peyote. And you could then. It was legal. There were no laws against peyote, so we sent off and for $15 we got 100 peyote buttons from Smith Cactus Ranch, which had some fame at the time in Albuquerque, New Mexico. Sure enough. In the mail they come in a big box. There's all these little green, rotty looking mushrooms, so we all sat there at night and just started chomping them down. We had absolutely no idea what we were doing, and you know, of course, about three days later . . . bleah! It was one of those total overdose numbers. I did about fifteen buttons of peyote. That was an impulse that took me years to get over. Although it was a very positive thing, because I don't believe in tripping if you're going to control it all. I don't see the point in these people who take a half a tab of half-assed acid. What's the point in it? I think a lot of people who don't do it should have at one point, you know?

Chronicle: What are your feelings about women's liberation?

Harrison: Well, I've gotten into an awful lot of trouble with those people, and not through any meaning myself. It's just like Diane Wakoski on my last novel—she's a very brilliant woman and she had felt I was condescending to women in there. But that was a fictional perogative. She knew from me myself that I wasn't particularly that way. But I've really gotten irrationally laced into by those people so often in reviews and so on that I always feel very beleaguered, that nothing I can say will be the right thing to say.

I've been married seventeen years—I'm absolutely for them getting every perogative that they can get, that any male has. I think that it's delightful in the sense that women are getting predatory like men used to be. I think it's very nice for them. It seems to be a saner situation than it used to be. American males are so basically assinine about sex. I mean, look at things like *Oui* and *Penthouse* and *Playboy*. It's just really startling if you try to remove yourself and think about it. It seems like they would really go after those people. Maybe they do, I don't know. All this new, radical scientific information about female sexuality is really startling. This new Hite book (Shere Hite's *The Hite Report*) that just came out. She just proves even Masters and Johnson were sort of a Rube Goldberg operation.

Anything that eases pain and frees people, I'm for. I hate to be blamed, though, for all the generalized repression, and I've gotten that at certain poetry readings. I was going to bring suit against one anthology because they used one of my poems to demonstrate male chauvinism. But they also used Yeats's poem, the one that's about No one could love you for yourself for not your beautiful hair and all that kind of thing. And they used Jagger's *Honky Tonk Woman.*

Chronicle: A good collection.

Harrison: Yeah, Waylon Jennings actually sings that better than Jagger, because you know Jennings has at least had sufficient amount of experience in the area, where Jagger doesn't sing it with great conviction. It's a lovely song. But, since I've freed my own self, I don't want to be blamed for anybody else's bondage. With women, it is a very individual case. They're really rapaciously throwing out dumb husbands now, which I think should have happened long ago. You notice how much more direct and aggressive women are compared to say, five, six years ago? And it's even gotten up here, totally. Women can go to bars alone now where they never used to. It's odd that it's all happened without people all noticing it.

Chronicle: In *Farmer,* Joseph's father, though dead, played a big part in his life.

Harrison: Well, I can't remember who this new lady is who is writing so much about death.

Chronicle: Elisabeth Kubler-Ross.

Harrison: Kubler-Ross, yeah. I talked to an analyist-poet friend of mine, who was at Michigan State for a while, about this situation. Death is about the most important thing that can happen to you mentally. I mean the death of someone you love very much. Because other than having the loved one taken away from you very abruptly, it also reminds you for the first time that you're going to die. I mean the utter reality of death. Well, (Garcia) Lorca said, what's there to write about except love, and suffering and death? They're the most notable things that happen in your life. In terms of Melville, they're about incomprehension. You come to that final black well when somebody dies because you basically don't comprehend it. You can't. Your animal body can't comprehend it. You think you know about it, but until it happens, nobody comprehends it at all.

Chronicle: In *Farmer* when Joseph's mother dies, the euthanasia bit was pretty subtle yet powerful. What about that?

Harrison: This tripey Jesuit at Notre Dame really attacked me for that in some review. Why sure, that's the hope for the naturalness of the book, of course. They're going to let her die and help her along, because that form of pain—that's why I picked stomach cancer—is the most brutal pain conceivable. You're never free from it. There's no pain like that. The body is literally rotting from the inside. That's what Mailer called the wild orgy of lost cells. Christ, it's up to the person, in my mind. When there's no recourse, some choose to live and some choose . . . I like that new California bill that lets people make that choice. These life support systems of course are so extraordinarily subtle now that they can keep you cooking until the last cell gives up the ghost.

Chronicle: What are your favorite motion pictures and who are your favorite directors?

Harrison: Directors, I like Bergman, Fellini, Truffaut. I like crappy movies. I have a great appetite for junk like Don Siegal does, like *Dirty Harry.* I loved it. I've watched it about four times. It was entertainment. You had a real villain. That guy had to be the nastiest human being in the history of

American fiction. Siegal does it so unfairly, it's really an extraordinarily fascist, junkie movie. He sets it all up. Once the guy pulls the girl's tooth out, everybody wants him to be blown away, when big Clint Killgood comes up with his 44. But see, people want Nicholson's character's rough. He knows how to choose scripts. He's a brilliant man. Did you see *Cuckoo's Nest?* A wonderful movie, I thought.

Chronicle: What about Robert Altman?

Harrison: I liked *McCabe. Nashville,* I thought, was horrid. I love country music. None of them were good, except Keith Carradine. That song was the only good song in there. The rest of them were sort of parodic rip-offs. Real country music doesn't have irony in it. When you let all of these flaky actors make up their own country songs, its abuse of freedom. I enjoyed it in the sense I enjoy all Altman movies just to look at, but as a movie it was too self-conscious.

Chronicle: You didn't mention Kubrick.

Harrison: I'm not too crazy about Kubrick. It's too self-conscious again. I liked *2001* and I liked that one he made out of the Anthony Burgess novel (*A Clockwork Orange*). That was a delicious movie. I didn't see that new one (*Barry Lyndon*). I understand it's very boring. I don't see how you can do anything with someone like Ryan O'Neal. I don't want to be reminded that we're seeing a work of art in progress. I want the raw meat thrown on the floor. I want the work of art there instead of it being self-actuating, like the least successful Truffaut movie to me is *Day for Night,* which is a movie about a movie. The only person who seems to get away with that is Fellini, because he has a marvelous sense of humor. . . . The same thing in a novel—I get tired of novels about professionals. *Wolf* is a novel about a professional, as opposed to the other two novels which were about people. But I don't know, that's a fine line. One of the great novels of the twentieth century was Joyce's *Portrait of the Artist as a Young Man,* so maybe I'm a little bit supersensitive about that. The most inspirational literature I ever read was Dostoevsky or Camus. Then I believe his assertions when he says you only have one choice in your life: it's whether or not to commit suicide. If you don't commit suicide, you have to treat your life with a great deal of energy and assertiveness. As a novelist, you don't want to withhold the evidence. I think that's the error in some of Hemingway's fiction as opposed to Faulkner, who had more of a tendency to allow them to be whole human beings. Hemingway had a tendency to the ideology.

Chronicle: What response to your work is most gratifying?

Harrison: I don't know. I think the best thing I ever heard was something Kafka said, "A book should serve as an axe for the frozen sea within us." If a book doesn't sort of break up your mind a little bit and give you a new sense of people, however small, then it's not worth reading.

Chronicle: What about John Gardner, John Barth, and Thomas Pynchon?

Harrison: Gardner I've never been able to read. Barth I could read—the early Barth but not the late stuff. By the time he got to *Giles Goat-Boy,* he sort of lost me. *End of the Road* I loved. I think that's the best Barth novel. And Pynchon, I didn't like *Gravity's Rainbow,* but what's the previous novel? *V,* yeah. I liked *V.* But you can't be nationalistic, you have to look far and wide for your reading interests. There's no sense of talking about thinking about Pynchon when you've got someone else who did the same thing so much better, like Gunter Grass in *Dog Years* or *Tin Drum.* Everybody can have reverence for Faulkner or reverence for Hemingway, but that kind of novel has stabilized. It's a static experience in the past, largely about heroics which no longer has a top. The world had a top for Faulkner and it did for Hemingway. There were those old eternal verities: duty, honor, love, pride, pity. But we don't quite live with that world anymore. It's much nastier in many respects and the lines have blurred much more than they were before. The literary brain now has a great deal less structure.

Chronicle: Have you heard they are making a movie of Hunter Thompson's *Fear and Loathing in Las Vegas.*

Harrison: I don't see how they can. I always used to believe his political articles because when he first heard about Watergate rather than rationalizing and making a big sentententious paragraph about it he said, what I really want to do is take a gunney sack full of dead rats down to the White House and throw it over the fence. As an image it's much more convincing than someone like James Reston going on pompously for pages and pages.

Chronicle: Why do you want to write a comic novel?

Harrison: I don't mean comic in terms of slapstick. I mean comic in the classical sense that everything is not tragic. In good comic novels people die. I just wanted to tilt my world. I never can bear to do the same thing in two books in a row.

Chronicle: Where do you want to be in ten years?

Harrison: I just want to write some more novels.

Contemporary Authors Interview
Jean W. Ross / 1981

From *Contemporary Authors, New Revision Series,* vol. 8, ed. Ann Evory and Deborah A. Straub (Detroit: Gale Publishing, 1983), 227–29. Copyright © 1983 by The Gale Group. Reprinted with permission of The Gale Group.

CA interviewed Jim Harrison by phone 7 October 1981, at his home in Lake Leelanau, Michigan.

CA: You've been away recently. Were you out promoting your new book, *Warlock?*

Harrison: No, I've been out to Los Angeles figuring out how I'm going to make this year's living. I don't like to do any book promotion. I've never done any.

CA: Being at home on your Michigan farm seems to be very important to you, yet you travel a lot, both for work and for pleasure. Is the contrast necessary to your writing?

Harrison: I think so. I live in northern Michigan, where I was born and raised. It's where I feel the best in the world, and it's the only place I've ever been able to write—I've never been able to write in transit. Also, I have a place further north here, a cabin on a river in the Upper Peninsula. My nearest neighbor there is five miles away. I like that sort of thing. If you have to go to Los Angeles and New York a lot where everything's enervating, it's nice not to have anything to do with that during other times.

CA: In his *Washington Post* article, Gordon Chaplin wrote about how much you enjoy telling stories. Was there a storytelling tradition in your family?

Harrison: To a certain extent, I would say, on both sides of the family. The families were large and basically rural, and such people are always storytellers. My dad could never bear to say the same thing the same way. You know, when people spend a lot of their lives based in some kind of oral tradition, they're much more careful about the words and they make a much greater attempt to make what they say interesting. They also have a lot of time to talk if everyone is poor and there's no television. I think you have the same thing in any rural region, even in the countryside of, say, northern France.

CA: How did your early interest in writing begin?

Harrison: I guess with a ninth-grade teacher who started giving me books that I couldn't ordinarily have gotten. But I didn't have anything specific in mind. Even when I ran off to New York and California when I was nineteen, I still didn't know what I wanted to write, so I wrote short stories at that time and then started writing poems. I wrote poems until I was thirty-one or thirty-two, then I wrote my first novel.

CA: Was writing poetry a kind of deliberate apprenticeship, as it is for some writers?

Harrison: Usually it is, almost inadvertently. For instance, the houseguest I have now from Alabama just gave me William Faulkner's first book of poems. Even Hemingway wrote poems; Sherwood Anderson did. I suppose it's partly because you have so many hormones in your twenties and thirties that you can't sit down for that long haul that's known as writing a novel, yet your feelings are inexpressibly intense at the time, so you take it out on poetry. I still write poetry. In fact, Delacorte is going to publish my selected poems next year. About a third of the poems will be new ones.

CA: You've been described as something of a nonconformist as an undergraduate at Michigan State. Was it hard for you to stay on for your M.A.?

Harrison: It was hideous. As an undergraduate I think I had quit half a dozen times. But the man in the scholarship office was sympathetic with my desire to be an author. I think he was Michigan State's first Rhodes scholar; he was interested in literature. So he'd always give my scholarship back to me when I came back. But then I sort of flunked out of the M.A. program. They rearranged the degree requirements for me when I published my first book of poems with Norton. They had to waive the language exams. I'm the only person I know of who actually got an F in a graduate course.

CA: Has the M.A. been worthwhile at all in your writing?

Harrison: Not at all. I never took any writing courses, except a course in writing essays when I was a sophomore. The teacher had the odd idea that the way to get people to write essays was to have them imitate other people, so we wrote essays in the fashion of Henry James and so on. That was good teaching. If you don't have an incredible playfulness about language, I think you tend to write boring novels. Auden talked about that. Being a writer requires an intoxication with language, an obsession with language. You get the meaning later, because you don't have a great sense of meaning when you're first finding this out—it's the hormones again.

CA: Very young children are fascinated by the sounds of language before they have any real sense of meaning, but that seems to be educated out of us.

Harrison: Oh, for sure. That's because of the banality of the school system. And literature isn't now and never was nor ever will be a popular taste. It's all a mistake to think that literacy has any real meaning other than a very functional one: most quasi-literate people only read the comic strips or the sports page. The importance of literacy in the United States is basically for people to know what they're signing so they won't be swindled.

CA: I noticed that *A Good Day to Die* had been published in Spain. Have you gotten much mail or other response from readers of the translation?

Harrison: Really quite a bit. I got an enormous sheaf of Spanish reviews, which I've never read because I don't read Spanish. That novel in particular seems to be perfect for them. *Legends of the Fall* sold better in England than it did here, oddly enough. One thing, I guess, is that Bernard Levin gave it a huge review in the *Times* in London, and his reviews have a lot of authority. It was certainly a more interesting review than I've ever gotten in America.

CA: *Legends of the Fall* brought financial success the earlier books had failed to bring. How were you affected by the rush of publicity that came with it?

Harrison: It was a real mess for a while, because I had been poor for about forty years, you know, and then I got really *not* poor. That was confusing for about two and a half years until I started spending a lot of my time with my family; then the confusion went away and I became sane again. But before I became sane again, I made a lot of dumb investments. I made no investment that I wasn't able to halve in one year—English gambling stock, Australian oil stock, a charter boat in Key West, a lot of personal loans to indigent friends, unsecured, written off for ever and ever. I don't care now.

CA: You've helped a lot of friends who were trying to get established as writers, haven't you?

Harrison: You try to, but it's very difficult. The only novel I think I ever helped immediately get published was Tom McGuane's *The Sporting Club*, just because I knew someone at Simon and Schuster. Tom had fired his agent suddenly. I took it to Richard Locke, who was then at Simon and Schuster, and he only took twenty-four hours to get it accepted there. That was fun.

CA: Commenting on the style of the title novella of *Legends of the Fall*, Vance Bourjaily wrote in the *New York Times Book Review,* "In compression, unexpectedly, lies credibility." Did it take a lot of revision to achieve the narrative leanness of "Legends of the Fall"?

Harrison: That's the one about which an unnamed publisher asked me wouldn't it be wonderful if I had written that in a 400-page form. Long books are popular because people think they're getting a good deal. It didn't take a lot of revision; I only took out one sentence after the first draft. That novella came sort of pouring out. I wanted to tell a tale like a romance, sort of like "Once upon a time. . . ." What you do is create the illusion in the first paragraph that this actually happened. You're very matter-of-fact about it.

CA: How are plans proceeding for the movie version of "Revenge"?

Harrison: "Revenge" is still owned by Warner, and they've got John Huston on it now. I think he's a fine director, when you consider the number of really good pictures he's done. He's not terribly popular with the studios, because he's such a wonderfully arrogant, powerful human being. He can get away with wearing a cape. I've had dinner a number of times with Orson Welles, and I like him too. "Legends" is owned by Twentieth Century-Fox. "The Man Who Gave Up His Name" is owned by Columbia.

CA: You've been writing screenplays on contract for Warner Brothers now for several years. Are you enjoying the work?

Harrison: I've finished my Warner Brothers contract. But the way it works for me is that after I finish a novel I have a big overflow of energy for about a year and a half, and that's the time I feel I can write screenplays with impunity. And they're actually sort of fun to write, because I've tried a number of times to write a play for the theater but have never been able to. I'm still trying, in fact; I've started another one this year. I suppose screenplays are an overflow too of that passion that started on my senior trip to New York when I saw Eugene O'Neill's *The Iceman Cometh*.

CA: Would you like to respond to the criticism that you sometimes portray women shallowly and in a chauvinistic way?

Harrison: It's OK as long as you don't say the word *macho,* which has literally driven me up the tree. No, I think in *Warlock* that's definitely not true. Someone told me, at least, that that was my first major woman. It's just that I don't suppose I ever knew them well enough. Certainly no one could present women as shallow as women novelists often do. Feminism as such has too many didactic tenets to expect novelists to follow now. Novelists write stories; they don't write tracts. When I've presented a shallow woman, it was because she *was* a shallow woman; she was no more shallow than the man—as in *A Good Day to Die*. Also, I certainly don't want to pretend to more knowledge about women than I have, just to curry favor. Most women are still like Tibet to me; though I've studied Tantric Buddhism at some length, I still don't feel I comprehend it. The only thing I really resent is *macho*. I know a lot about Mexican culture, and as I've pointed out, macho is when you throw a rattlesnake in a baby carriage or bite off your mother's toe—some kind of overpowering violence.

CA: You work in a very concentrated way—long hours—on a specific project, then rest when it's done. Are you able to free your mind of writing during the periods of rest?

Harrison: Of course not, but generally you're so exhausted that you can't write any longer. Since I was born and raised here a lot of my preoccupations are with hunting, fishing, things like that. (And that may be one reason I'm so highly criticized by the feminist press.) Some New York critic said that the people in *Farmer* couldn't have actually existed. That's because people on America's dream coasts—both East and West—don't largely have any comprehension of the Midwest. Or the deep South; the fashionable opinion is that any white Southerner is ipso facto a bigot.

CA: You care a great deal about nature. In an *Esquire* article you wrote, "If the next good country doesn't exist it's because we pillaged the last one we so stridently walked through." Do you play an active role in any organized conservation movement?

Harrison: No, I don't, because I can't bear them, but I just won a big environmental suit that cost me in the five figures personally. I didn't take donations because I just wanted to win the suit and I didn't want it to be messy.

CA: What kind of suit was it—or do you want to talk about it?

Harrison: Not really, because it's a sore point up here. It was about an illegal and totally unwarranted dredging activity. So I pursue conservation to that extent. But I find that conservation groups are very busy with language: they think if they get the language right, then everything's OK. But that's not what it takes. You have to have power, and you have to have power resources equal to those of your opponent; so you have to organize yourself some way, either with cash or dynamite, to win. There's no sense sitting around convincing the convinced. You have to go after them with usually every legal means possible, and very immediately—there's not much time for meetings.

CA: Are there present or future projects you'd like to discuss? Anything you'd like to say for the record that's gotten left out of other interviews?

Harrison: I have started another novel, but it's a long one, my first long one, so it takes a long time.

CA: I know you've been unhappy with some of your interviews. Is there anything you'd like to add to this one?

Harrison: No, I don't think so. It never was any kind of inclusive or specific thing. I don't think I actually enjoy talking about myself. I don't mind talking about my work, but I've consistently turned down interviews that were based on personality. That's why I have a big sign in my front driveway that says, "Do not stop here without calling. This means *you*." I don't understand writers who want to be in some publicity-oriented limelight, because it's never based on people who are actually interested in the work.

An Interview with Jim Harrison
Kay Bonetti / 1984

From *The Missouri Review,* 8, no. 3 (1985), 65–86. Reprinted in *Conversations with American Novelists: The Best Interviews from* The Missouri Review *and the American Audio Prose Library,* ed. Kay Bonetti, Greg Michalson, Speer Morgan, Jo Sapp, and Sam Stowers (Columbia: University of Missouri Press, 1997), 39–55. Also available in a longer, unedited version with additional material as an audio cassette from American Prose Library, P. O. Box 842, Columbia, MO 62505, (1-800-447-2275). Reprinted by permission of Kay Bonetti and American Audio Prose Library.

Interviewer: Could you tell us about your publishing history? You published a whole book of poems without ever having a single poem published.

Harrison: I'd heard Denise Levertov read and I never published anything in my life. So I sent her poems and she wrote back that she'd just become the consulting editor at Norton and if I had more poems like this she would publish a book. After I got the book contract, I sent some poems off and they came out about the same time as the book, but that was true. It was an accident.

Interviewer: What happened with *Wolf?* How come you moved from three volumes of poetry to the novel?

Harrison: I fell off a cliff. I was in the hospital for a month and went into a coma and almost died. I sort of woke up and I couldn't do anything. I had to wear a body corset because I'd torn the muscles away from my lower spine. So Tom McGuane called me up and says, "Now that you're laid up, why don't you write a novel?" I said, "Jeez, I don't want to think about writing a novel." "Write a sort of autobiographical novel," he said and I said, "Okay, goodbye." Then I started writing the novel. I wrote *Wolf* in six weeks or a month. I sent it off the day before the mail strike, years ago, and the only copy of it was lost for a full month. I didn't even think it was important, because I didn't think of myself as a novelist. I wasn't very attached to it. I'd sent it to my brother to make a copy because we were real broke. So he finally went into the New Haven post office and dug it out of the pile of mail there. I don't know how he managed that, but he's authoritative. Then the publisher got it and took it.

Interviewer: You also wrote some novellas . . .
Harrison: I always loved the work of Isak Dinesen, and Knut Hamsun,

who wrote three or four short novels, so I thought I would have a try at it. I called the first one "Revenge"—my Sicilian agent gave me a little motto that struck me: "Revenge is a dish better served cold." The second of the novellas is called "The Man Who Gave Up His Name." I wrote it in a time of extreme mental duress. I envisioned a man getting out of the life he had created with the same intricate carefulness that he'd got into it in the first place. I suppose I was pointing out that if you're ethical you can't just disappear.

Interviewer: You've described yourself as a sensual Calvinist.

Harrison: Maybe that's true. I wrote a poem in which I said John Calvin's down there under the floorboards telling me I don't get a glass of wine till four o'clock. Not 3:57, but 4:00. I was talking to Kurt Ludkey last night about how if you're a total workaholic and you also drink too much you tend to control it, but that doesn't make you less of an alcoholic. It's just that you never, never have more drinks than you can remember.

Interviewer: Can you really drink like that?

Harrison: I have done that for years. I had a little trouble in my early thirties with it and then I began tightly controlling it. I went down to a Mexican fat farm in January because I was so exhausted from my novel. And I felt grotesque, I felt about like I do right now. So I didn't drink anything. I expected it would be awful and nothing happened. I didn't feel anything. Reagan's immigration chief was at this fat farm, and I said to him "don't you realize that you guys are hassling the greatest writer in the world about getting in and out of the United States?" I was talking about Marquez, who's the only writer on earth that I admire without qualification. He said, "Oh I didn't know that, what's the guy's name, we'll see what we can do."

Interviewer: Have they been denying him a visa?

Harrison: Yeah, they've been giving him trouble because they know he stops and sees Castro. But you know what he and Castro do all the time? Cook. They cook all night. He gets there and he has fresh stuff he's picked up in Caracas or Mexico City. They cook veal and chicken, everything like that. And drink of course.

Interviewer: Your books are full of great cooks.

Harrison: What I always liked in Boswell is the idea that if you're obligated to eat two or three times a day, you may as well do a good job of it. I once stopped to see John MacDonald and Betty Friedan was there and she asked me why I was so obsessed with cooking. I said, "Why, I cook to avoid adultery." And she says, "My God! are you a mess. To say such a thing." But it's sort of true. When I started cooking frequently, at least three times a week, my wife enjoyed it because it's no fun cooking if you have to cook all the time. And I could also avoid going to the bar when I finished my work day.

Interviewer: A lot of writers seem to have problems with alcohol. Do you think there's anything necessary about the life of the writer that leads to extreme pain?

Harrison: Well, no. I think it's partly the profession. You're alone most of the time. You're creating other worlds all the time. And it's what Walker Percy talks about in that last book of his—it's the reentry problem. You know how I say, or, I have my narrator say, "It's your return to earth like some kind of burned out satellite." Something like that. Alcohol is the sedative when you finish the day's work—it helps you to re-emerge into the world.

Interviewer: Would you say that your personal life has been something of a stabilizing force?

Harrison: Oh my, yeah. You know I've been married twenty-four and a half years. Not in the clingy sense, it's just the way I prefer to live. Every time I think I'm a mess, a total mess, I sort of look around and find out that I'm not quite a total mess. It's like McGuane said, that alcoholism is a writer's black lung disease. Which is sort of true. But even that I seem to have under control. I suppose that's a moralistic urge. Just to control. To control it.

Interviewer: You have that passage in *Sundog* where Strang says something about having made up rules when he was a kid. The narrator, Harrison, says, "I love rules." Can you tell me some of the rules?

Harrison: Do I have any fresh rules? Yeah. I was on page like 197 of that novel manuscript before I realized I was writing about my alter ego, and it blew one writing day. It totally terrified me.

Interviewer: How so?

Harrison: Strang worked on eleven dams, and I'd written eleven books. I mean it got that bad. And I felt utterly crippled. Just like Strang's been crippled by his work. I said, "Oh my god! Can I go on?" Well the energy of the novel had taken over, so it didn't matter.

Interviewer: The book is, by no means like, but reminds me of, *The Secret Sharer*. You wonder at the end about the secret sharer. Whether or not it's one person or two.

Harrison: That's giving me goosebumps. James Hillman, who's a Jungian psychiatrist, said that thing I quoted "The notion that there's a light at the end of the tunnel has mostly been a boon to pharmaceutical companies." I love that.

Interviewer: Would you explain that?

Harrison: Well, tranquilizers and everything like that. It's because people think they can't bear the nowness of now. They can't bear the present tense. In Zen terms they're either rehearsing something they've already done, to make it come out right. Or they're expecting something to occur in the future. Or trying to change the past. It's like somebody might say, I'm revising my memoirs. I mean something ludicrous like that. A person like Strang is free from dread because he's consented totally to the present. Whereas the narrator, which is another portion of me, can't, can't accept anything.

Interviewer: Where did you get the character Strang?

Harrison: My brain. I met a few people, in an outward way, that did what he did. And I tried to create the kind of person they would become. On frequent trips all over the world, I would meet these men sometimes in hotels, and I'd ask them what they do. I met one in Costa Rica that was a foreman on a huge construction project, and in charge of 32,000 workers on this dam in the Amazon Basin. He was self-educated, from Tennessee. I became more and more interested in these people and then the character took shape. I wanted to create a hero who was free from dread. Dread and irony have gotten to be literary addictions. And I noticed there are some people that live without it. So I created this character named Strang. When I was thirteen I read about King Strang over here on Beaver Island. He was a Mormon apostate, and he had fifty girlfriends or wives. When you're thirteen you're horny as a toad and you don't even have one girlfriend and here's a guy that's got fifty. So this is what I had in mind. A man free from dread. Maybe that's what I wanted—to be free from dread. I mean besides wanting a drink, I also want to be free from dread.

Interviewer: It has been said that Strang is the metaphor for the artist. How much do you use yourself, in your work?

Harrison: Strang isn't me though.

Interviewer: What about the sub-title, *As Told to Jim Harrison.*

Harrison: That was just to have fun. Like Nabokov, I did that to throw people off the track. It is a little bit myself, but I had to have a contrast to

Strang. I had to have somebody coming from way outside, coming into this world. And I had to know both people. You could say they're almost extremities of the right and left lobes of the same head.

Interviewer: You wrote this novel as a para-journalistic escapade.

Harrison: I was just pissed off. Everything is a novelty. Somebody's most utter and terrible grief is a minute and a half of the evening news. That kind of thing. I was thinking of David Kennedy at twelve sitting in that hotel room watching his father die. He didn't ever get over it.

Interviewer: Strang says almost immediately, "Tell me something bad that you've never really gotten over."

Harrison: I forgot I said that. But that's it. Like his niece can't get over being raped, any better than Karl can get over it. Karl was a strange character. Some people wanted more of him but Karl's effective because there's not more of him. He's the kind of guy that's terribly sensitive but often verges on being the town bully, because he is so eccentric. Karl on a surface level is very attractive to some people for the same reason they like Clint Eastwood. He got back at them. Tom McGuane had a motto over his kitchen door saying "Getting even is the best revenge." And that's okay, but Steve McQueen was out there and he looked at the motto and he said, "Tom, even *I'm* not that bad. That's really going too far."

Interviewer: In many ways that book is as much the narrator's book as it is Strang's.

Harrison: Well, it's unpleasant because everything the narrator could say is true to my experience. But you need a contrast. Strang isn't Strang if the whole book is Strang. The narrator comes to Strang. It's almost like that notion of monkey brain. You can't often evaluate yourself because it's your own brain that's evaluating your own brain. Supposedly what removes us from animals is that we can stand back and look. But it's sometimes confusing. My cabin is the cabin that Strang is living in. So I go up there and I say, "Oh, my god, now I'm living in this novel, and I'm not sure which one I am."

Interviewer: And you took a swim like Strang, to test that swim.

Harrison: Last summer I did. I swam down the river.

Interviewer: Are you that strong a swimmer? Can you swim like Strang swims?

Harrison: Yeah, I used to swim. I remember when I was ten I swam twelve miles. When I was seven, there was a loon on our lake, and I never could get close to it so I thought, "I'll trick the loon, go out at night and try to catch her." So I snuck out of the cabin, off I went in the dark. When I was getting ready finally to write that novel, I did something similar for that last scene. It's two o'clock in the morning, I've had a few drinks. I locked my dog in the cabin, went down the steps to the river, took off my clothes and swam with the current way down the river, and over two log jams in the middle of the night so I could get that feeling. It's very strange to swim down a river at night alone, naked. But that enabled me to imagine that last scene, say Julian and his son were down there, you'd see those lights off the trees, just the car lights way down.

Interviewer: The narrator and Strang are two sides of one being, together, it seems like. And the telling of the tale is the revelation of the wedding.

Harrison: What the narrator was finding in Strang is maybe what I found in the left side of my brain. And the tape device amplifies it, which is fun, because you have the more formal narrator, then you have the narrator off-the-wall. And some of the inserts have the narrator wondering what he's going to eat, wondering how he's going to get laid. Textural concretia, the "thinginess" of life. That's an old rule I have on the wall. Make it vivid.

Interviewer: Did you feel like you were taking a chance by letting in the possibility that Strang and the narrator really are brothers?

Harrison: No, I was flirting with that. No one will ever know. The only one that knew died.

Interviewer: The narrator is flirting with it. He wants to play with it and he doesn't.

Harrison: It was just an interesting possibility. But of course it's true.

Interviewer: They are brothers?

Harrison: It doesn't matter if they're blood brothers or what kind of brothers. That was all sort of unconscious. You write and you don't even know what you're writing when you're writing it. It just emerges.

Interviewer: At what point did you start realizing that you had a subject out of writing from what you know?

Harrison: Well, death did it to me. You can see it in my first book, *Plain Song*. If people die then you better get down to business.

Interviewer: This was your father and sister? They died in a car accident.
Harrison: That was part of it. That was when I was twenty-two and I'd been writing since I was sixteen. I wanted to write poems like John Keats.
Interviewer: You started out wanting to be a poet?
Harrison: It was all the same to me. I'd read those romantic novels about artists like Vincent Van Gogh and I was thinking that's what I want to be. I wanted to be a wild artist and have lots of love affairs and live in strange places. I have.

Interviewer: But I take it you've found out it's a lot more of a discipline than you thought?
Harrison: Oh, that's all it is. It's what Stevens said: technique is the proof of your seriousness.

Interviewer: Are you happy with *Sundog?*
Harrison: I don't know. It wouldn't occur to me to be happy with something I wrote. It's not healthy to even think about it.

Interviewer: After you've done it?
Harrison: Nope. It's all gone. I mean you're making me think about it now and it's not unpleasant. It's sort of interesting to get somebody else's point of view.

Interviewer: So you don't worry about judging or assessing your work?
Harrison: I don't think I'm very competitive about it. I don't see it as a horserace, the way some novelists are always rating each other. You know how in New York every day they take each other's temperature to see who's hot. I don't think that way too much.

Interviewer: You don't look back on a book and say I learned this problem in this novel?
Harrison: Oh, yeah. You do that to some extent. You write sometimes to find out what you know.

Interviewer: Do you think that the skills you learned in writing poetry transferred into your novels?
Harrison: Very much. Trying to bear down on the singularity of images. Movement. Those suites were good training for moving from image to mood to mood. It's like Mailer says, "Boy if you're worried about getting people in and out of rooms, you've already blown it." The reader can get anybody they want in and out of rooms. They don't need your help.

Interviewer: You often use animals in your work.

Harrison: It's the same idea that the Indians had. One is naturally drawn to certain animals more than other animals. Now I like crows and coyotes and pigs for some reason.

Interviewer: Have you ever thought that out?

Harrison: I could pretend that I don't know what the associations are, but I do. The coyote is a sorceror amongst animals. He's the trickster, he's the humpbacked flute player. He's an animal of immaculate, precise and varied means. Intense curiosity, but cagey. I think I like that idea. And a crow is a garrulous semi-predator, semi-scavenger. Sort of foolish, but smarter than other birds. He just likes to fool around. Squawk all the time.

Interviewer: You mentioned pigs. . . .

Harrison: Yeah, I had a pet pig when I was a kid. But you know they're all going to get killed in November. It's a bit of a disappointment. Was it Hugo that said, "All of us are condemned to death with an indefinite reprieve"? A sort of catchy idea. He says that the ultimate that a human leaves is his skull.

Interviewer: You use the animal point of view without it being a pathetic fallacy. To use one of those school terms.

Harrison: As Strang says, "What's the sense in drawing conclusions about human behavior from animals when you can draw conclusions about human behavior from humans?" There's a danger of extrapolating, but they're our fellow creatures and always have been. What's the sense of ignoring them? I'm writing now about the drama of an English department. Lots of writers are going to start writing about Government intervention in the arts. It's quieted literary magazines a great deal, you know.

Interviewer: You want to talk about that?

Harrison: I've just noticed it. Just like all the writers' schools have created less variety—there's a sameness. I said once that the Iowa Writers School on a yearly basis outproduces the English Romantic movement. It's all a delusion. What are you going to do with 4,000 MFA's? It's ludicrous.

Interviewer: You did pay your dues though. You went through and got a Masters yourself, didn't you?

Harrison: In Comparative Literature. I never took a writing course of any sort. In my life.

Interviewer: Do you advise against that across the board?

Harrison: No. Sometimes they're good. Look at Wallace Stegner's thing out there. I mean, my god, look at the people he got out. Kesey, Robert Stone, McGuane. But you know what he did. They sat around and talked a little and he just sent them off to write.

Interviewer: You have a lot of friends who are writers. And then there are writers who avoid that sort of thing.

Harrison: Well, I don't see them that much and I think a lot of other writers partly like me because I'm not competitive. I simply don't care. Frankly, I mean I don't ever think about being number one or number seven or number three. Self-publicity or valuation isn't a productive thing for writers. Mailer's *A View from Here* was marvelous because it just totally pissed everybody off. And it was also so on the money. I love novels like his *Barbary Shore* and *Deerpark*. But the critics were totally unpleasant; those novels weren't part of the nativist tradition. That's why a lot of people hated *A Good Day to Die*. Kazin told me these are simply the nastiest people, they don't exist. I says, "Alfred, they're all over. It's just that people don't write about them." *Sundog* came out of my conviction that the American literary novel as opposed to a more commercial kind of novel tends to ignore about seven-eighths of the people. The literary novel often concentrates itself on people in New York, Los Angeles, academic and scientific communities. People don't write about the Strangs of the world because they don't know any of them. You're not going to meet any in Cambridge or New Haven. People like Strang don't loiter around universities and they don't feed at the public trough.

Interviewer: So you think that the academy has had a negative effect.

Harrison: I think I would agree with Faulkner when he said, "A writer can't be ruined by having a swimming pool if he's a good writer. If he's a bad writer, it doesn't matter if he has a swimming pool." So I don't think it matters, but it's had a tremendous leveling effect.

Interviewer: On the kinds of books written?

Harrison: Yeah, they're not as idiosyncratic. They've lost a charm and a self-taught aspect. These people keep track of their credits and that's how they get jobs. They say, "I have been published in *Shenandoah, Sewanee, Lust, Spook,* etc, etc." Where I pointedly have no notion of where I published anything, or little memory of it. I've never kept track.

Interviewer: So you'd approve of someone like Wallace Stevens, who sold insurance and wrote.

Harrison: It's important to know something. Knowing literature is different. Hollywood's always making movies about making movies. Or the movie business. Well, that doesn't play in Kansas. Who gives a shit? It's like making movies about dope. They think everybody does dope. Well, very few people do dope. Why do people in Topeka want to go see a movie about cocaine? They don't know shit from cocaine. Why should they? It's a sense of fungoid self-congratulation that you see in academic communities.

Interviewer: You think it leads to a more narrow vision in literature?

Harrison: Well, that's true. Its just like academic types who say to me, "Oh Jesse Jackson, yuk, oh he's fascist." "Oh stop," I say, "He got jobs for 200,000 blacks in Chicago, what have you ever done? He's a great orator. So he's a little spooky in some areas. But why are you talking about this man this way?"

Interviewer: Henry James said experience is never limited. It's the atmosphere of the mind.

Harrison: Well, that's true. You make your own environment wherever you go. I don't like to be exclusionary. I don't like art which, I think Williams says, cuts off the horse's legs to get him in the box.

Interviewer: You taught once, didn't you?

Harrison: [indelicate sound]

Interviewer: You felt like the town clown, is that what you said?

Harrison: No, it's just that teaching is overrated. It's just not very interesting. You're never done with the job, time's never your own.

Interviewer: As somebody who's worked as a journeyman writer for films in order to survive, what do you think about books being made from films, or movies being made from books.

Harrison: I don't have any feeling about it; they're different mediums and you're a fool if you don't realize that. Even when I write an adaptation of my own work, I like to feel free to change it as much as possible to adapt it to another medium. My ambition is to write a good movie; I want desperately to write a good movie.

Interviewer: Does it bother you that none of your books have become films?

Harrison: I only have one regret. John Huston and Jack Nicholson were going to do *Revenge* and Warner's backed out because they didn't want John Huston to direct it. I felt badly then because I thought he would do a good job.

Interviewer: They pay you a lot of money, don't they?

Harrison: For some things they do. One time Sean Connery had read "Revenge" in *Esquire* and wanted me to write something for him. He found I was under contract to Warners and Warners got excited and says, "You gotta come out here." I says, "No, I'm not coming back out there, ever!" They sent a plane all the way from Burbank to Traverse City Airport and I got on it with a bottle of whiskey and a six-pack of beer and some deli sandwiches they'd got me and flew out there on condition they would fly me back the next day at noon. They'll do anything for you. It's curious isn't it, all those years when people were saying, "Poor Faulkner, he had to go to Hollywood." He wasn't nearly as unhappy as he pretended to be, because he had that dancing girl out there all that time. Though Blotner refused to acknowledge it in his biography. Where she said, "Billy liked to take baths together and sometimes we'd buy toys like rubber ducks" and you think, this is William Faulkner. I loved it. Faulkner for awhile was getting $3,000 a week during the depression to write screenplays. That's good money now, that was great money then.

Interviewer: Is the writing you do for the movies your substitute for teaching? I mean in the sense of surviving.

Harrison: Yeah. It is about the same thing and sometimes worse and sometimes better. It's better because it pays better.

Interviewer: Does that mean you can do it less often? or less frequently?

Harrison: Maybe, but you get greedy. Somebody gives you $150,000 for a screenplay, you think, well why not write two. Get more. And then you say, well why not write three, and get even more. And by then, you're retired.

Interviewer: Does writing for the movies drain you?

Harrison: No. In the last twelve months I wrote three screenplays and that novel, and I don't think the three screenplays detracted from the novel. Just makes you tired generally. And I'm the most tired I've ever been in my whole life, right now.

Interviewer: You say that when a book comes out you get depressed.

Harrison: Uh huh, I don't like judgment. I can't stand criticism.

Interviewer: Not even good criticism?

Harrison: When Bernard Levin of the London *Times* decided I was immortal, I says, "Does that mean I have to take out my laundry in 300 years?" No, it's okay. If you work very hard, what's wrong with getting admired.

Interviewer: But there's something in you that doesn't think that's right?

Harrison: Well, it's because people you love died, and they didn't get admired. That's part of it. It's stupid. I mean, you ought to be able to be valedictorian once in a while. It's like pursuing a beautiful model and seducing her and then feeling real bad after you'd literally been thinking about doing it for seven or eight years. Why bother? Why should I kill myself writing a book if I don't want to at least accept one pat on the back for what I'm doing?

Interviewer: What about the sense of place for you? It seems to me that you're a writer that has to be grounded in place.

Harrison: I think everybody does. I wrote *Locations* partly from that sensibility. But I'm no more a rural writer than Judy Rossner is a New York writer.

Interviewer: And yet, Northern Michigan is pervasive in your work.

Harrison: Yeah, that's because that's where I was born and raised. When I get away from there, I don't think the writing is necessarily weaker as long as I know the other place.

Interviewer: Do you think there's a basic superiority in that "heart of the country" notion?

Harrison: I think what I believe most is actually, as Rilke said, "It's only in the ratrace of the arena that the heart learns to beat." I think you have to do that. It's hard to find more small-minded people than you can find in some areas of Montana, in the most gorgeous part of the United States.

Interviewer: But they're also in New York City.

Harrison: Well, sure they are, but I mean the country in and of itself isn't going to do anybody any good.

Interviewer: It's what you bring to it.

Harrison: I was being evasive. I was thinking about an uncapped city water well that I almost fell into in Reed City. Memories are evoked by a location, and I was thinking of San Francisco, the bridge. Six hundred and ninety-three people have jumped off that goddamned bridge. There'something sort of haunted in the air there. Nobody would do that in Missouri, and they don't do it in Northern Michigan. But in New Orleans, and San Francisco, these apparently perfect places where everybody's so happy, well that's why there are 400,000 homosexuals there. I mean, what the hell's going on? It's a spooky place, but very beautiful. Maybe it attracts them from the midwest. None of those people ever even want to come to the midwest, ever.

Interviewer: In *Farmer* the doctor tells Joseph that, yes, Robert's a homosexual and not to worry about it. He'll go to the city and find other people like him.

Harrison: Homosexuals will gather in one place, for the same reason that the rich all want to be in Palm Beach or Beverly Hills, or Grosse Point, or farmers all go to the Grange. I mean it's natural. And it's not all bad. Think of jazz clubs. If you have 300 Sonny Rollins nuts and half are black and half are white, then there's no barrier left. It's the same with literature. I'm not a nationalist. I don't want to hear about American literature. It's world literature. And all this sniping about who's good in America is nonsense when you've got Gunter Grass, and Gabriel Márquez. Who is good is who is good wherever they are.

Interviewer: You're a wonderful reader. How much do you write for the ear?

Harrison: I don't consciously, but as a poet you do. Yeats would think of the entire rhythm of the poem before he would fill in the words. You know he says, " 'I am of Ireland and the Holy land of Ireland and time runs on,' cried she." You say Jesus Christ, I don't know if it makes any sense, but its beautiful. I think it comes from my early addiction to Stravinsky or Sonny Rollins or Miles Davis or Thelonious Monk. And that's finally the music you hear in your head and you hear word music in that way. I think I was seventeen when I read Joyce's *Finnegan's Wake* four or five times. I used to carry it around with me. It was my main sexual reading, I still think it's the sexiest book I've ever read. So *Hustler* magazine doesn't work with me at all. *Vogue* is better than *Hustler*.

Interviewer: Do you think your reputation as a macho writer is the source of the negative criticism your work has gotten?

Harrison: It's just faddism. When Prescott owned *Newsweek* rather than talking about my book he used me as an object lesson in what's wrong with contemporary writing because, he said, I had none of the new feminine sensibility. He's talking about a public movement, a woman's movement, that I don't think has anything to do with the novel. I mean you write novels. I'm not trying to get out the vote when I write a novel. A novel's a novel. Everybody can't be everything. I don't like to be attacked for reasons anterior to my work.

Interviewer: Do you think it's because you so often seem to use the stuff of yourself in your work?

Harrison: You are what you are. I'm not going to pretend that I'm a Manhattan restauranteur when I'm not. But it's the illusion, too. I've worked very hard to create the illusion. Wouldn't I be something if I was all the people that people think I am in all these books. God, what a mess.

Interviewer: Does the misunderstanding bother you?

Harrison: I don't actually care. I pretend to be more upset. *Esquire* offered me a case of whiskey if I would write two paragraphs answering a review. I wrote that it's a misuse of the word. Actually what macho is in Spanish is someone who would fuck a virgin with a swan or throw a rattlesnake into a baby's carriage. Screw his mother. You know, cut his sister. So that's macho. I don't know what it has to do with me. I don't care about being misunderstood. I'm not pretending that I'm right and there's not a lot of my stuff that might be terribly cheap and wrong. That's neither here nor there if that's what they're dealing with. I don't want to be attacked for my failures as a supporter of the woman's movement. Because I'm a novelist.

Interviewer: Where do you find your characters? Do you use people whom you really know?

Harrison: Just modifications of them. There's such a crazed variety of people that you can take an eighth of this and a third of that and make a human being. In *Legends of the Fall* I found the character William Ludlow in journals; he's actually my wife's great grandfather. But I've changed all the details of his life except the initial ones. He did lead an expedition into the Black Hills with Custer as his adjutant; he also did loathe Custer. And in real life he ended up owning some copper mines in Northern Michigan, but I'd read his journals and was fascinated by the kind of man he was.

Interviewer: You've complained someplace about the fact that there's so little useful information in novels, nowadays.

Harrison: I mean useful to, as Robert Duncan would say, your soul. Life information without which we cannot live. Like Pound says, "Poetry is news that stays news."

Interviewer: Larry Woiwode says he's read that most writers are manic-depressive. Have you ever thought that you might be a manic-depressive?

Harrison: Oh, absolutely, but not to the point where I would need lithium and not so much in recent years. About ten years ago I went through a self-taught Zen training. I had severe colitis from a parasite I got in Leningrad and I thought I was going to go insane with the mood swings combined with physical problems. I got rid of the colitis by sitting. Usually I would go sit on a stump and then on a rock for three or four hours. For some reason that eased all that out, I'm still not sure why. Psychosomatic maybe. For instance I've had a chest cold off and on for a month and a half. I know I have it because I have a novel coming out. No one in the history of my family, including my father, was successful, and I have a lot of questions about whether it's proper to be successful. It's like the craving for anonymity—I've already blown the anonymity shot, but I'm still looking for it. I'm like the kid hiding under the bush or behind the barn. I've gotten so weary or strange about interviews because I've been too trusting on a couple of occasions. The trouble is anything you read about yourself seems to be sort of inaccurate; well, maybe everything that everybody writes about everybody is inaccurate. I've never been really keelhauled, but I read once an article about McGuane in *Village Voice* where they really did a job on him.

Interviewer: That can lead to the "gunfighter syndrome." Whenever a celebrity goes to a party you know that somebody there is going to became an asshole and you never know who it's going to be. I've seen people literally get up in Norman Mailer's face and stand on his feet.

Harrison: They never do that to McGuane who's 6'4" and weighs 220. It's because Mailer's shorter.

Interviewer: You said someplace that to be an artist you have to be able to hold a thousand different contradictory notions in your head all at once.

Harrison: I was thinking about that when you brought up that question on *Sundog*. Hillman said, "What have we done with this other who is given us at birth?" Well that's like that Secret Sharer idea or Rimbaud talking about my "other" and so on. The unrevealed heart of your personality.

Interviewer: Does that relate to the idea that the essence of all art is the ability to recognize paradox, irony?

Harrison: Or to be able to accept that good art does not specialize in cheap solutions.

Interviewer: Do you think, at least in the sense that Pound used the words, that all art is didactic?

Harrison: It's didactic, but boy you better hide it. I can't stand art that's preachy. I think Pound's best poems are free of obvious didacticism. The test is the aesthetic test. If somebody tells me has things he wants to say, I say "Well, I don't care, everybody has things they want to say." It's like Philip Roth puts it, anybody on the subway usually has a better story than an artist does. Because they're intensely occupied with life. Whereas we can't see a cow without saying cow. I want to get to the point where I see a cow without saying cow. It's never going to happen in my life. My particular burden is to make sentences. My wife and I saw a man commit suicide in San Francisco last week. We were down under the Golden Gate Bridge and this asshole jumps off. I had a driver that day, sort of an elegant, faggy character, much better dressed than I was. He and my wife and I were standing down under the fort looking over this area, nothing was there. I was watching a man fish. Then I heard a gargle, we looked back and a man had just jumped off the bridge, missed the water by twelve feet and his head was even gone. You know the impact of three hundred feet onto cement, your head vaporizes. My wife and the driver were contorted with horror, and trembling, and I immediately started making sentences. That's my only defense against this world: to build a sentence out of it.

The Man Whose Soul Is Not for Sale: Jim Harrison
Hank Nuwer / 1985

From *Rendezvous with Eight Contemporary Writers,* Special Issue of *Rendezvous: Idaho State University Journal of Arts and Letters,* 21 (Fall 1985), 26–42. Reprinted with permission of Dante Cantrell and *Rendezvous.*

Jim Harrison is a Lake Leelanau, Michigan, country gentleman with a 100-proof reputation as a poet and novelist. He's a solid man through the chest and arms, but a trace of paunch shows beneath the red Long John-model shirt he's wearing. Dark hair, a coffee-strainer moustache and a pleasantly malevolent grin give him the look of a man younger than his forty-eight years. All his parts work except for the left eye which was poked with a beaker by a young girl when he was in grade school. He is a man rooted to the earth. He loves good sipping whiskey, fine wines kept cool in his two wine cellars, spices that enrich without overpowering good food, and being left alone, not necessarily in that order. Pelts of fox, beaver and raccoon hang from crossbeams in his farm granary-turned-office where this interview takes place. Hundreds of books, including many of his own in foreign editions, indicate that a man of letters lives here. A handwritten admonition to "Keep it Vivid" is tacked to one wall.

Harrison's work is marked by playfulness, invention and chance-taking. His poetry varies from *Outlyer and Ghazals,* which uses a lyric form perfected by the ancient Persians, to the epistolary prose poems of *Letters to Yesenin. Wolf,* his first novel, is a romance in which a protagonist named Swanson seeks the solace of northern Michigan to serve as buffer from the corrupting conditions in urban America. *A Good Day to Die,* often compared to Edward Abbey's *The Monkey Wrench Gang,* pits two men against a dam they see as unnecessary and destructive. *Farmer* is a long mood piece, telling the tale of a man of inaction whose physical cravings threaten to suffocate his existence. *Legends of the Fall* is a collection of three novellas; the title story is a historical western, and some of its characters are derived from his wife Linda's ancestors. *Warlock* is a detective novel in which Harrison creates a sinister world of deception and desertion. His latest novel, *Sundog,* is the story of a crippled but courageous character who is forced by a journalist who interviews him into a remembrance of things past.

Though it may disappoint those who think a writer functions best if he endured a hostile, neurotic childhood, Jim Harrison maintains that his young life was happy. He came from a big, close-knit family of readers. Harrison attended a small, agriculturally oriented high school, winding up as class president and linebacker on the football team. He took undergraduate and graduate work at Michigan State, later teaching for a time at SUNY–Stony Brook. Harrison married Linda King, his high school sweetheart, and the union produced two daughters.

The versatile Harrison is now working on a screenplay. Just as Faulkner is identified with Mississippi, Thomas Wolfe with North Carolina, and Walter Van Tilburg Clark with Nevada, so too, Jim Harrison is Michigan's proudest literary son.

Nuwer: What's that [taxidermied] bird there on your wall?
Harrison: A ruffed grouse. A friend gave it to me. He just hollowed it out.

Nuwer: The way its neck looks I thought it was a bittern—
Harrison: —It does have that neck. And this here is a blue heron wing, somebody found a dead blue heron. It's funny, but on the day I got this wing, I got this postcard from John Irving [with a bird's wing picture on one side] which is an odd coincidence. It's a German wing, but there's a resemblance. And this one here is my bird. I never say it in my book [*Sundog*] but his [a character's] middle name, Corvus—Robert Corvus Strang—is *Corvus,* the American crow. It's a bird that I like the best.

Nuwer: Ever read Ted Hughes' book *Crow*?
Harrison: Yeah, I didn't like that very much, because I don't like English contemporary poets. There aren't many that I like very much. I like images of the natural world that seem to rise naturally, rather than some M.F.A. from Iowa, or Compton State Junior College of the Creative Arts, deciding that he's going to go out and look at nature during his summer vacation. The biggest presumption in the current educational system is the production of M.F.A.s. Eventually they'll all live in Ohio and each one will be given a Xerox machine. It's uncharitable, but it [the M.F.A. degree] is meaningless. It's a pyramid scheme, see? You can have M.F.A.s if you can then have M.F.A.s that will teach more M.F.A.s. And they keep publishing in these little, little magazines, and they keep track of that. But sometimes it works.

There's no use in jumping on Iowa's ass when they've been the best at it, along with that Stegner fellowship [for writers] at Stanford. Some very good people have been helped—Kesey, McGuane, Robert Stone—I mean there's no question that some it's helped. Stegner—I like a couple of his early novels really well—he somehow has really had some kind of benign or helpful influence on some of these young graduates, even on the ones he didn't like and who didn't like him. I don't know how well Stegner and McGuane got along together, but there's no question that that [fellowship to Stanford] was a good thing for Tom at the time. I never had any writing courses of any kind, but that was by choice. I finally realized only last year that writing, or art as I'd just as soon call it, had absorbed the transference of all my religious impulses at age sixteen. Up to sixteen I wanted to be a preacher, and then one day I did a whirlwind: I jumped from Jesus to John Keats in three days. That kind of thing: to Rimbaud, to Dostoevsky, to Appollinaire, to Lorca, you know, your Shane who gives you strength, who gives you the blood transfusion. You want to know what makes one writer better than another? One writer says "I am growing old"; the other says, "Devouring time fluff now thy lion's paw." (*Laughter*) Give me a break. One poet says, "I am tired, I'm depressed, I can't take it any more." This is a graduate of Iowa! It's one of those workshop poems that they publish. Another says, "I want to dream the sleep of apples far away from the tumult of cemeteries."

Nuwer: Did teaching [at the State University of New York at Stony Brook] strike you as meaningless?

Harrison: Oh, no. But I'm too evangelistic. I would use all my energy as a teacher to get them to read this stuff that I love. I thought they didn't know enough, so I wrote down a reading list of 118 books that I thought were the core of modernist tradition and asked them to read them. I got rid of some students like that, but they're still attracted to someone who gives them that much energy. But I could see that I couldn't be a writer and teach because I couldn't control myself. I would give it all away. Which is what you're doing in a novel anyway—you're giving it all away between covers. I don't feel I owe anything beyond that.

Nuwer: Did you want to be a Mennonite preacher?

Harrison: No, Baptist. I spoke a lot at youth groups and so on. So I did that to my hero in this novel [*Sundog*]; that's what I did to him. It was only until I was on page 270 of the manuscript that I realized I was writing about my other half. James Hillman says, "What have we done with the other that we abandon at birth?" The other in the Yeatsian or Rimbaudian sense. But that's how unconscious it is, this process. I couldn't believe it. I blew a whole day thinking about it. Oh, God, no. That I have two parts of the human being. But then you always do that in novels. Before, my only sort of spiritual autobiography was that novella, "The Man Who Gave Up His Name." That was the closest. In fact, you only think of the therapeutic aspects afterwards. Goethe, I think, said, "Such a price the gods exact for song to become what we sing." So when I wrote that, I felt better after I wrote that. That's why I have this keyring here [picks up large ring]. None of these keys fit any door, and I have a green janitor's suit, too, because I know that's the complete escape costume—a green janitor's suit, black shoes, and this keyring—because nobody ever pays attention to janitors. Once you've got the green suit and a keyring, you can go anywhere. You get the idea?

Nuwer: Yeah, you're anonymous.

Harrison: (*Laughter*) Yeah, totally anonymous. I have Strang say in the novel [*Sundog*]: "We are, in totality, what we want to be, or we wouldn't be like this." [Note: Harrison is paraphrasing in the previous sentence.] It's a kind of nasty existential point. The yearning you feel for another life which gets transubstantiated into the idea of a will to do something else—well, it takes a lot to get you to do something else. That's why it's very hard to write novels. Because when you start a novel, there's this incredible sense of vertigo. Even if the composition time doesn't take that long, you're off on a two-year tangent.

Nuwer: Your mind shifts.

Harrison: Yeah, there's a downshift or upshift. No matter what else you're doing, your job or whatever, you're always pretty much thinking about that [novel].

Nuwer: Just reading a novel can give me vertigo. I have to come back to the world after reading sometimes.

Harrison: It does to me, too. People send me galleys sometimes, and I have to send them back if I'm writing myself at the time—I mean, I can't read any novels when I'm writing. When you're ready to write a novel, you're in a state of absolute vulnerability. Everything nails you. That's what Walker Percy in a marvelous book called "the re-entry problem." How do you get back to earth? Now I had envisioned in this essay I wrote—it was only five pages but it was an essay—that one usually returns some kind of burned-out satellite that's performed its function, and now you're tumbling back. By the time you hit earth you'll be a twenty-two-pound block of coal. You're the spiritual equivalent of what Marilyn Monroe is in the grave now. Well, I thought there's got to be a better way to get back than that. That's why I went to a Mexican health camp [after completing the writing of *Sundog*] rather than go out and trash the shit out of myself as I usually do. I went off to this Mexican health camp, because I found out at my advanced age the realization that at certain points I can no longer take care of myself. After finishing that much work, I was totally geeked out. That's the right word for it. So I went down there where everything is taken care of. But that's a case rather than having some totally fatal habit, I just over-rev.

Nuwer: How does your family regard the fact that you're a writer?

Harrison: We were always a close, larger family. In my family it was easier because nobody in it had ever made any money. If you were making even a living as a writer, that was incredible. My father was a college graduate. He thought it was wonderful that I wanted to go off to New York and be a writer because he read a great deal. He liked Faulkner and Erskine Caldwell and Hemingway. He became a county agent, but what he really wanted to do was own a big farm, which was, of course, impossible. So, naturally, I have a big farm, which was, of course, impossible. So, naturally, I have a big farm that I'm not too interested in. That's how it works.

Nuwer: How did you and your wife Linda meet?

Harrison: I met her when she was fourteen, and I was sixteen. She seemed very beautiful. She was wearing riding pants and boots at the time. I thought, "Isn't she fine?"

Nuwer: Growing up in the far North as you did, did you have storytellers in the same tradition that [author] Harry Crews enjoyed as a pup in Georgia?

Harrison: That's true up here. My background from both sides of my parents is heavily rural and poor. We never even had a TV until I was a senior in high school. So, it was much more verbal-oriented then, just as it is in the U.P. [Upper Peninsula]. Commercial fishermen, all retired, are up there, and they have coffee every morning at ten o'clock. They tell each other the same stories but with different little items in each one.

Nuwer: Have you been tempted to use your own postage stamp's worth of soil in Northern Michigan as a basis for many books the way Faulkner did with his Yoknapatawpha County?

Harrison: I almost actually have done that with the Midwest, but no, never to the extent he did. People actually are very different who come from here. I have a number of characters who are basically Scandinavian in origin who come out of this milieu. Faulkner, to a certain extent, no matter how beautifully he did it, occasionally cut off the horse's legs to get him in the box. It's a selective reality, but that's understandable because it's the only way it works. [Thomas] McGuane made a brilliant comment once about Faulkner. Contemporary to Faulkner's Snopes from Yoknapatawpha County, there probably were people from Jackson going down to Miami Beach and dragging along the Atlantic in Buick convertibles, who were probably doing coke and listening to Cole Porter.

Nuwer: All things considered, would you rather live in a palace or a cabin?

Harrison: Cabin! (*Laughter*) It's charming if you have a little money coming in to live in a cabin as I do with no electricity—I have an old Coleman generator. I'm on a river about five miles from my nearest neighbor up in the U.P. I bought it four years ago when I reached a state of absolute panic and depression that came from making money finally when I was thirty-nine. That frightened me a great deal, so I bought the cabin to retreat; it's tended to detoxify me from other pressures. I could go in twenty-four hours from Los Angeles to my cabin where there are only ravens and bobcats and coyotes around.

Nuwer: So you don't get societal bends?

Harrison: Well, I did at first get a lot of bends. It's something all writers supposedly go through once things start working well. You spend your whole life on this principle of violently up and violently down. It's like life on a shuddering elevator. It's not that you're manic-depressive; it's just that it's built into the situation. I remember having lunch with Vonnegut years and years ago. He said that it's unfortunate that a writer—I mean a literary artist—either makes a little or a lot. There's no middle ground. You're either just barely scraping by, or you get a lot. There's no sedate middle ground that you'd be better off with.

Nuwer: Wallace Stegner is always talking against New York literary establishment.

Harrison: He should be. They go by that Steinberg cartoon of America: there's New York, there's the Mississippi, and there's L.A. It's like the way the movie companies call everybody in the Midwest "flyovers." Will the flyovers like this? I love the idea of being a flyover. I have never felt competitive in that sense. I think it's because I started by publishing a number of books of poems and did OK that way; then I wrote novels. I don't want to have to think whether or not I'm what they call a quote-unquote important novelist. If somebody wants to be an important novelist, let him be an important novelist. That's for Bernard Malamud, Philip Roth and all those people. If I thought of myself as an important novelist, it wouldn't help me write novels; I would hate to think I was only what the consensus of media opinion says I am. So, therefore, I *don't* think that's what I am. I love it when I get a good review in, say, the *London Times,* because they're not so topical as a lot of your reviews are here. You actually run into people who've read all your novels instead of just the last one. But I don't think these reviewing mediums have any more power than you want to ascribe to them.

Nuwer: Critics don't have the power over you [a poet/novelist] that they have over a playwright.

Harrison: Yeah, that seems extremely cruel, but [then] there's so much regional theater now, fuck 'em [the critics]! I like what Takahashi, the Japanese poet says: "If you want to write well you have to give up the idea that there is art, that there is success, that there is anything like that. That's when you write the best."

Nuwer: You never think of an audience in any way, shape or form when you write?

Harrison: No! Oh, never. I don't want to think that I have an audience whom I have to confirm their taste with me.

Nuwer: When you travel from place to place, are you, in effect, creating your own destiny?

Harrison: I told a rather snotty younger novelist that he was going to have trouble eventually because he won't talk to people. I think it's very helpful to talk to everyone. You don't know what's going to happen. I think academic writers have that problem of insufficient exposure because they're stuck in one place for at least nine months of the year. Now I was shocked that [John] Updike gave a negative review to [Bill] Trogdon [AKA William Least Heat Moon, author of *Blue Highways*], implying that he would have been better off to have stayed in one place, which is what Updike has done. But personally, I think it would behoove Updike to spend a year in Walla Walla, Washington, and see what he comes up with. That's a Thoreauvian idea that everything [in life] can be extrapolated from one area. I don't think that's true at all.

Nuwer: Are you a dinosaur, so to speak, because you went out as a young man bumming around the country to collect experiences? Student writers now think getting experiences means traveling to Iowa to attend grad school.

Harrison: You don't go out because you want to write about something. You go out because you're full of curiosity. If you fish in Equador or Africa or travel in Russia or all over the United States, it's your interest that takes you there. I had one of my characters say—think about this now—that the most exhausting thing in another human being is a lack of curiosity, because that's what leads to the most ubiquitous disease—boredom. Some people have a favorite TV series they watch and when it's canceled, they're fucked—that kind of thing. I don't have any reason to go anyplace else, except that I get curious. But it's not travel as novelty, because I love it here [Northern Michigan]. It's a more interesting way to live [as I do].

Nuwer: You're not restless when you're here at home?

Harrison: No, not in those terms. I want to know what Leningrad is like, so I go there. That's the beauty of Least Heat Moon's book. Twelve years ago I wanted to go all the way to Montana on county roads. I got a compass for my car, and then I got in a hurry. It's that thrill of seeing cities you've never seen or going down roads you've never seen. The brain is inventive.

Nuwer: When you invent a scene in your mind, is it better than [when it goes] on the page?

Harrison: No, not usually, because it hasn't been flushed out yet. It's still on the fantasy side. You acquire the tools to pretty much get down what you're thinking. If you can't do that, it's because you didn't do well enough acquiring your tools. Or, as [Robert] Graves said, you valued some other form of experience higher than your art—which you dare not do if you're going to be an artist because that's adultery.

Nuwer: NASA is looking for writers and artists to go up into space. Interested?

Harrison: Not in the least. I wouldn't get on a fuckin' space vehicle and go at gunpoint—I feel alienated driving a car. I'm not good at machines. There's only one person to go and that's Mailer, because his imagination is willing to make the experience something he can handle. He would maximize it to make it something he can handle. Mentally, not necessarily in the novels, he's always way out there on the edge. I hope they don't think he's too old to go. There's no question he's the one that should be sent. I'm not saying that he's our smartest novelist, because certainly Bellow is the bear of largest brain, as Pooh would say—there's no question. There's nobody with the mental equipment that Bellow has.

Nuwer: Did you need the stamp of publication to tell you that your work was good? Did you have doubts that you were spending your hours in a way that you could better spend doing something else?

Harrison: No, this is the religious thing again that I've only lately understood. When I was sixteen I read Joyce and Faulkner addictively. You feel a calling just like you feel a calling to be a minister. I was lately rereading Joseph Campbell's masks of god thing about mythology—

Nuwer: —*The Hero with a Thousand Faces*—

Harrison: —Yeah. And what it is, essentially, is that I didn't have any choice. I wanted to be a poet. That's what I was going to do, although I had to do all these other things to make a living. Oddly enough, I published quite by accident when I got my first book contract from Norton for my first book of poems. I had never published a poem, but it happened that I met Denise Levertov, whom I didn't know. We enjoyed talking to each other, so she said, "Let me see some of your poems." So I sent her thirteen poems—short ones—they're in *Plain Song*. She wrote back she wrote a huge long letter back, which was wonderful. That was the first break. Actually, no one had ever seen the poems but me. She said, "Look, I'm a consultant at Norton. If you have fifty pages of writings like this, I can get you a book contract." So I did. I only had about twenty-eight pages—I was unemployed at the time and living with my brother in Boston, because my sister and father had just been killed. I wasn't doing anything, so I wrote twenty-two pages more of poems and sent them in; they turned out to be the first book. Then after that I started publishing poems in magazines. And then the novels I started writing. I wrote *Wolf* because I'd fallen down a cliff, and I was in traction. I was in a coma, because I'd gotten penicillin poisoning. And McGuane wrote and said, "You can't do anything else, so why don't you write a novel?" I used to think of writing a novel all the time when I was eighteen or nineteen years old. Then I was twenty-nine, and I had just written poems. OK! And then I wrote *Wolf.* I sent the only copy off, and then they had a mail strike. I'm sure at the time I didn't have enough money for a Xerox. The only copy was lost for about a month. I wasn't even terribly upset. At the time, I didn't think it probably would be published anyway. And my brother John finally found it in the post office.

Nuwer: They let him into the post office?

Harrison: Yeah, they let him dig around and find it. It was a college town as it had to be for a postal clerk to realize the enormity of a lost manuscript of which there was no copy. It probably was stupid of me, but I wasn't taking myself seriously. The novel was mostly writing an autobiography. I've always denied that it is autobiographical, but it is, of course, [*Chuckles*] ninety-four percent of it.

Nuwer: Do you ever have dreams or night thoughts that wind up in your writing?

Harrison: Dreams? Sure, everything is in one piece. It's a sense of reality that enters. That's why I stopped drinking so much. It got so it ruined my dream life. It's no longer a source of energy because alcohol is basically a sedative, a very inelastic sedative. Among your friends, the more they drink, the less elastic they get as human beings, the less fluid. It's very corrupting that way.

Nuwer: What really destroys my friends who are hard drinkers is the accompanying self-pity.

Harrison: [Peter] Matthiessen, who's not a close friend or anything although we write back and forth, wrote me a note warning me that self-pity is the most injurious emotion there is, the most energy gobbling. Not jealousy, not anything, is like self-pity. It's ruinous for a writer because it makes him whine and makes him more housebroken, too. The most housebroken writers I know are the hard drinkers because they have no latitude to do anything else. As McGuane said beautifully, alcohol is the writer's black lung disease. With Yeats the heart was more dangerous than alcohol—that's true to an extent—but when I understood about that paralysis, I began to drink less.

Nuwer: I wonder why it is that writers seem to drink.

Harrison: It just is. It's the loneliness of it. What's the main way a writer re-enters the world? It's alcohol. He sedates himself to re-enter the world.

Nuwer: I think it's because writers are really strong. You get everything else in your life through sheer force of will, but you cannot beat a drinking habit that way.

Harrison: The worst people to cure from drug or alcohol addiction are doctors because they think they know everything. It's the same thing you're saying about writers. You're a loner. You're the Lone Ranger—absurdly, absurdly the Lone Ranger. People change so gradually they hardly notice their own disintegration—that's the danger. It's what the Buddhists call "Monkey Brain." You don't sense yourself falling apart because it's your own brain observing your own brain. Your own brain is in a state of disintegration or deliquescence. You can't see your disintegration until it's too late. You really must try to stand aside. You come to the point where you say it's not interesting to be drunk, and, if it's not interesting, what's the point? When cocaine ceases to be interesting, why bother doing cocaine any more? I'm not going to be moralistic about it. I can't imagine life without wine and garlic, but that doesn't mean I'm interested in being a drunk.

Nuwer: Do you have to stand vigilant to protect yourself from being swallowed up as an individual while advancing the good of your career?

Harrison: Why sure, why I don't like to do interviews and don't do them much, for instance, unless they're solid things—this thing [current interview] for instance—is that I don't think publicity is the proper function of the artist. I was talking with McGuane who is one of my oldest friends. He says that our main problem, the thing that hurts us the most, is ordinary human greed. You've been poor so many years; in my case the first eighteen years of my married life I averaged ten or eleven thousand dollars a year. When your daughter is getting ready to go to college that becomes insupportable. You're depressed all the time because you can't make enough for your family to live on. When I talk about the yo-yo and shuddering elevator, I mean it would have been nice if I could have gone modestly, but that's *not* how it worked. It's boom or bust like miners. But so far as being swallowed up, everyone is swallowed up. Now an actor I know says what happens when you've sold your soul, and I said, well, you figure out a way to buy it back. You get it back in pieces. I've often thought about professors who've been mildly critical about my work. They've been wallowing in the public trough for twenty-five years. It's a little easier when nobody wants to buy your soul. Jack Nicholson—I've worked quite a bit with him—is the one who gave me a break. Do you know that story?

Nuwer: No.
Harrison: *Farmer* didn't sell any copies at the time I met Nicholson, although now it's doing very nicely. We started corresponding, and he said, "If you ever think of an idea for me, let me know." But I never did, of course,

not realizing at the time that I was *supposed* to, of course. I didn't understand how it worked. So then, when we were at our worst, our most destitute, I went down to see him in Durango, Mexico. He found it offensive that an artist he liked couldn't make a living at it. He advanced me enough to write the book I was working on at the time, which was pleasant—

Nuwer: —What was the book you were working on?

Harrison: *Legends of the Fall.* I had this idea for the three novellas before I went down there.

Nuwer: Couldn't you farm them out to *The New Yorker* for money?

Harrison: After I wrote them, *Esquire* published the entire *Legends.* But no, I couldn't write for *The New Yorker,* although I read it occasionally when it has McPhee or Matthiessen or Ed Hoagland. *The New Yorker* doesn't publish stuff that has food and sex in it which leaves me out. There's no food or genitalia in *The New Yorker,* because that isn't the kind of magazine they want it to be. But I don't care. In fact, there are no magazines now that I'm interested in publishing in, although maybe I'll try to do something on gluttony for *Vanity Fair.* Only in the Midwest is overeating still considered an act of heroism.

Nuwer: If you do an article for *Vanity Fair,* don't wear a skimpy red wrestling uniform like they made John Irving wear.

Harrison: I don't really know him. We've met a couple times, but I enjoyed talking with him. He never really goes out in New York; I sort of wonder why he lives there. He likes to cook, too. [Pause] See we give [Gabriel] Marquez this heat—our government does—about his visa because he knows Castro. But as an interview pointed out, Marquez, when he visits Castro—basically, all they're doing is cooking. They enjoy cooking together. Can't you imagine Marquez coming in? He's met by a limo and he's off to the presidential palace. He's got some *veal* with him, he's got some *shrimp,* he's got some *chickens.* These deep revolutionaries are going to *cook* a meal and threaten Reagan. (*He pronounces the name REEE-gun.*)

Nuwer: That's funny. Sounds like a Max Apple story.

Harrison: Uh, huh. It's funny.

Nuwer: How did you get the nickname of "Brown"?

Harrison: As in brown [gestures to his dark coloring]. Nicholson can't stand ordinary language by being in the movies. He's very inventive. Conversational. He speaks in kind of shorthand sometimes. Warren Beatty's called "The Pro" because he's obviously just simply *the* pro. (*Harrison's dog comes up to him with a favorite toy and looks at him pleadingly before dropping the toy at his feet.*) I'm not throwing the ball now, darling. I'm busy. This is a literary talk. (*Rummages about the office*) You'll like this here. This is a shoe. This is a great reminder of when I was living in Palm Beach that one winter to try to write a cookbook with this friend, a French count. I went down to the beach one day and right in front of the DuPonts' house on the beach, a Haitian boat had landed with these malnutritioned people. After the police hauled them away, I found this little Haitian shoe in the boat, and I said, "Boy, oh boy. If there's ever a magical object to remind me and give me balance, it's to look at that shoe." The Haitians—the pathetic part of it—was that two of them dropped to their knees and covered their heads, because they assumed when the police came that they were going to be shot. So I felt sorry for this policemen who was explaining to this one guy that he could get up, that he wasn't going to be shot in America. And that's when they let them stay here, too. (*Chuckles*) "NO . . . BULLETS!" And that's when he finally got up.

Nuwer: Do you know who your readers are?

Harrison: I'm getting a sense of them slowly because there are pockets of them in odd places that I hear from, like Oregon, Washington, Montana, New Hampshire.

Nuwer: What does your mail indicate about your readers. Are the letter writers intelligent?

Harrison: Oh, a lot of them are. Sometimes it [the mail] is off the wall. Some books that didn't do well at all like *Farmer* brought an enormous amount of mail. It takes a lot to get people to the point where they're going to write a letter. And you get hate mail, naturally. You get weird hate mail, too, from literary people who want you to do something for free. Oddly enough, after the Traverse City bookstore, the store that sells the most of my books is in Oxford, Mississippi. I was really quite surprised. I don't like to be handicapped by having a sense of a certain type of reader, but I suspect it has something to do with agrarianism of some sort. I don't think I do terribly well in New York City. A lot of letters are from doctors and career Air Force officers, people you'd never think you'd get letters from. That's true—I *do* know who my readers are—because I can tell through the mail. But I don't have any composite picture, because I don't think there is one—a lot more women than I would have thought, because I've been reviewed badly in that respect under the aegis of quote-macho-unquote, which I find totally nuts. If you were born and raised in a family to whom hunting and fishing was a preoccupation, it seems no more [macho] to me than stickball or basketball is in New York City. It's just what you do from the time you are very small, starting from when you are four, you go fishing with your father. Now, of course, the country is so bifurcated in so many ways, that they don't realize that this is still true in rural areas. People hunt and fish all the time, and it's a main form of our recreation.

Nuwer: Can you expand upon what you mean by the "theory and practice of rivers" in *Sundog*?

Harrison: It's actually the title of a poem I'm working on. I like rivers and I like watersheds. When I find a creek I like to walk up to where the creek starts in a seep or a spring. I like to have a topographical view of any area, including my life. I like to know the relationship of the land mass. The theory and practice of rivers that this man [Strang] has given his life to is almost an Oriental idea about the nature of water, and how humans—you—at your best, live like the river does. All water on earth moves. You remember Blake's *Marriage of Heaven and Hell*. He says that still water breeds pestilence. So, when I was recovering from a crackup three years ago, what I basically did for five months at my cabin was to stare at a river from the deck every day, most of the day. That's why, I'm sure, I wrote this novel. Although it didn't occur to me while I was writing it, now I'm sure that's why it was.

Nuwer: Are you aware of the genesis of other of your stories?

Harrison: Not usually until later. I don't think about my novels after I've written them. And I never reread them unless I have to write a screenplay, and that's very upsetting. I prefer not to write a screenplay from my own work.

Nuwer: What have you based screenplays on?

Harrison: "Revenge" and *Legends of the Fall*. And years ago I did a screenplay for Fred Wiseman, the documentary filmmaker, of *A Good Day to Die,* which was easier, whereas *Legends* was tremendously difficult. It was an emotional problem of living again with these people that I'd gotten rid of in the process of the novel. To go back and have to live with them again was very painful. "Revenge" wasn't so painful because it was a story I could hold at arm's length. I think novelists get mistaken for intellectuals, but they're a lower form. They're distinctive. They want to tell tales. In *Legends* I wanted to tell three tales like "once upon a time," that kind of thing. It's funny when critics misunderstand and think that I, personally, the writer, am every character in my books—that when a character says something, that's what I'm saying. A novel isn't a didactic form at its best. You're not out there preaching. I've never known a novelist who didn't want to write a screenplay. I've read Thomas Mann's screenplay which was good. When I was working for Warner's, they got me out half-a-dozen Faulkner screenplays. Oddly enough, they weren't any good at all. I mean, they're interesting because Faulkner wrote them, but they weren't good screenplays. People don't like to talk about the seven years he was out there, but at one point during the Depression, he was making $3,000 a week, which would be the equivalent of ten grand a week now. Poor Billy in Hollywood was supporting at least thirteen people that depended upon him back home in Mississippi, his dead brother's family, his alcoholic brother's family, his own wife, and a couple black retainers. He was supporting all of them. Then there's that marvelous toe dancer Meta [Doherty] Carpenter, who was Faulkner's girlfriend out there—which was obviously his morale factor, just as surely as mine is eating.

Nuwer: I can identify with your narrator in *Sundog* who is always talking about gout. There's a doctor in Clemson [Dr. Bill Hunter] who I think was a model for Barry Hannah's doctor in *Ray*. He believes gout is associated with creative people who then invariably attain an overload of purines. In *Sundog*, your narrator couldn't even touch the gas pedal.

Harrison: Yeah. Of course that guy I did the way I did because I wanted a real representative of the modern world. He's a radically, radically altered version of myself. You had to have a contrast between those two [main] male characters [narrator and Robert Corvus Strang]. The guy whose paintings I select for my whole series of books, Russell Chatham—

Nuwer: —the man you dedicated *Sundog* to—

Harrison: —yeah, he's perhaps the greatest cook I know. I'll give you Chatham's number; you'll like his sense of food. He gets that same veal that I get from Wisconsin, Provini prime veal, and he gets great lamb. This one bar has the best restaurant in the Rockies—Chico Hot Springs outside Livingston, Montana, and I know the cook there, Larry Edwards. He cooks you what you want to eat. Chatham, the painter, lives down the road, and he eats there all the time. Fabulous food! We shot grouse, and they did a special grouse dinner for twenty-eight people.

Nuwer: Can you tell me a bit about Russell Chatham?

Harrison: He's a very dear friend and very close to my hero in *Sundog* in a metaphorical sense because he never gave up as an artist even when he was living out of a van for two years. He's doing very well now because a lot of people are buying his paintings and for good money. Jack [Nicholson] has five or six of them.

Nuwer: Do you have a friend or editor who reads your work before you send it out?

Harrison: No. Nobody touches what I write. Although when I was at Viking on *Farmer* I had a marvelous editor who has since gotten married and moved on south. She said, once, "Jim, do you realize that if we switch chapters three and seven it makes a lot more sense?" YOU'RE RIGHT! That kind of thing. But I consciously think about it [a novel] a long time and then I write a draft. I write each day, and then before I give it to my secretary Joyce [Harrington], I correct that. Then she types it up; I correct that. When I'm done, I recorrect that and give it to a typist who is also a copy editor—she lives out in Kalamazoo. So by the time I submit the novel it's really clean copy, just exactly what I want, and I don't change things in galleys because I think that's stupid. Novels are very tentative that way. I also think it was a mistake for [W. H.] Auden to rewrite some of his earlier poems.

Nuwer: You don't think the same way as an old man that you did when you were younger.

Harrison: Yeah. [Walt] Whitman did the same thing. I think it's unhealthy to think about your previous work.

Nuwer: Did you know that you have a lot more commas in *Sundog* than in your other books?

Harrison: Oh, I did that on purpose. I hate commas. But the book becomes more instinctual as it goes, but setting it up was less so. I decided to be painfully clear.

Nuwer: How do you organize things while working?

Harrison: When I'm writing a novel and get confused, I do a whole linear chart and paste notes all over that. I put it up there, and I don't get lost. I work off that. (*Gets a bulky package*) Here are fifty pounds of notes for the novel [*Sundog*], most of which I didn't refer to at all.

Nuwer: I thought it ironic that you had a character blow up a dam in *A Good Day to Die,* and in *Sundog,* you had a dam builder.

Harrison: That is funny. I never, at first, thought of that at all. I was almost all done [writing *Sundog*] when that occurred to me. The reason I wanted to write about someone like this is because they never get written about—people who know what they're actually doing. The misrepresentation of businessmen or executives is incredible both in novels and in films. It's almost like parody. It occurs to you over the years that as opposed to the notion that these people are silly and captious, you must be somehow very smart to make six or seven hundred grand each year in the world—you really do. But I don't think the crop of MBAs in recent years is as interesting as the old type, the self-made man. That's why this guy [Strang] who's an epileptic never goes to school; he's totally self-educated. A lot of perceptions that we have about the world he doesn't have at all. I like that notion because it gives me more freedom as a novelist. That way he can say or think anything that I want him to, up to a point. And when I was traveling around South America and Central America and Africa, I'd meet this kind of person on R&R in bars. When I was in Costa Rica I talked with one who said he was a foreman on a big Brazilian hydroelectric project. He's from Indiana. A lot of these guys are from places like Kentucky and Indiana, because they're the guys who grew up on a farm like I did, studying maps. You know, I can't wait to see the Pacific Ocean; then I'm going to see the Atlantic.

Nuwer: I associate one's forties as a time when friends and family are dying. What do you associate your teens, twenties, and so on with?

Harrison: Hmmm. The teens? That's when you dream the most. I think of a nineteen-year-old standing on the roof of a house or building in New York, dreaming his largest dreams. I spent my whole year at nineteen hitchhiking all over the country. There's a sense of amplitude at nineteen because everything is at the same moment impossible-improbable and possible-probable. You know the there where you want to get to, but there doesn't seem to be any way to get there. You're just full of Unutterable Yearnings. I suppose your twenties are when you are learning how to live this dream. You have so many hormones and emotional violence in your system that you can't do it. That's almost the same way with the thirties. By the thirties you better have a pretty good idea or you never are going to take off. And I suppose forty is the big exception. Writers and artists realize that you can't be a better artist than you are, assuming you've given all your energy to it. There aren't any miracles. The fifties seem to me to be a little more pleasant. Although it's now too early [for me]. I still have to figure that one out. I like the idea, the old philosophical thing from college, ontogeny recapitulates phylogeny. Your own process of evolution as a human imitates the process of evolution itself. It's an odd thing, because you see it in art, too. For a writer it's at the structure. You're surprising yourself. I wanted to create a character [in *Sundog*] who has almost totally emerged from dread, but the only way to emerge from dread is to live within your own system and exhaust yourself. It's simple-mindedly doing the very best you can, when you give it your heart and soul, but it's only going to be as good as you are. Dread depends on possibilities that you just barely entertain, and when you entertain the possibilities, dread disappears because you've done everything you can. If it doesn't work, too bad.

Nuwer: Can you tell me one bad thing that you've gotten over?

Harrison: No, I don't think so—I think you have a lot of things that you've successfully encysted in scar tissue. (*Laughter*) I like that. I said to a guy who was making a deal once; he wanted me to do it for less and I said, "No! At this particular age I am a stone wall that's been mortared together with scar tissue. Therefore, it's not possible for me to do anything that I don't want to do." [Pause] Can you think of anything you've really gotten over?

Nuwer: Yeah, a first marriage.

Harrison: What you've done is diffused it somehow. In terms of forgiveness or compassion or basic instincts that have to be nurtured, you finally have to forgive everyone else and also to forgive yourself, or else you become paralyzed. I have to constantly forgive myself for not being as good as I'd hoped to be. Even though I couldn't work any harder than I have, I still think somehow it should have been better.

The Art of Fiction: Jim Harrison
Jim Fergus / 1986

From *Paris Review*, 30, no. 107 (1988): 52–97. Reprinted with permission of George Plimpton and *Paris Review*.

This interview was conducted over a five-day period in mid-October of 1986 at Jim Harrison's farm in Leelanau County, Michigan. It was the middle of the bird-hunting season, and his friends, painter Russell Chatham and writer Guy de la Valdene, were staying with the Harrisons, as they have every fall for the past thirteen years. Harrison chose this particular time for the interview because it was essentially his only free time of the year, and because, as he put it, it is a time when he "tends to be intensely voluble and cheerful." Both Harrison and his wife of twenty-seven years, Linda, are accomplished cooks, as are Chatham and de la Valdene, and this is also, it must be said, a fattening time. An enormous portion of each day is devoted to planning, shopping for, preparing, discussing, and finally eating one breathtaking meal after another, at the end of which preliminary discussions and preparations for the next meal begin almost immediately.

A threatening sign outside, DO NOT ENTER THIS DRIVEWAY UNLESS YOU HAVE CALLED FIRST. THIS MEANS YOU, is belied by the inside of the farmhouse, a hospitable home with bookcases lining the walls, dogs and cats comfortably reclined on the furniture. I arrived in the evening, just in time to participate in a dinner party for twelve, so there was even more activity in the kitchen—the soul of the house—than usual; a lot of tasting from saucepans by guests and chefs alike, a certain amount of pilferage off the butcher block countertops by the pets, and much good natured squabbling, giving of orders and unsolicited cooking advice, mostly ignored. There is a brief uproar when Harrison discovers that someone has tampered with his game sauce; he demands to know who and why. For dinner we are being served an appetizer of woodcock, with grouse as an entree, as well as sundry side dishes, including marvelous garlic mashed potatoes, for which Linda has poached thirty cloves of garlic in butter.

Jim Harrison is a dark-skinned, robust man, with a Pancho Villa style moustache—oddly Latin in appearance, although he is of Scandinavian heritage. He's been described as looking like a block layer (which he indeed was), a beer salesman, and a sumo wrestler; he bears himself with a most unique kind of physical grace, indescribable except to say that it has something to do with a style of movement which is not precisely linear. His eye—blinded in a childhood accident—is sighted off on a different plane, increasing the feeling that Harrison is a man with his own unique sense of balance.

Harrison is the author of seven books of fiction, including the novels *Dalva* (1988), *Sundog* (1984), and *Wolf* (1971), and the collection of novellas *Legends of the Fall* (1979); but he began writing as a poet, and has published six collections of poetry, most recently *The Theory and Practice of Rivers and Other Poems* (1986).

Because he prefers to be on the move, out of a total of almost fifteen hours of taped conversation only about two hours' worth was conducted in any kind of a formal interview fashion—seated in Harrison's office, a converted granary near the house, or at my room in a nearby lodge on Lake Michigan, a room in which he had written much of *Legends of the Fall*. The rest was conducted informally, in conversation with the tape recorder running while touring the northern Michigan countryside in his car, or walking through the woods and fields with his bird dogs. Sometimes he carried a shotgun, although considerably more talking was done than hunting.

Conversing with the poet-novelist is somehow akin to watching his dogs work the cover for birds. They race off on tangents, describing broad loops and arcs, or tight circles, always returning in a controlled, if circuitous, pattern that is at once instinct, training, ritual, and play.

Harrison is a man of prodigious memory and free-wheeling brilliance and erudition, as well as great spirit and generosity, lightness and humor; so the reader should imagine wild giggles and laughter throughout, and supply them even when they seem inappropriate—especially when they seem inappropriate. Imagine, too, the sounds and the textures in the background of the tapes: the easy talk of friends and hunting cronies, the light, cold drizzle of the wettest fall in Michigan history, sodden leaves and branches underfoot, and always the ringing of the dogs' bells, sometimes nearby, sometimes barely discernible, fading into the woods.

A final editing of this interview was accomplished over a two-day period at his publisher's house in Key West, Florida, where Harrison with his family, was taking a much-needed ten-day break from work on his novel *Dalva*.

Jim Harrison: I wrote this in my notebook: "My favorite moment in life is when I give my dog a fresh bone." That comes from being the blinded seven-year-old hiding out in the shrubbery with his dog, whom he recognized as his true friend.

Interviewer: Do you think your childhood accident when you lost sight in one eye gave you a different way of looking at things?
Harrison: Probably. I understand they believe that in other cultures, especially when it's the left eye.

Interviewer: You seem to have a remarkable memory for the events of your childhood, which you use a lot in your work.
Harrison: It's nondiscriminate and that's why you have to work hard at it. In terms of classic Freudianism, if you have a knot in your past that stops the flow of your life, it's a psychic impediment. Your memories enlarge in ways proportionally to how willing you are to allow them to enlarge.

Interviewer: Do you believe that a good memory is an essential attribute for a writer because it gives one a deeper well to draw from?
Harrison: Sometimes I wish I could forget more things. I have to make a conscious effort to free my mind, open it again because memory can be tremendously rapacious. Was it to you that I said jokingly that I had to go out and collect some new memories, I'm going dry? That's why I like movement.

Interviewer: This idea of movement and the metaphor of the river, seem to be central to your work.
Harrison: It's the origin of the thinking behind *The Theory and Practice of Rivers*. In a life properly lived, you're a river. You touch things lightly or deeply; you move along because life herself moves, and you can't stop it; you can't figure out a banal game plan applicable to all situations; you just have to do with the "beingness" of life, as Rilke would have it. In *Sundog,* Strang says a dam doesn't stop a river, it just controls the flow. Technically speaking, you can't stop one at all.

Interviewer: But you have to work at it, make a conscious effort so that your life flows like a river?
Harrison: *Antaeus* magazine wanted me to write a piece for their issue about nature. I told them I couldn't write about nature but that I'd write them a little piece about getting lost and all the profoundly good aspects of being lost—the immense fresh feeling of really being lost. I said there that my definition of magic in the human personality, in fiction and in poetry, is the

ultimate level of attentiveness. Nearly everyone goes through life with the same potential perceptions and baggage, whether it's marriage, children, education, or unhappy childhoods, whatever; and when I say attentiveness I don't mean just to reality, but to what's exponentially possible in reality. I don't think, for instance, that Márquez is pushing it in *One Hundred Years of Solitude*—that was simply his sense of reality. The critics call this "magic realism," but they don't understand the Latin world at all. Just take a trip to Brazil. Go into the jungle and take a look around. This old Chippewa I know—he's about seventy-five years old—said to me, "Did you know that there are people who don't know that every tree is different from every other tree?" This amazed him. Or don't know that a nation has a soul as well as a history, or that the ground has ghosts that stay in one area. All this is true, but why are people incapable of ascribing to the natural world the kind of mystery which they think they are somehow deserving of but have never reached? This attentiveness is your main tool in life, and in fiction, or else you're going to be boring. As Rimbaud said, which I believed very much when I was nineteen and which now I've come back to, for our purposes as artists, everything we are taught is false—everything.

Interviewer: How did you think at age fourteen that you might want to be a poet?

Harrison: Those years, fourteen, fifteen, sixteen, are a vital time in anybody's life, also a tormenting time. I wanted to be a preacher for a while, but then it seemed to me that whatever intelligence I had wouldn't allow it. That again would be a question of leaving out the evidence. So I think all my religious passions adapted themselves to art as a religion.

Interviewer: Did you always read a lot?

Harrison: Yes. My father was a prodigious reader and passed on the habit. He was an agriculturist but he also read all of Hemingway and Faulkner and Erskine Caldwell. He read indiscriminately. Both my parents did.

Interviewer: That had to have been valuable training for you.

Harrison: A large part of writing is a recognition factor, to have read enough to know what good writing is. Finally, what Wallace Stevens said, which I love and which is hard to explain to younger writers, is that technique is the proof of your seriousness.

Interviewer: Did your rural background in any way prepare you to become a poet?

Harrison: My background used to embarrass me. I'd think, I want to be like Lord Byron, or Vincent van Gogh. And then I'd realize, how can a boy from a little farm town do that?

Interviewer: Didn't that give you more incentive to break out?

Harrison: And I think more power. I think the years I spent at manual labor as a block layer, a carpenter, a digger of well pits, have given me more physical endurance for later in my life. And in an utterly corny Sherwood Anderson way, it makes you think those long thoughts. If you're unloading fertilizer trucks for a dollar an hour all day long, and dreaming about New York City, it really means something. I remember a month before my first book of poems came out, I was working on a house foundation and the lumber truck couldn't get close enough to the excavation, so I had to wheelbarrow 1200 cement blocks for about seventy yards, load them and unload them. It was a cold, icy, early November day and it took me about nine hours to do it. That day I manually handled thirty-five tons worth of cement blocks, and that was for two and a half dollars an hour. When I got home I was hungry and tired, and what I had to show for it was right around twenty-five dollars. But you got a lot of thinking done.

Interviewer: Do you think that the physical endurance you developed in those years somehow translates onto the written page?

Harrison: I've never thought about that. What it does do for you is, if you can hoe corn for fifty cents an hour, day after day, you can learn how to write a novel. You have absorbed the spirit of repetition. When you look at my wife's garden you understand that; the beauty of the garden—the flowers and the vegetables—that's how an artist is in his work. And I think the background that at first nonplussed me—that rural, almost white-trash element—stood me in good stead as an artist, in the great variety of life it forced me into, the hunger to do things. Joseph in *Farmer* wanting to see the ocean—that's a reflection of my background. I can't tell you the thrill I had when I hitchhiked to California to look at the Pacific. And then the same way with New York City. Our family had no money—there were five children—and I accumulated ninety dollars and my dad gave me a ride out to the highway. I had my favorite books and the typewriter he'd given me for my seventeenth birthday—one of those twenty-buck used typewriters—and my clothes, all in a cardboard box tied with a rope, and I was going off to live in "Greenwitch" Village. I was going to be a bohemian! I think I'd seen pictures of bohemians in *Life* magazine, and that's what I wanted to be. Also the girls looked really pretty. They had straight black hair and they wore turtlenecks. And my dad thought it was all fine. He wasn't insistent about me finishing college at the time. He knew that Hemingway and Faulkner didn't go to college.

Interviewer: What were the books you took with you?
Harrison: Rimbaud's *Illuminations,* in that Louise Varese translation, Faulkner's *The Sound and the Fury, The King James Bible,* Dostoyevsky's *Notes from Underground,* Joyce's *Finnegans Wake.*

Interviewer: Having begun your career as a poet, how did you make the transition to fiction?
Harrison: I fell off a cliff while bird hunting and hurt myself, and I had to be in traction for a month. I had a long convalescence. Fortunately, I had the Guggenheim that year, or we would have been bankrupt. Tom McGuane suggested I write a novel while I was convalescing, and that's how I wrote *Wolf.* I sent it off and for a month it was lost in the mail strike. It was the only copy. When they accepted it for publication I was somewhat surprised. I thought, oh good, here's something else I can do, because the dominant forces in my life had always been novelists, along with a few poets.

Interviewer: In its form, *Wolf* is quite unconventional. It has a very personal, almost confessional quality. Does that reflect your background as a poet?
Harrison: At the time I hadn't written any fiction other than juvenilia, so naturally *Wolf* was a poet's book. I even have grave doubts whether it's a novel at all. That's why I called it a false memoir. I certainly came to the novel backwards, because poets practice an overall scrutiny habitually, and what's good later for their novels is that they practice it pointillistically. You read some reasonably good novelists who tell a story well enough in terms of a flat narrative, but they never notice anything interesting, whereas a poet has folded and unfolded his soul somewhat like an old-fashioned laundry girl with the linen. His self is his vocation. As. W. C. Williams said, "no ideas but in things."

Interviewer: *Wolf* is a very angry book.
Harrison: *Wolf* reminds me somewhat of a heartbroken boy up on the barn roof, just sort of yelling. I've certainly become a nicer person over the years.

Interviewer: Do you think you've become nicer, or less angry, as a result of age?

Harrison: I don't think it's a result of age because, if anything, people get angrier as they go along. I think it's the result of a particularly long effort to make myself sane, at least on my own terms. As Ortega y Gasset said, "With no standard nothing has merit and man is capable of using even sublimity to degrade himself." An artist has to evolve some standards, because nobody's asking you to do this, and what you think of as your muse is really a couple dozen violent bacchantes.

Interviewer: Along these lines, Faulkner once said that nothing could ruin a first-rate talent, to which Normal Mailer replied that Faulkner made more asinine remarks than any other major American novelist.

Interviewer: Except for Mailer, I think Faulkner was always defensive and he gave Chinese answers. And that question of the formation and disintegration of personality is such an enormous subject, an imponderable thing. Of course alcohol and drugs, marriage, jobs, everything can ruin talent if allowed to. But these are inscrutables, and finally Mailer is right and Faulkner is right, and the fact remains that Faulkner really ruined his talent later in his life with whiskey. I certainly know when I'm doing so. For instance, the whole first section of this new book I'm working on, *Dalva,* is written from the voice of a woman, and I can't get into her voice if I've had too much to drink the night before; I can't slip into her persona because it requires a conscious effort every day. The best thing I've ever read on the subject of alcohol and the writer was by Walker Percy, who defined it as a "re-entry" problem. The writer works in this totally solitary universe, and to re-enter the world he has to have a couple of belts, then a couple of belts on top of a couple of belts. And most people drink for no other reason than that they started drinking. It's essentially a sedative, and if you're a manic depressive in the first place, which is basically my configuration, you sometimes need a lot of sedation. But this is not a profitable question in the long run, because what Faulkner called the raw meat on the floor is whether you do the job or not, and eventually everyone knows if you did the job or not. The fact is, I can only think of one American in our time who's lived up to the full promise of his talent, and that's Saul Bellow. He's the only person who brought his talent to the fruition that seemed promised way back with his first work.

Interviewer: After *Wolf,* your next novel, *A Good Day To Die,* took a more traditional form as a narrative. Was that a natural progression from poetry into fiction?

Harrison: No, I think it was the influence of Raymond Chandler and John D. MacDonald. I wanted to tell one of those simple tales that has a great deal of narrative urgency, propelled by characters who, once you've met them, you know it's going to be a godawful mess. These are people that nobody wants in their living room . . . except maybe Sylvia, in her white cotton underpants.

Interviewer: I can see where some people might find these characters objectionable. That's a disturbing book.

Harrison: The book came out of the feeling of the late sixties. In a sense it was the first Vietnam book. A critic in New York told me that such people don't exist, and I said, well, I'm afraid they do, in enormous quantity, as we were to see later.

Interviewer: Do you think the fact that you often write about people who are not exactly "mainstream" type characters has hurt you in terms of critical acceptance?

Harrison: It's occurred to me that some of the awkwardness I have in reception—not that I can't write badly—is because the kind of people I write about are utterly alien to almost everyone in the reviewing media.

Interviewer: Has it been a problem for you being labeled a "Michigan" or a "midwestern" writer?

Harrison: What I hate about this notion of regionalism in literature is that there's no such thing as regional literature. There might be literature with a pronounced regional flavor, but it's either literature on aesthetic grounds or it's not literature. In the view of those on the Eastern seaboard, everything which is not amorphous, anything that has any peculiarities of geography, is considered regional fiction, whereas if it's from New York, it's evidently supposed to be mainstream. I told my agent, Bob Dattila, years ago that it struck me that the Upper East Side of New York was constitutionally the most provincial place I'd ever been. As far as interests go, it's as circumscribed as say, Fergus Falls, Minnesota, which is a Catholic farm community—it's that specific.

Interviewer: Do you think that it's still more difficult for a writer working in a different part of the country, with the possible exception of the South, to be recognized in New York?

Harrison: It's only a question of contiguity, population density and literary friendships. Think of all the column inches the Mets got when they weren't very good. The media loathed the World Series between St. Louis and Kansas City. It's the same way with novelists.

Interviewer: You make forays into New York, but you've managed to maintain a certain isolation here at your farm and at your cabin in the Upper Peninsula.

Harrison: I'm lucky to be rurally oriented because I save myself a lot of problems by being where I am, by being that remote. I'm not overburdened by the regional concerns of New York. I think of Mailer or Vonnegut, and these are brilliant, brilliant people, and somebody's always pushing a microphone in their faces. Writers aren't trained that way. In terms of wisdom, we're usually not much smarter than the modern living page of the daily newspaper, and we can't always come up with something on the spot; so we're often made to sound stupid when forced to react spontaneously in a media situation.

Interviewer: Did you participate in the recent international PEN conference?

Harrison: No. My feeling about that is that there's nothing I can say about those issues that someone like Doctorow can't say better. Politically I'm clumsy and full of rages. Mailer, who tends to be a very genuine creature, arranged literally the best conference ever. He even got Donald Trump to pick up the room rates so these threadbare writers were living better than usual, and then they all jumped on him. What I particularly don't understand is that ignorance—when they had Shultz come in and speak and a lot of them booed him. If the purpose of PEN is to get imprisoned foreign writers out of jail, you'd think the first thing they'd do is tend to be a little polite to those in a position to help. Instead they booed him. They did that because most of us are terribly compromised people and we pick these little items to try to maintain our integrity. They get in a snit over George Shultz, who's a pushover, right? I would want to subdue my notion of integrity and get some writers out of jail.

Interviewer: I know you taught for a year at Stony Brook, and that you disliked it. You've remarked in the past about "academic" writers. Anything more to say about this?

Harrison: That's probably an old horse that doesn't need to be beaten any more. It wasn't very profitable in the first place. Certainly there are some very good writers who perforce teach, and they're not academic writers.

There's the old notion I loathe of the writer as some kind of hysterical Ichabod Crane—the oddball on campus. That's a very comfortable existence, but I don't know if it's good for you finally. Certain professors will say, "I'm glad to see you're still writing poems," as if you've left the essential integrity of the teaching profession to defile yourself. I said a nasty thing in an interview once: "I'm always being lectured on integrity by professors who've spent a lifetime slobbering at the public trough."

Interviewer: Early in your career as a poet you received a National Endowment for the Arts grant, and then a Guggenheim. In terms of encouragement, how important was that to you?

Harrison: It was fine as long as it lasted but then it was absolutely grueling for years and years. I had a bit of a drinking problem which didn't make it any better. Those kinds of problems emphasize your basic manic-depressive tendencies. You had a boom-or-bust mentality. You'd make a little money, then you'd run down and buy a bottle of whiskey and some steaks, and everybody would be happy. It's how most blacks and Indians have to live.

Interviewer: As humiliating as it is to have to live that way, is there finally anything strengthening about it?

Harrison: How are they going to kill you if you've been through all that? You tend to take everything that passes afterwards with a grain of salt. The idea of getting bad reviews is not nearly as bad as getting no reviews, frankly. And it never stopped me from writing poems and novels, it didn't slow me down a bit. That comes from too deep a source. It's something you have to do. And at any given time during those fourteen or fifteen hard, impossible years I could have taken a well-paid teaching job, because I had that cachet as a poet and a novelist, but I refused to do it.

Interviewer: Did you ever get to the point where you thought you were just never going to make it?

Harrison: Yes, I did. *Wolf* actually did quite well for a first novel, and *A Good Day To Die* did all right, but the heartbreaker for me was the absolute failure of *Farmer*. That was something I couldn't handle because it just slipped beneath the waters. I think Viking took out one one-inch ad for it. That was a difficult period and I couldn't maintain my sanity. I had a series of crack-ups. I was at the point where I couldn't pay my taxes, which were a feeble amount. My oldest daughter won a full scholarship but I couldn't fill out the forms because I had no IRS returns to show what I made. That was the period out of which I wrote *Letters to Yesenin,* which is the book I've gotten the most mail on.

Interviewer: *Letters to Yesenin* deals with the consideration of suicide. At the end you come out against it as a valid option in your own life. Did you know right then that it was totally out of the question?

Harrison: I knew I'd been thinking about it during that bad period in the back of my mind, but I finally couldn't entertain the thought because I'd seen it in my circumstances as an utterly selfish and stupid thing to do, and then I evolved this theory that even the next meal is worth waiting for. Also I wrote, "My three-year-old daughter's red robe hangs from the doorknob shouting stop."

Interviewer: Do you think that so many artists, perhaps poets in particular, commit suicide because they've painted themselves into a corner?

Harrison: Sure, and they don't have any resources left to get out. A metaphor isn't a free lunch, and you get the kind of metaphor that keeps you alive not that often. Sometimes you have to stay alive merely because you are alive. Of course, people commit suicide in a state of derangement where they don't realize that this is the last chance—they're not quite aware of it at the time. It seems a temporary measure.

Interviewer: After you'd made that decision, "decided to stay," as you put it at the end of *Letters to Yesenin,* what happened then?

Harrison: Curiously, things kept going downhill. I would get cheated on the most minor little screenplay. I'd write one for money and then they wouldn't pay me. These things kept happening. My older daughter is still angry about what we went through, and I must admit I am occasionally. But there's nothing unique about it, and all it does is make you enormously cynical. At the end of that ghastly time I met Jack Nicholson on the set of McGuane's movie, *The Missouri Breaks.* We got talking and he asked me if I had one of my novels with me, and I had one, I think it was *Wolf.* He read it and enjoyed it. He told me that if I ever got an idea for him, to call him up. Well, I never have any of those ideas. I wasn't even sure what he meant. I think he said later that I was the only one he ever told that to who never called. A year afterwards, I was out in L.A. and he called up and asked me to go to a movie. It was really pleasant, and I was impressed with his interest in every art form. It was right after *Cuckoo's Nest* and all these people tried to swarm all over him after the movie. Anyway, later he heard I was broke and he thought it was unseemly. So he rigged up a deal so that I could finish the book I had started, which was *Legends of the Fall*.

Interviewer: After your initial financial success, didn't you blow a tremendous amount of money and get yourself back into trouble?

Harrison: The first seventeen years of our marriage we averaged less than ten grand a year; so I was a babe in the woods, and the money junkies—the lawyers, brokers, accountants—can see you coming a mile away. For two years I was simply the Leon Spinks of the literary world. One morning, during the first year of success, I was reading the *Detroit Free Press* and I sort of got the shakes because it suddenly occurred to me that I'd gone from making ten grand to making as much money that year as the president of General Motors. Well, how are you supposed to be sane? Now that it's calmed down it's nice. I'm not making a third as much money, but at least I have a nice life. And that's what we all want, isn't it? Who wants to be crazy? I don't.

Interviewer: In the last few years you've done a good deal of screenplay writing. Does it worry you that you're spending too much time at it, to the detriment of your fiction?

Harrison: Naturally, I worry about that. But it's the only way I can make a living. I don't have any other way of getting any money. I have no other gifts except what I can pull out of my hat, my imagination. I made a very conscious choice between teaching and the film business. If I hadn't made a mess of my life, I could make a reasonably good living off my novels. I'm close to it.

Interviewer: Do you enjoy writing screenplays?

Harrison: Yes, I always have, but just lately, going from one to another, I'm getting tired of it. But nobody made me do it. McGuane and I had a talk about this. The reason that writers get submerged in the film business is simply a result of ordinary human greed. There's nothing literary about it— it's just greed. Why should I blame Warner Brothers for my own greed? Faulkner always presented himself as this martyr to Hollywood. Well, bullshit. His family evolved such a high nut that he had to keep doing it, because he was supporting seventeen people—his brother's children, retainers, aunts, uncles, an alcoholic wife—and whether old Billy wanted to go to L.A. or not they stuck that sucker on the train and shot him out there to make some more money.

Interviewer: Wasn't there at one point a deal where John Huston was going to direct the screenplay you'd written of your novella "Revenge," and Jack Nicholson was going to star in it?

Harrison: My major disappointment in Hollywood was when that deal fell apart. But now, as I get older, that sort of thing doesn't bother me so much.

Interviewer: Do you still keep in touch with Nicholson?

Harrison: Sure, we're friends. He's an extraordinary person, really literate and intensely perceptive. I don't know any novelists who are more perceptive than he is, which after all is central to his profession too—to be perceptive about character. He's always aware of how people around him are changing, just as he's changing. He never tries to locate people or make them stay in one place.

Interviewer: This is perhaps another old horse that doesn't need to be beaten any more, but you've been accused of being a "macho" writer. Anything more to say about that one?

Harrison: All I have to say about that macho thing goes back to the idea that my characters aren't from the urban dream-coasts. A man is not a foreman on a dam project because he wants to be macho. That's his job, a job he's evolved into. A man isn't a pilot for that reason either—he's fascinated by airplanes. A farmer wants to farm. But you know what it's like here and up in the Upper Peninsula. This is where I grew up. How is it macho that I like to hunt and fish? I've been doing it since I was four. I have always thought of the word "macho" in terms of what it means in Mexico—a particularly ugly peacockery, a conspicuous cruelty to women and animals and children, a gratuitous viciousness. You don't write—an artist doesn't create, or very rarely creates—good art in support of different causes. And critics have an enormous difficulty separating the attitudes of your characters from your attitudes as a writer. You have to explain to them: I am not all the men in my novels. How could I be? I'm little Jimmy back here on the farm with my wife and two daughters, and, at one time, three female horses, three female cats, and three female dogs, and I'm quite a nice person. So how can I be all these lunatics?

Interviewer: Nevertheless, there is clearly a lot of you in many of your protagonists, and though they are very different people in many ways, with different backgrounds and professions, you can almost see them growing from one to the next. More recently, you seem to be coming off that a bit.

Harrison: I think so. That's what I've become exhausted with. The reason I revere Faulkner is that he was such a pure storyteller, in the Conradian sense. He created a whole world, a whole reality, and any time you don't aim to do that, you're somehow involved in contemporary gossip. I don't want to piss myself away on that kind of nonsense. And it's always this hyper gossip that turns out to be the most popular in any given age. Frankly, I can't imagine a nastier or more exhausting profession because in the long run you spend your life pulling everything out of your ass. Remember Coleridge's great quote: "What webs of deceit the spider spins out of his big hanging ass." That's in Coleridge's notebooks. I love that.

Interviewer: Has there been a conscious progression from the intensely personal material of your first novel to what you're trying to do now?

Harrison: Hopefully. This time, in *Dalva,* the first third and last third of the book are written from the voice of a woman. Why that's been brutally hard is that you don't get to use any of your easy accumulation of male resonances.

Interviewer: How do you give yourself the voice of a woman?

Harrison: It's taken about three years of hard work and, as such, is a trade secret.

Interviewer: As long as we're on the subject, who are some of the women novelists you admire?

Harrison: I don't think of women novelists but writers. Who do I read when they have something coming out? Denise Levertov, Joan Didion, Joyce Carol Oates, Diane Wakoski, Renata Adler, Alison Lurie, Toni Morrison, Leslie Marmon Silko, Ellen Gilchrist, Anne Tyler, Adrienne Rich, Rebecca Newth, Rosellen Brown, Gretel Ehrlich, Annie Dillard, Susan Sontag. Those come immediately to mind. Also Margaret Atwood.

Interviewer: You have said that you can't be a good artist unless you have a very well-developed feminine side.

Harrison: That's largely unaccepted but absolutely true. It comes from an idea in the area of psychology. The work of a man named James Hillman, an unbelievably brilliant man, has helped me to understand certain things. He asks, what have we done with our twin sister who we abandoned at birth? A man usually gives up the feminine because of our culture.

Interviewer: When you're writing about something that you can't know personally, is there ever any question of cheating?

Harrison: No, because you live through it in your imagination and you have to trust the truth of your heart's affections and the imagination.

Interviewer: You've always written your novels very quickly. Are you changing your work habits on this one?

Harrison: Writing out of this woman's voice has been so enormously difficult. I've never had more than a three-page day with her. It makes you feel like an ineffective bulldog, you keep worrying it and worrying it and nothing has come fast at all. And you have to wait until the bread comes fresh from the oven. I don't know if she's going to talk to me today or not. It's been sort of spooky.

Interviewer: Does the speed with which you usually write your novels have something to do with the poetry process?

Harrison: Yes, because you've already thought and brooded about it a lot. I think I wrote "Legends of the Fall," the title story, in about ten days. "Revenge" in about ten days. "The Man Who Gave Up His Name" was a little slower, that was probably two weeks. It just came that fast, it all came at once, and I couldn't "not" write it down that fast. Of course, those were some real long days—some eighteen-hour days. And I've never done that before or since.

Interviewer: Do you keep to a specific schedule when you're working?

Harrison: With this woman, I've had good luck starting very early in the morning which I've never been able to do before. My optimum hours are between two and four in the afternoon. I don't know why and it aggravates me. It's a circadian rhythm I can't avoid. And then between eleven and one at night. I always work a split shift.

Interviewer: Does it require a discipline to maintain that schedule?

Harrison: After you've been it this long there's no such thing as discipline. You write it when it's ready to be written. And I've tried several times to start novels when they weren't there and that's tremendously discouraging and anguishing. It's dogpaddling, and fraught with the stupidest kinds of anxieties.

Interviewer: What do you do when you can't write?

Harrison: I wonder, when a writer's blocked and doesn't have any resources to pull himself out of it, why doesn't he jump in his car and drive around the U.S.A.? I went last winter for seven thousand miles and it was lovely. Inexpensive too. A lot of places—even good motels—are only twenty-five dollars in the winter, and food isn't much because there aren't any good restaurants. You pack along a bunch of stomach remedies and a bottle of whiskey.

Interviewer: Is the gestation period a conscious process?

Harrison: Much of it, although the best things seem to arrive unconsciously, somewhat in the manner that your dreams invent people you don't know.

Interviewer: You said earlier that one's dream life is the foundation of art.

Harrison: It is for everyone whether they like it or not. Or that sleeping/waking period early in the morning. Your brain has spent the night evolving a sequence of metaphors that allows you to survive the day, and sometimes it comes out in such poignant, distinctive terms.

Interviewer: Hemingway spoke about stopping work when it was going well and then not thinking about it until the next day. Can you actually shut down the process at the end of the workday?

Harrison: Not altogether successfully. You wanted to give it as much chance to occur as possible, but not too much. It's similar to that Faulknerian notion that if you grovel before the muse, she'll only kick you in the teeth. You have to court her, do little dances, all these things you do to keep right with her.

Interviewer: Don't you also do very little rewriting?

Harrison: That's just an artificiality. The people who do a lot of rewriting haven't thought about it for three years. Some writers work it out on paper and I work it out mentally beforehand. It's only a habit.

Interviewer: I know that you allow very little, if any, editing of your work once it goes to the publisher. Why is that?

Harrison: Because I know what I want to say. If they want to publish the novel, fine, if not, not. I've been over it four or five times, so why should I let them fool with it? They're not writers.

Interviewer: I don't know many writers who don't feel they couldn't benefit at some point from sound editorial assistance.

Harrison: A woman at Viking, Pat Irving, did an extraordinary thing. On *Farmer* she suggested that chapter five should be chapter three and chapter three should be chapter five. So I switched it around and she was totally right. That's wonderful.

Interviewer: Does your publisher, Seymour Lawrence, ever ask you to accept editorial advice?

Harrison: No, he doesn't. But I might need some editing on this novel because I'm in a whole different area, and my editor who works with Sam Lawrence, Leslie Wells, is improbably alert and I would certainly listen to anything she had to say. But where this comes from, too, is the poem. Editors don't change poems.

Interviewer: You've always seemed interested in form, and in experimenting with form.

Harrison: I diagrammed the form of *Wolf* before I wrote it—just a picture of the form, no words. In *Farmer,* for example, I tell the reader how the book is going to end in the first two pages, then attempt to make the reader forget. It's similar to a Greek tale that people listen to two hundred times and still enjoy. The idea is that you make little suggestions, little parts to suggest a whole.

Interviewer: Did you ever have any formal training in music?

Harrison: No, but it was always very much of an interest. When I was in college, many of my friends were in music. That was pleasant because they taught me how to read scores, so when I was working as a farm laborer I could play Stravinsky's "Petrouchka" in my head. Stravinsky was a hero of mine. Now I'm planning to write an opera with the composer, Nicholas Thorne.

Interviewer: Dancing frequently seems to have a place in your work.

Harrison: When I was nineteen in New York I went to see dancing all the time. Up at Lewisohn Stadium, you could go for sixty cents and see Eric Bruhn or Eglevsky and the New York Ballet Company. I've always been fascinated by physical limitations. And I like it in the sense that kids dance before they're taught to. That's how the mind works. Part of it's from Yeats, who believed that the primary thing is to see life in terms of dance. To me, along with the river, the best metaphor is the dance. As Nordstrom said in "The Man Who Gave Up His Name," maybe swimming is dancing in the water. It's also a tantric motion, all those tantric Gods who are always dancing, they're always caught in a movement, no matter how ornate. They have a belt of snakes and a head of fire and seven eyes, and they're dancing. Those old myths keep coming up.

Interviewer: One reviewer called *Sundog* "a novel teeming with ideas." How has your interest in philosophy influenced your work?

Harrison: I think ideas are as real as trees. *Sundog* is actually a philosophical novel. I live around that structure although those ideas tend to emerge in my work as sort of irrational and metaphoric. What Bergson called *elan vital* interested me very early. You can see me as a fifteen year-old reading Kant's *Critique of Pure Reason,* wondering why I didn't understand every bit of it. Then I went from Kant to Kierkegaard, to Bergson, to Nietzsche. Those questions started very early in my life, once I gave up temporarily on the Bible, though I still seem to write totally within a Christian framework in an odd way.

Interviewer: In what way?

Harrison: Well, I realized a couple of years ago that never has it occurred to me not to believe in God and Jesus, and all that. I never questioned it particularly. I was quite a Bible student, pored over and over it, both the Old and New Testament in the King James Version.

Interviewer: Do you feel that your style has evolved or changed in any particular direction?

Harrison: Well, I'm no longer interested in anyone getting fancy for the wrong reasons. I'm not interested in showing off anymore. I think what's important in style, which of course is someone's voice finally, is that you have a firm sense of the appropriate. There's a temptation to enter into rhetorical sections because they're fun to write. That's probably a problem William Styron has, particularly as he's so good at it. It was very difficult for me in "Legends of the Fall," the title story, to subdue that impulse, because I think I'm pretty good at it too when I cut loose, and I had to consciously subdue my more grandiose impulses.

Interviewer: So sometimes you have to consciously hold a style in?

Harrison: Absolutely, because you want the style, in that book especially, to burst at the seams. One editor told me that if "Legends" was four hundred and fifty pages rather than one hundred pages, I could make a fortune. But the whole reason it works is that it's only a hundred pages. Tristan isn't Tristan if he's babbling. And the grandeur is in people's minds.

Jim Fergus / 1986

Interviewer: Will this new book be longer than your others?

Harrison: This will be the first time I've written a novel that's five hundred pages.

Interviewer: Was it your intention from the beginning to try a longer work?

Harrison: No, but this was a larger idea and I couldn't do it in less. And what I did again is I over-researched it. That seems to be a nervous habit I've been involved in recently.

Interviewer: Do you dislike didacticism in literature?

Harrison: I hate it. I can't use most of what I know but I think it should be there as a resonating board. You should read enough to know what's going on throughout the world. Poets should know the history of the United States and South America. Congressmen certainly don't know any of it. That's why we're down in Central America when we have no business there. They don't even know that those countries down there think of themselves as separate entities. They keep referring to "Central America." Well, try passing that off on the Panamanians, the Costa Ricans, the El Salvadorans. It's amazing to me, for instance, how few people know anything about nineteenth-century American history. They don't know what happened to the hundred civilizations represented by the American Indian. That's shocking. I'm dealing with that in this book. To me, the Indians are our curse on the house of Atreus. They're our doom. The way we killed them is also what's killing us now. Greed. Greed. It's totally an Old Testament notion but absolutely true. Greed is killing the soul-life of the nation. You can see it all around you. It's destroying what's left of our physical beauty, it's polluting the country, it's making us more Germanic and warlike and stupid.

Interviewer: Does it ever discourage you that the artist can do so little to prevent this?

Harrison: No, he's doing all he can by writing well.

Interviewer: You have said that you thought it was dangerous for an artist to embrace causes.

Harrison: I think it's terribly dangerous. I think Mailer's "The Steps of the Pentagon" was terrific, but I don't know if it was worth what he put into it. I liked better that little novella he wrote, *Why Are We in Vietnam?* which was exactly why we were in Vietnam. For my purposes, I believe what

Kierkegaard said, that you have to work out your own salvation with fear and trembling before you can get on with anyone else's program.

Interviewer: And yet the artistic sensibilities of many of the South American writers, for instance, are very much seasoned by the political climate.

Harrison: There's a danger in our lush society that the artist won't be taken seriously. For people as a whole it's been a fabulous system, but it's shit on certain people and continues to do so. I asked a group recently—and they got very angry when I brought this up—to try to explain to me the difference between apartheid and the Indian reservation system as it's been maintained by the Bureau of Indian Affairs. As far as I'm concerned, there isn't any. I went around to a half-dozen reservations last year and if you think these Indians are any better off than the blacks in Soweto you're full of shit. Some people think we got their land fair and square because of the Dawes Act. Well sure, but none of those Indians had M.B.A.'s. Red Cloud had never been in a bank. Read Mari Sandoz's book on Crazy Horse. I visited the actual murder site and it was closed because of budget restrictions! I was the only one there. All the tourists were over in the Calvary horse barns, which I wanted to get a bunch of Sioux to invade and torch. Can't you see them—a thousand mounted Sioux—riding out of the hills to destroy Fort Robinson? I think that's a magnificent idea. I'd be glad to join up as a nickel-plated Indian for that one. That area of our history is just ugly, ugly. I know this lawyer who worked for nine years as a volunteer at Pine Ridge. One night about three A.M.—we were drinking—he took me downstairs. Way back in the corner was a safe, and in the safe was a little pouch that belonged to this old woman. In the pouch was a stone that Crazy Horse had given to her mother, and this guy showed it to me, and he let me touch it. It was such a strange thing. You know, when the Sioux were being driven hither and yon by the Army until Crazy Horse's daughter died of pneumonia, he lay next to her on a burial platform for three days and three nights. Am I supposed to think that Ronald Reagan is as interesting as Crazy Horse, when he's not? What does it serve us to take these people seriously and not listen to what Black Elk said? And of course there's a grandeur in that area so hopelessly lost. Think of being a Sioux and knowing that. I can't imagine anything more painful than being an American Indian, and I'm dealing with some of those issues in this book. It's a mystery to me how we could be so generous in defeat to the Japs and the Germans, and yet so neglect and disregard the Indians. When so many are starving to death, the BIA was spending an average of six thousand dollars a year per Indian. Why don't we simply give them six thousand dollars a year in a monthly allowance and then they wouldn't starve? They don't raise their voice in their own defense anymore because they have for over one hundred years and nobody payed any attention. Why should they continue trying to talk? A Sioux told me that one reason they get drunk, other than that they're alcoholics, is because it's the only insulting thing they have left to do to us. Our doom as a nation will be unveiled in the way we have treated the blacks and Indians, the entire Third World. Washington is a flunked Passion Play.

Interviewer: You've never been afraid of poking fun at yourself in fiction, have you?

Harrison: Who wants to read about another nifty guy at loose ends? There's not a lot of self-knowledge in those novels which are published by the hundreds.

Interviewer: Are there any of your own novels that you like better than others?

Harrison: I actually never think about it. I'm always interested when reviewers compare my current work unfavorably to work that they never reviewed at all, like *Farmer*.

Interviewer: Do literary prizes mean anything to you—say, winning a Pulitzer Prize?

Harrison: No, not really. Any kind of prize is pleasant—especially to your mom, your wife, and kids—but I never got one. After you've written novels or books of poetry for a long time, your concerns become very different. That's just what you do, you've given your entire life over to it, and luckily it's panned out to the extent that they're printing your books. So as far as reputation goes, I'm not interested in any reputation that has to be sought. If there's anything more gruesome than Republican politics, it's literary politics.

Interviewer: So you don't feel any pressure at this stage in your career to write the "Big Book"?

Harrison: I feel absolutely no pressure of any kind. People don't realize how irrational and decadent an act of literature is in the first place, and to feel pressure in a literary sense is hopeless. I always think of an artist in terms of his best work, which I think is what he deserves. If he can do this, if he's taken the trouble, then this is what I think of him. The before and after is always there, but so what? He wrote well and nobody should wish to take it away from him. That's what people forget about James Jones, who wrote far and away the best war novel I can imagine. Why did they flog him senseless for the rest of his life? I always felt, strangely, a real kinship with Jones, whom I never met, being from the Midwest.

Interviewer: They also did it to Steinbeck, particularly posthumously.

Harrison: I think *The Grapes of Wrath* is a monstrously underrated novel, and Steinbeck has been neglected. But that's O.K., because he's Steinbeck and they're not. Where's their *Grapes of Wrath?* They didn't even write *The Grapes of Goofy.*

Interviewer: Do you feel any sense of competition with other writers?

Harrison: I don't know what that would be for I can't see the art processes as being a sack race. I've thought that over as part of the idea that when people whom you love very much die, why would you get in a sack race over the novel? And I think sometimes that bitterness of competition leads people to write the wrong kind of novel, the kind of novel they wouldn't otherwise write. I think Keats is still right in that the most valuable thing for a writer to have is a negative capability.

Interviewer: In what sense?

Harrison: Just to be able to hold at bay hundreds of conflicting emotions and ideas. That's what makes good literature, whereas opinions don't, and the urge to be right is hopeless. Think of the kind of material Rilke dealt with all his life. It's stupefying. Did you read Stephen Mitchell's new translation of *The Sonnets to Orpheus?* You see that the depth of his art is so dissociated from what we think of as literary existence. Your best weapon is your vertigo.

Interviewer: Is that a characteristic that might be somehow easier for a poet to cultivate than a novelist?

Harrison: Why? Look at Knut Hamsun's novels, or the best of Isak Dinesen. The best of Faulkner. It had nothing to do with that fractionated, dry, cold cliquishness of any given period. As Thomas Wolfe pointed out writing about Greenwich Village in the thirties, at any given time the most highly-regarded artist in New York is very likely to be a puppeteer. That's always been true. In my formative years, when I was eighteen or nineteen, my religion was Joyce's *Finnegans Wake.* I wore out two copies. I was insane for that book. Now it seems to me that so much of the post-modernist movement is intensely worn out, looking to European models for emotions that

Americans never get to have. For instance, I was looking at Kundera, who's not my kind of novelist but he's certainly a very good writer, and he's earned his feelings; he's been through the complete bifurcation, the destruction of his country. For someone at the Iowa Writer's Workshop to use him as a model is absurd. That's how wrung out they are when they're hoping to use a European model that has nothing whatsoever to do with any feeling they could possibly have for their own country. I remember something Yeats said, and I was going to use it as an epigraph for my novel: "What portion of the world can the artist have who has awakened from the common dream, nothing but dissipation and despair."

Interviewer: You admire Márquez a great deal, don't you?

Harrison: He's simply done things that no American novelist has shown himself capable of. Look at *Chronicle of a Death Foretold*—it's such a strong juicy death, a death in primary colors. It's not a pastel death with a film of snot over it—chichi snot at that. It's right there. That's an aspect of Lorca's poetry I've always admired. I was in a snit the other day over the infantile mechanics of minimalism, the extreme posture of fatigue. Minimalism is that old cow, Naturalism, rendered into the smallest of print.

Interviewer: Can you name some of the younger novelists you admire?

Harrison: David Martin, who wrote *The Crying Heart Tattoo*. That's a fabulous book and so is Russell Banks' *Continental Drift*. James Welch, John Calvin Batchelor and Charles Baxter are also very good. I wish Barry Lopez would write novels.

Interviewer: Anybody else?

Harrison: That's all I can think of right now. There's no sense in plugging one's friends because most of them don't need it anymore, frankly. What, am I supposed to give McGuane a plug? Of course you read your friends. In terms of sheer verbal wit and brilliance, I don't see anybody in our generation of his size.

Interviewer: Do you have any advice for younger writers?

Harrison: Just start at page one and write like a son of a bitch. Be totally familiar with the entirety of the western literary tradition, and if you have any extra time, throw in the eastern. Because how can you write well unless you know what passes for the best in the last three or four hundred years? And don't neglect music. I suspect that music can contribute to it as much as anything else. Tend to keep distant from religious, political, and social obligations. And I would think that you shouldn't give up until it's plainly and totally impossible. Like the Dostoyevskian image—when you see the wall you're suppose to put your hands at your sides and run your head into it over and over again. And finally I would warn them that democracy doesn't apply to the arts. Such a small percentage of people get everything and all the rest get virtually nothing.

Interviewer: Hemingway said something to the effect that the further along you go in writing, the more alone you become. Has that been your experience?

Harrison: He was a marvelous writer but a bully, and bullies tend to become lonely souls. You're only as lonely as you want to be. Scott Fitzgerald said this very whiney thing, that in your forties friendship can't save you any more than love could in your thirties. That's preposterously stupid and self-serving. Many times, because of certain arguments, McGuane and I could have broken off our relationship, but we never did. We always overcame it one way or another, and have been corresponding weekly for twenty years.

Interviewer: Many of your protagonists seem to be seeking escape from their lives. Joseph in *Farmer* laying his farm to rest. Nordstrom in "The Man Who Gave Up His Name" very deliberately disassembling his life. Lundgren in *Warlock* trying in his fatuous way to fill the vacuum. Is there some metaphor at work here through which the artist can then move on to something else himself?

Harrison: I think part of that is a literary device. You don't want to catch the man on the job, you want to catch him quitting the job, because when he's on the job all he gets to do is work. You have to think of him as escaping into life rather than from it. Somebody gives you the most banal and demeaning life in the way of making a livelihood, and if you abandon that, you're escaping—well, you'd have to be a nut case not to abandon it. It's that whole notion that Strang has of meaningful work. If you're an intelligent human being and you don't have meaningful work, then you'd better find it because your death, in those spooky terms, is stalking you every day. What those characters have in common, I suspect, is that they all want more abundance—mental heat, experience, jubilance. As a young man, Henry Miller saved my neck by offering these qualities.

Interviewer: And does that quest for abundance satisfy a similar need in the artist?

Harrison: The closest I've come to a perception of it keys off that prime metaphor of Neruda's—the interminable artichoke, the unfolding, a process which never stops. What people forget is that this is not a goal-oriented operation. The Buddhists say the path itself is the way. It's a matter of not stopping your perceptions and of the courage involved in following them. It's why you have to think of Rilke as the most courageous poet, and certainly Rimbaud, potentially, in terms of the sheer daring of his consciousness. But that's an interesting question, to tell you the truth, I've never thought about it. What you've done is created these people who fascinate you, created them perhaps because they'll try to answer some questions that you deeply need to be answered. Frankly, a writer should be a hero of consciousness.

Interviewer: Is there any sense of resolution for the writer at the end of a novel?

Harrison: I don't think you get a resolution so much as you've expanded your universe. At any point as an artist, like the universe itself, if you're not expanding you're contracting. It's an integral part of the life process. There's no stability involved, nothing ever stops, so the biggest problem as an artist—and it's been a problem all my life—is that of vertigo; and that's probably the source of the drinking, because, being a sedative, alcohol stabilizes. Though only on a temporary and somewhat destructive basis.

Interviewer: Do you have any problems with depression when you complete a book?

Harrison: No, just exhaustion. The last time, I had to go to that clinic in Mexico because I was exhausted. I'm trying to avoid it this time by approaching it more rationally, but I don't think I'll be able to. I'll probably have to go back to the clinic, or if I can't afford it, to my cabin.

Interviewer: Have you noticed your stamina decreasing as you get older?

Harrison: Actually, it's increased over what it was ten years ago. I usually dance a half-hour a day to Mexican reggae music with fifteen-pound dumbells. I guess it's aerobic, and the weights keep your chest and arms in shape. You know that group Los Lobos? They go from ordinary rock music into this crazy border music which I love.

Interviewer: Will it be difficult for you writing this new book through the winter months, a time when you've habitually had mental problems?

Harrison: I think it will help me beat the rap. *Sundog* did it for me that one year because I wrote through that period, which was a conscious attempt to fight it. Then three weeks after I finished *Sundog* I went to Brazil. I defy anyone to be depressed on their first trip to Brazil. It's such a gorgeously strange place, and the music element is overwhelming. They were having an anti-nuclear march when I was there, holding up their signs while they marched to samba music. It was extraordinary. I stood there on the street corner with my hair standing on end. They said to me, "O.K. you fucking American, why are you going to blow us all up? You going to blow us up before Carnival?" I said, "I'm sorry. I'm not doing it. I'm not even a senator." I was thinking that all the rest of the world is a victim of us and Russia.

Interviewer: Let me ask a question about where your passion for food and cooking enters into your life as an artist.

Harrison: I think it's all one piece. When you bear down that hard on one thing—on your fiction or your poetry—then you have to have something like cooking, bird hunting or fishing that offers a commensurate and restorative joy. It comes from that notion that the way you eat bespeaks your entire attitude toward life. Consequently it can become obsessive, especially this time of year when Guy and Russell are here, because they're both such good cooks. And sometimes you can temporarily exhaust it, just as you can exhaust yourself with writing because you work so hard. For instance, in the last few years I've really tried to lighten up on this whole cooking thing when I'm at my cabin.

Interviewer: Does the metaphor of dance translate to play?

Harrison: I used to have second thoughts about my sporting life until my wife pointed out to me that where I really get into trouble is when I lose my sense of play. In one of Rilke's poems, he talks about this overdeveloped sense of heaviness that an artist acquires. It's what I put under the heading of "lugubrious masochism." You walk around and you feel like you're literally so heavy that you might fall through the crust of the earth. For this reason I've always been a fan of Peter Matthiessen's, in a peculiar, spiritual sense. He and Gary Snyder are writers who seem to live outside the whole framework of literary reputation and ambition. When I've run into them they seemed to have an air of being content with what they were doing that other writers don't have. Reputation is volatile and a writer will despair if he thinks he is, at any given time, a consensus of what the media thinks he is, because if the media's not thinking about him at all then he disappears. Surely you need some encouragement as the years go by, but if you look too far outside yourself you're going to forget what the original dream was when you were nineteen.

Interviewer: Can you really preserve that dream?

Harrison: Just of being an artist—in the old sense of the word. More a painterly notion of an artist, or a poet, than what we think of as a novelist. My first passion was to be a painter, but I was without talent.

Interviewer: A question of maintaining a sense of purity?

Harrison: Yes, the integrity of the total mission. It's a "calling" in religious terms. You feel called to be an artist, and the worst thing is the refusal of the call.

Interviewer: It would seem that that almost childlike integrity is constantly assaulted in an artist's life, especially in this age. How can you maintain it?

Harrison: That's why you keep yourself apart. The reason I have my cabin is that it's easier to suffocate now in this culture than it's ever been, in terms of sheer, continuous bombardment, and you're not supposed to suffocate if you're an artist.

Interviewer: Isn't there a danger of being too separate, too isolated?

Harrison: Absolutely. What is it that Rilke said, and it's the truest thing I remember about being an artist? I think he said, "It's only in the rat race of the arena that the heart learns to beat."

Interviewer: So it's necessary to enter into that world and then be able to get out of it unscathed?

Harrison: Intact. It's the Zen metaphor of the ox, the ten stages of the ox, to finally have no fences and to be able to return to the city. The whole point is not to need any strictures and to still maintain balance and grace, and if you can't the danger is a life-and-death thing.

Interviewer: Metaphorically as an artist, or literally?

Harrison: Both. There are lots of ways of being killed. One of the main ways a person is killed as an artist is when he becomes mechanistic and repeats himself. Then he's dead. It's killed him as a human being and as an artist.

Interviewer: Isn't that something that all artists must eventually face, as there is a limit to one's experiences and capabilities?

Harrison: There's a limit to one's resourcefulness, but how do you know the limit? You have to push out and not do anything you've ever done before. It comes to that. The notion of change in fiction is that a train has to stay on its tracks, and animals, even more than we, are creatures of specific habits, which is why, once you learn their habits, they are quite easy to hunt. But a man can stop his car, get out; he can dive in a lake and swim across, and then climb a tree. So don't tell me you can't change your fiction. Habit is what destroys art. I've always been struck by those Cheyenne who did everything backwards when they were bored. There's a longing, a craving to know more than we get to know, sort of a Faustian notion that you want a lot of interesting things to occur before you die; and it strikes you that rather than wait around for them to occur, you're going to have to arrange most of them.

Interviewer: And your new novel pursues that longing?

Harrison: I think you design something, whether it turns out that way or not, that's very nearly impossible in terms of your own talent and then you try to do it. Here's something I wrote this summer. I was characterizing my new novel, what I wanted the mood, the feeling of it to be: "A novel written from the cushioned silence, out of the water, the first light, twilight, the night sky, the farthest point in the forest, from the bottom of a lake, the bottom of a river, Northern Lights, from clouds, the loam, also the city at midnight, Los Angeles at dawn when the ocean seems less tired having slept in private, from the undisturbed prairie, from attics and root cellars, the girl in the thicket, the boy looking the wrong direction for the moon . . ." That's all.

Interviewer: Do you think that this *Sports Illustrated* swimsuit calendar that you have above your desk is sexist?

Harrison: Yes and no. However, as a tree hung with apples bespeaks God's plenty, so does that model. It's an old Protestant trick.

Interviewer: What is this strange mobile hanging over the desk?

Harrison: That's a crow's wing I found. This is a toy pig my daughter gave me because I like pigs. Then someone read *Letters to Yesenin* for the first time this year, thirteen years later, and sent me this anti-suicide button. Here's a grizzly turd Douglas Peacock sent—that was a hard one to figure out how to hang. That's a pine cone from the forest where Lorca was executed. A Haitian baby shoe—that was found on the beach after the Haitian boat lift. A beaver pelt . . .

Interviewer: Those are talismans?

Harrison: Yeah, they are, aren't they?

Interviewer: And you have these little signs up on your bulletin board "Mortality." "The Glass Coffin." "Reality."

Harrison: Those are just little reminders. My wife put that "reality" sign up there when I was entering a depression. I never mentioned it, but it's her handwriting. And the glass coffin—I was dreaming that all these people were in glass coffins in a procession down the street and this brown person who looked like me but turned out to be my daughter went out and broke my glass coffin with a club and I popped out. She was bringing me awake to her difficulties and my own.

Interviewer: You have a ritualistic way of going about things, don't you?

Harrison: It's a bit embarrassing, isn't it? One night in my cabin I saw a flash of light and thought somebody was entering my driveway. I was so angry that I jumped out of bed and hit my head on the iron chandelier. I heard this horrible howling and yowling and I smashed through the back door to look for the car, but it was just a lightning storm. I was covered with sweat and my nose was distended, and I had long teeth and there was hair all over me. Obviously a little attack of lycanthropy, see? My dog wouldn't speak to me for two days. Perhaps it was all the anger finally coming out of me because I'd heard a wolf down in the delta, and three days later I saw the wolf right on my two-track. Two days later, I dreamed I found the wolf on the road and her back was broken, and I hugged her and she went all the way into me, and I remember thinking humorously in the dream—God, I've been trying to lose weight all summer and now I have to carry this she-wolf around in my body. How can I ever hope to lose weight? But she didn't seem too heavy.

Interviewer: In *Wolf,* Swanson was trying to see a wolf, and in *Farmer,* Joseph was trying to see a coyote. And in your own life you finally did see a wolf after many years of looking for one. What's the importance of that?

Harrison: It's a shamanistic thing, a process that occurs in your dream life. It's very primitive because our brains are primitive in a Jungian sense. From the time I was a little boy I admired bears and wolves, and it became important for me to see one in the process of my life rather than going off and seeing one as a tourist. I know what we'll do. Grab your recorder and let's walk out here and see how many of the aspen hybrids I planted have survived . . . I'm going to get about five thousand of them and make a little woodcock covert right here, so I can have a singing woodcock in my backyard. Then I got this other idea, which is to fill up this whole pasture with planted and transplanted wildflowers, just keep planting them every year until this whole thing is a jungle of wildflowers and bushes. It's hard to think about but by the time I die, if I make it another twenty years, wouldn't it be wonderful to stand out here hidden from view in this big jungle of bushes and wildflowers? That's my idea of a nice thing.

Publishers Weekly Interviews: Jim Harrison
Wendy Smith / 1990

From *Publishers Weekly* 237.3 (3 August 1990), 59–60. Reprinted with permission of *Publishers Weekly*.

Though he spent brief periods in New York and Boston during his restless youth and though his riotous visits to Key West, Fla., and Hollywood with his friend Tom McGuane have been the subject of numerous journalistic accounts, Jim Harrison's home has always been in northern Michigan. He and his wife, Linda, live on a farm about fifty miles as the crow flies from Grayling, where he grew up. It's only a short drive from their house to Lake Michigan, across which lies the Upper Peninsula, even more rural and remote, where Harrison has a cabin he retreats to in the warmer weather—"Summer," wisecracks a character in his new book, *The Woman Lit by Fireflies,* out this month from Houghton Mifflin/Seymour Lawrence (Fiction Forecasts, June 1), "being known locally as three months of bad sledding."

The initial reason Harrison decided to return to the Midwest was financial. "After my first book was published [the poetry collection *Plain Song,* in 1965] we had nearly fifteen years where I averaged only ten grand a year," he says candidly. "I needed a place with a low overhead."

But there was more to it than that; when *Legends of the Fall,* a trio of novellas released in 1979, added a measure of economic security to his already established critical reputation, he chose to remain in Michigan. "Ever since I was seven and had my eye put out, I'd turn for solace to rivers, rain, trees, birds, lakes, animals," he explains. "If things are terrible beyond conception and I walk for twenty-five miles in the forest, they tend to go away for a while. Whereas if I lived in Manhattan I couldn't escape them."

He steers clear of urban literary life for the same reason he has steadfastly turned down academic jobs. "I had this whole heroic notion of being a novelist," he says. "I wanted to be a writer in the old sense of staying on the outside. I can live for about a year on the proceeds from the first draft of a screenplay, which sometimes takes only six weeks, and I think that's more fun than hanging around some fucking college town for ten months waiting for summer vacation."

Like his characters, the author is blunt and outspoken, with an earthy sense of humor and a boundless supply of charm that take the sting out of his sallies. When he's said something especially outrageous, he glances slyly at *PW,* inviting us to share his enjoyment of how wicked he is. Yet he also sprinkles his conversation with quotes from Yeats, Camus, Santayana and Wittgenstein—Harrison is a complex man, by no means the macho figure some critics have taken him for.

This complexity can be seen in his work, both in the poetry collected in such volumes as *Returning to Earth* and, most recently, *The Theory and Practice of Rivers,* and in the series of novels and novellas for which he is best known, including *A Good Day to Die, Warlock, Sundog,* the remarkable *Dalva*—in which he definitively refuted the claim that he couldn't create believable women—and his latest. Though Harrison writes of such contemporary subjects as the rape of the natural landscape and the search for a meaning beyond materialism, none of his books can be reduced to a simple, one-sentence thesis. There is a mystery at the heart of each, a sense that beneath his beautiful, deceptively simple language lie deeper truths that can only be hinted at with words.

All of his ideas, he says, come to him in the form of images. The heroine of the title story in *The Woman Lit by Fireflies* first appeared as "a lady of about forty-nine climbing a fence behind a Welcome Center in tennis shoes. I had been thinking about Clare for years, worrying about her—you make somebody up and then you worry if she's going to be okay. I usually think about a novella or a novel for three or four years; all these images collect—Wallace Stevens said that images tend to collect in pools in your brain—and then when it's no longer bearable not to write it down, I start writing."

"The images emerge from dreams, or the period at 5:30 in the morning between sleeping and waking when you have that single durable image, like 'Nordstrom had taken to dancing alone' [the opening line of "The Man Who Gave Up His Name" in *Legends of the Fall*], which totally concentrates the character. I think you try *not* to figure out what they mean at that point, because what you're trying to do in fiction is reinvent the form; I want every fictional experience I have to be new. Once it gets didactic, then I say, Well, why not just write an essay? You don't create something so that people can draw conclusions, but to enlarge them, just as you have been enlarged by the experience of making it up. Art should be a process of discovery, or it's boring."

Harrison's own life has been a process of discovery. At age sixteen, in

1954, he decided he wanted to be a writer and headed for New York City, where he stumbled on "what I at the time called Green-wich Village," he says, pronouncing it like the color and laughing. "That's when I knew I wanted to be a bohemian; I wanted to meet a girl with black hair and a black turtleneck—and I did! Then I lived in Boston when I was nineteen; I went up there because I'd heard Boston was America's St. Petersburg, and my biggest enthusiasm in my teens was for Russian literature." He managed to squeeze in an education around his voyages, graduating from Michigan State in 1960, a year after he got married.

"I started out as a prose writer," he says, "Prose, poetry, I never separated them. But in your first notebook stage you tend toward poetry, because it's easier at that age. I tried to write prose, but I was never any good at the short story." In his mid-twenties, while living in Cambridge, Mass., with his wife and baby daughter, "I discovered the Grolier Bookstore, where I used to hang out with other poets. I'd written some poems and sent them to Denise Levertov, who was the only poet I'd ever met. My friends at Grolier had mixed feelings when I arrived one Saturday with my first contract for a book of poems—that wasn't supposed to happen for a long time!"

But the proceeds from poetry weren't sufficient to keep Harrison in the East after a year at Stony Brook convinced him he wasn't cut out to be a teacher. By 1968 he and his family were settled in Michigan. It was nearly two years before he made another try at prose, prompted by his friend and fellow Michigan State grad, novelist Tom McGuane. "I fell off a cliff birdhunting and hurt my back. Tom said—he barely remembers this—'Well, you're not doing anything else, so why not write a novel?' I thought, Yeah, that's the ticket, and so I wrote *Wolf;* I had a Guggenheim, which made it easier. I sent my only copy to my brother, who was the science librarian at Yale, because I didn't want to pay to have it copied, but I sent it away two days before the mail strike, and it was lost. He went down to the main post office and finally dug it up. I had a book of poems [*Outlyer and Ghazals,* 1971] coming out with Simon & Schuster at the time, and they took the novel too, so I started out with a bang."

Alix Nelson at S & S was the first in a long line of nurturing women editors for Harrison. He speaks warmly of Pat Irving at Viking, who published his third novel, *Farmer,* and Pat Ryan, "who saved my neck, because she would give me assignments to write outdoor pieces for *Sports Illustrated,* and they paid well enough for us to live up here for several months."

The period after *Farmer* was published in 1976 was a difficult one, however. "It sold only a couple thousand copies—it sold ten times as many copies last years as when it came out—and it was a terrible disappointment. I thought, If this is the best I can do, and it's utterly and totally rejected, then I don't know where I'm even supposed to be. There didn't seem to be any room for what I wanted to do; what I valued most, no one in the literary community valued. I went into a long clinical depression, but I gradually recovered."

Professional salvation came in the form of Seymour Lawrence, then affiliated with Delacorte, who made *Legends of the Fall* Harrison's first commercially successful book. "I had written these three novellas, and my agent at the time said, 'No one's going to publish these; they're not short stories and they're not novels.' I thought, Sam Lawrence has a good record for taking literary writers and giving them a shot, so I sent them to him. Then Clay Felker did the whole of "Legends of the Fall" and three-quarters of "Revenge" [the third novella] in *Esquire*."

If *Legends* didn't exactly make Harrison rich, it did make him much more widely known; the sale of film rights to all three novellas enabled him to buy land in Michigan and launched the screenwriting career that now allows him to attend to his real writing with a minimum of distractions. Since that book, Harrison has followed Lawrence from house to house. "Sam's mostly a publisher and a very acute reader," he says. "The kind of author he wants is someone who knows his stuff."

For the line work every novel needs, the author has relied on his eldest daughter, who reads his manuscripts before anyone else, and two editors associated with Lawrence. "Leslie Wells edited *Dalva* at Dutton, and she is so pointed. I tend to organize something dramatic and then back away from it, and she can always see it. The first sexual scene between Duane and Dalva was too emotional for me to write, and both Leslie and my daughter said, 'Hey, let's let 'em really do it!' Now there's a wonderful girl who works for Sam, Camille Hykes, who's a good editor too." His financial negotiations are handled by "my Sicilian agent, Bob Dattila, which obviously means 'from Attila'—so he has always been my main protector!"

In recent years, Harrison's ride on what he describes as "this shuddering elevator that is the writer's life" has been relatively smooth. Though he considers poetry and fiction his primary work, he doesn't disdain the movies. "I'll keep writing screenplays even if I don't need the money, because I want to write one really good one. You can't write novels all the time, and I'm intrigued by the screenplay form." He is polite about the recent film made from "Revenge," starring Kevin Costner. "John Huston wanted to direct it twelve years ago, with Jack Nicholson, and Warner Brothers turned him down. It was disappointing to me at the time, but when they finally made it, it was almost a real good movie—almost. It did well in California, the South and the Midwest, but not in New York. I doubt your average yuppie would think much of somebody dying for love—it would be out of the question."

There's a certain combativeness in Harrison's attitude toward the New York literary establishment but, he says, "It would be pompous of me to feel ignored when all nine of my books are in print. It's just that the nature of my books isn't by and large the kind of thing that interests Upper East Side New Yorkers.

"I like grit, I like love and death, I'm tired of irony. As we know from the Russians, a lot of good fiction is sentimental. I had this argument in Hollywood; I said, 'You guys out here in Glitzville don't realize that life is Dickensian.' Everywhere you look people are deeply totemistic without knowing it: they have their lucky objects and secret feelings from childhood. The trouble in New York is, urban novelists don't want to give people the dimensions they deserve.

"The novelist who refuses sentiment refuses the full spectrum of human behavior, and then he just dries up. Irony is always scratching your tired ass, whatever way you look at it, I would rather give full vent to all human loves and disappointments, and take a chance on being corny, than die a smartass."

The *Diddy Wah Diddy* Interview: Jim Harrison
Aloysius Sisyphus / 1990

From *Diddy Wah Diddy* [Jackson, MS], 6 (October 1990), 6–7. Reprinted with permission of Aloysius Sisyphus and Malcolm White.

Jim Harrison, the author of some of the best poetry and novels of the last two decades, visited with our own dear Aloysius Sisyphus recently, having just completed a promotional tour for the newly released and widely acclaimed *The Woman Lit by Fireflies*.

DWD: Are you presently working on anything that would be published in the next year?

JH: No, not in the next year, I don't like a book to come out very often. Oh, actually my collected journalism will come out, but . . .

DWD: The food columns?

JH: Yeah, well, we're not sure whether to wait on those. Terrell McDonald called and we got squeezed out of *Smart* and he's going to be the editor in chief of *Esquire* now, so I'm going to move my column over to *Esquire*. In the food column, I just talk about the theory and practice of food, eating.

DWD: That was a poem you had out a long time back that listed a lot of different types of things you had eaten that day and ended with "I'm still trying to lose weight."

JH: [laughs] Yeah, well, I lose weight frequently, every time I go to the bathroom. My last column was about fasting, it's intriguing, it's not out yet, it begins with the sentence "Throughout the long night I ate nothing."

DWD: Do you think you'll let *Esquire* print portions of the novel you've been working on?

JH: No, uh, it's strange about that, I got in an argument with the *Esquire* people ten years ago and I told Lee Eisenberg that I was going to give him the hip out of a nineteenth-story window, and I wouldn't have anything to do with him. He's a swine, but now Terry's there. No, *Legends of the Fall*, two of the novellas were in *Esquire* and then this new one was just in the *New*

Yorker, but it's hard to find a magazine, well, we didn't try, that will commit to that length. And I'm not going to condense it.

DWD: Are there any periodicals that, every now and then, you will release poems to?

JH: No, I tell you, I've gotten old and cranky, I just don't like anything about publication of anything. [laughs] It's an uncomfortable time, because of my essential modesty, I don't like to be the center of attention.

DWD: Do you think American poetry is very strong these days?

JH: Oh, the poetry situation today is miserable. There's a Red Guard sort of effect in America. There are about 6,000 of these MFA types wandering around muddying the waters of everything, writing their teeny nature poems or their teeny college poems, you know. It's like the civil service, actually, American poetry now, so, I lost interest in it, except to do a book once in a while. Never has so much rancor been raised over so little, the poetry world.

DWD: When you did the *Letters to Yesenin* why did you focus on him?

JH: Because when I was a young man I was obsessed by the prerevolutionary and revolutionary Russian poets, probably because I had that Yarmolinski anthology. So when I went to Russia in the early '70s, when it was sort of decidedly unfriendly over there, I visited the apartment where Yesenin committed suicide. And despite all these warnings I became interested in actresses later. [laughs] I should have known you know, 'cause he had that thing with Isadora Duncan, which helped precipitate his suicide and you know that was in the early '20s, and he had a tremendous cocaine problem.

DWD: When you started out writing, did you start out with poetry and then go to novels?

JH: No, I started, in high school, I wanted to be a novelist, and then all I could write was poems, 'cause I had an attention span something like Richard Nixon's, very brief; poetry is a young man's form in a sense.

DWD: Do you think there's merit to the argument that the reason you are such a good novelist is because you are a poet?

JH: Oh, I think a little bit; a story alone doesn't interest me, I can read novels only if I like the prose. You know, it's like Philip Roth said that wonderful thing, ah, "anyone on the subway has a better story than a novelist." I mean there's something to that, especially where I live in a rural area, it's a very verbal culture, in fact most people don't watch television at all.

And then, people actually look at each other when they're talking and they listen to the other person and they don't interrupt; it's a lot, like down here, it's very slow, and then one person tells a story, it might be the same story they heard thirty times but everybody's respectful and now he's told his story and [laughs] . . . well, it's like Faulkner in deer camp, when that guy said he was the worst storyteller at deer camp, 'cause he'd jump to the punch line or something like that. 'Course I've never been able to tell a joke, but I can tell a novella, though [laughs].

DWD: Where you live, are you able to get away from things pretty much?

JH: Well, totally, yeah. I live on a farm half the year and half the year I live in a cabin which is quite remote, no one in the little village near the cabin will tell anyone where I live, and they enjoy that kind of thing, you know, it puts them in on the conspiracy. This one woman that runs the newsstand and this old hotel where the rooms are five dollars, there are only eight rooms, she just likes to howl, "He doesn't want to see the likes of you, that's for sure!" you know, and it's a visiting journalist who's *supposed* to come up there, so . . ." Why would he want to talk to you, that's what I'd like to know!" That kind of thing.

DWD: Is there an Indian culture up there, or where did you get your knowledge about the Indians?

JH: Oh, since my childhood, where my farm is there's a small Ottawa reservation about six miles from me and, of course, the whole Upper Peninsula is basically Chippewah territory, and still very active, and these are the people who kicked the Sioux out of Minnesota, so they're tough people. And to survive up there for a couple thousand years is something.

DWD: Before you began to sell stories or actually got a contract did you have any occupation other than just carousing and stuff?

JH: [laughs] Yeah, I worked, that carousing talk is all gossip; I worked as a foreman at a couple of big horticulture farms, and then I was a union block layer for awhile.

DWD: Were you submitting things, trying to get published?

JH: Yeah, somewhat, but I was messed up because at the time my father and sister had been killed in a car accident which caused a lot of mental problems for the next thirty years or so.

DWD: When did you first get some inkling from any publishers that they were interested?

JH: Oh, when I was about twenty-six. What happened is I'd written ten poems, that's all, and I met Denise Levertov, the first person I ever saw read. I gave her my poems, and I thought she was sending poems back but it was big long letter saying she was the new poetry editor for Norton and would I send her my manuscript. She said if they're like the poems you sent me, I'll publish your book. Well, I didn't have but ten poems, so I got busy and got the rest of them written out. [laughter] Then Norton published that book, and it got good attention, so I tried to teach for a year at Stony Brook.

DWD: What did you think of that?

JH: That didn't work at all, I was no good at it. I think I was good at it, but it took up all my time and I wanted to be a writer, and I didn't want to be around these people all the time. It's like when I get offered a job as a writer in residence, which has happened a lot, I always use the same line, "Someone has to stay on the outside."

DWD: Did you tell your publishers you had other things that you could give them other than poetry?

JH: Oh, that happened by accident. Tom McGuane was an old friend of mine, and he had gotten back from Spain; I had had a hunting accident, I fell off a cliff and I was convalescing, and he said well, now you have to sit still, why don't you write a novel, so I wrote *Wolf,* my first novel.

DWD: Do you still spend a lot of time in the woods?

JH: All the time, I've been in the woods all summer, since late April.

DWD: Does that do anything to help center your frame of mind?

JH: Well, it does that. You know, I used to think it made you better able to handle the world, but it doesn't, it makes it worse. Everybody says if you go on a retreat, then you're fresh for the world, well, bullshit. You just see it, you see that everyone's suffocating in lint.

DWD: Do you think a writer should look for various reference points?

JH: Well, I don't know; I try to change. I think anytime you tackle a work of art where you don't try to reinvent the form, you're just adding to the clutter. You should present yourself with a formal challenge, in terms of aesthetics, and also, a more humble basic motivation is that I just can't stand to repeat myself. I don't even like to cook the same thing the same year; that's a little manic, I know.

DWD: Do you get any resistance or surprise from people when you take on different viewpoints?

JH: Yeah, every time you sort of lose some people and you gain some people. It's odd, some people resent it, "Why didn't you write *Wolf II* or *III?* And then they all have favorites, "Why don't you write *Legends of the Fall* again or *Legends of the Fall Goes to the Philippines?*" or something like that. No, I like to write different things, I would be crazy with boredom if I didn't. And you don't have to be just one thing. What was that Buddhist quote, "To study the self is to forget the self, you can be anybody. You can be a woman, in a woman, when you write, a tree or a creek. There's a cultural tradition for that kind of behavior that's 60,000 years old, you know, a novelist is just basically a storyteller, a culturally transplanted medicine man; I don't mean an herbalist, but what the Sioux call a *wakasa wanka,* which is a storyteller and a spiritual man, so if you don't that's your option. You can be anything you choose to be; that's why you have an imagination.

DWD: Do you think any of your other stories might go into screenplays?

JH: Oh, sure, I mean all of those in *Legends of the Fall* have been under options.

DWD: With those options do you retain control over them?

JH: Oh, no, you have no control over anything they do.

DWD: I assume you didn't have control over *Revenge* (the movie)?

JH: Yeah, [laughter] that's a euphemism. I had done several versions with Nicholson and John Huston eleven years ago, and then when that went under, I had nothing to do with it.

DWD: I saw a review that said it was too much Kevin Costner and not enough Jim Harrison.

JH: Well, but, Hollywood doesn't think that way, and they probably shouldn't because when you sink twenty-three million bucks in it, you want to get your money back. They had everything in the book *except* the spirit of the book. And that's because the director was English and likes jets and racing cars; he didn't understand love, he didn't understand love and doom. [laughing] They should have gotten a director from Mississippi, where that was in the air. And Huston would have done a good job of it, because he understood love and doom.

DWD: Do you have plans for putting together some screenplays now?

JH: Oh, I write them now, but I'm looking. Ed Sclicht [sic: Edward Zwick], who did that movie *Glory,* which is pretty good, he owns *Legends* now, and I think he's going to try to get it together. I think he's finished the screenplay and is going to try to shoot the film starting later this year.

DWD: A lot of people have compared you to Herman Melville. Did you see that influence before you heard it said about you?

JH: Oh, I love Melville, but I don't see any connection but, then, it's not my business to come up with these things, maybe they'd only read Melville and it was convenient that way. [laughter]

DWD: Do you do a lot of revision of your work as you go?

JH: Just in process, 'cause I write long hand, but my secretary, we have a computer over at her house, so I get to see it several times. Then I sent it to my oldest daughter, she goes through it. She's my best editor. Always has been since she was eighteen.

DWD: Does she edit it blind or discuss it with you as she goes?

JH: No, she just looks at it and tells me, well, in *Dalva*, I tended to back away from certain sexual aspects, and she told me I was chickening out, and I knew I was. She's a brilliant girl and she's much more violently critical than anybody I've ever run into in New York.

DWD: You don't expect to change publishers at anytime in the future?

JH: If Sam (Lawrence) retires, I'll probably get paid what I'm worth, [laughing] 'cause I stick with him for reasons of sentimentality. The flattering thing about being with Sam is he has such credibility in Europe, and I like to have my books all come out all over Europe, too, in different countries, It makes up a lot of the difference between what I get from Sam and what I would get from Random House or something like that, that European exposure.

DWD: Does the poetry translate well?

JH: No, they have never translated it. Well, some of the poetry has been translated into Spanish.

DWD: When you read the Russian poetry, did you not think that it translated poorly?

JH: Well, it depends on who it is, as Samuel Johnson said, "If you translate something into English, what's the point if it doesn't read as a poem in English." That's the beauty, I think, actually, Lowell's best book is *Imitations*, now that all the crap has settled about Robert Lowell, his best single book will be *Imitations* and then maybe *Life Studies,* 'cause they were such marvelous renditions of foreign poems.

DWD: Some reviewers said you and Saul Bellow are really the same person, what do you think about that?

JH: That's some raving psychotic. [laughter] No, I admire Saul Bellow, I never even met the guy, just because he stayed in Chicago and stuck to it, and he made New York eat it on his terms. You know, when Saul Bellow deigns to go to New York, he has dinner with all the critics at once, he cons them into saying what he wants and goes back to Chicago on the morning flight. How could it be better than that? The guy's a bearer of a very large brain, as Pooh would say. Certainly he has the best equipment, mentally, of any American novelist. For sheer prose I like people like McGuane, just like I like Nabokov, just to read for reading prose, it's brilliant.

DWD: Have you read any of the new people that are coming out from Eastern Europe?

JH: Well, I've read Kundera, but I always liked the Latin Americans and the South Americans. Of course, to me, the great European novelist is Günter Grass, still. In fact, I'm not much for regionalism or nationalism. I mean, Norman Mailer is fine, but he certainly isn't in the league of Gabriel Marquez. I mean, who cares what country they're from, I care about the art form. When you look at novelists' politics, they generally don't have very interesting politics, just very quirky and self-serving, so I try to stay clear of all that. But it is interesting to learn about different places.

DWD: Well, we sure do appreciate you visiting with the *Diddy* while in Jackson.

JH: Thank you, too.

A Man Lit by Passion: Jim Harrison
Tom Auer / 1990

From *The Bloomsbury Review*, 10 (November/December 1990), 1, 16.
Reprinted with permission of Tom Auer and *The Bloomsbury Review*.

If you were to see Jim Harrison on the street, you would probably step aside quickly. His bulk, his muscularity, and the sternness of the face behind the thick, droopy mustache would no doubt inspire fear in most pedestrians. He is not tall, but he's as wide as a truck and probably just as strong. In fact he looks more like a bodybuilder than the author of six books of poetry and seven works of fiction or the Guggenheim Fellow that he is.

Harrison has a deep, earthy voice, which sometimes slows to a drawl; you would not expect that voice to quote long passages from literature, as he often does. Hearing him speak, you might think he is a farmer. And you would certainly never guess that this man, whose mere presence exudes a gritty masculinity, would also be an expert cook and food columnist for *Smart* magazine. Appearances, as powerful as they may be in this case, do not make this man.

More than likely, you would not see Jim Harrison on the street, anyway. You might find him on a trout stream or hiking through some canyon or across a desert or maybe on a western highway, headed nowhere in particular. Most likely you'd find him at his home in the woods of northern Michigan. Chances are, he would either be writing or reading or cooking or eating. These are a few of the passions that make this man.

One might safely say that Harrison lives a full life. His fondness for good food and wine, the wildness of his youth, his love for the natural world, and his disdain for academia are all well documented. Like many writers, his career has been a roller coaster ride of critical successes and agonizing disappointments, financial and otherwise, but he has always managed to remain in control of his own life and destiny.

Academic life never quite suited him, but he eventually received both a B.A. and M.A. from Michigan State University, but just barely. "I'm the only one I know to ever flunk a graduate course and still get the degree," he admits. Before bowing out of the ring of academe, he taught for a year at the State University of New York at Stony Brook. But he has not bowed out completely. His reviews and essays continue to appear in the best literary journals.

In between his novels and novellas, poems, critical writing, and food columns, he writes screenplays. While only a few have been produced as films (many more have been optioned), he has managed to make considerably more money writing for Hollywood than for book publishers or periodicals. Writing screenplays, he says, "is just a downshift. And I only will write originals, so then I get to have the fun of making them up. And I can't write novellas all the time. It seems soporific." Screenwriting has also kept him in food and wine and books, and has allowed him to buy land around his farm to maintain his privacy and sanity.

For most of any given year, Harrison lives on the land where he was born in 1937. He makes his home in the northern Michigan woods with his wife of thirty years, Linda, and they have raised two daughters, the youngest now nineteen. The farm and the woods provide the tranquility required to turn out a good story—or a culinary feast. Harrison also spends some of his time at a cabin not far from the farm and five miles or so from the nearest distraction, where he does some of his writing.

Jim Harrison passed through Denver in August of this year on one of his infrequent book tours. His new collection of novellas, *Woman Lit by Fireflies* had just been released by Houghton Mifflin, and he was on a promotional tour that would take him to Seattle, Minneapolis, Birmingham, Milwaukee, and Jackson, Mississippi, after Denver—by no means the standard East Coast-dominated author tour. Harrison knows where his readers are.

Perhaps like Harrison himself, his most recent characters are all facing the perplexity of age and maturity, and reckoning with lives they have led and not led. *Woman Lit by Fireflies* presents three widely different stories of arriving at, and in some cases escaping from, the muddle of middle age. "Brown Dog" tells the story of a rural rascal with a religious background but a far from spiritual lifestyle who manages to find a variety of troubles through his weakness for the joys of the flesh and his attempts to both exploit and protect some Indian burial grounds. "I haven't tried to write anything comic for a long while, and the character Brown Dog, that's sort of the way I grew up. I liked that somewhat opportunistic scoundrel. He's likable, but he's finally swindled by the anthropologists through his own fatal flaw. But he tries."

In fact, Harrison's own upbringing was very religious. "When I was fifteen I wanted to be a preacher," he explains. "My parents were Congregationalists, so I was a Baptist . . . before my rebellion. I did some preaching at Youth for Christ. And then a terrible thing happened. I ran off to Estes Park, Colorado, and worked as a busboy at the Stanley Hotel and met a girl—I was only sixteen, but I was a fibber. She was a senior at the University of Kansas and she took me way up in a fire tower, and she started taking off her Levi's. It was wonderful, I'll tell you, but I lost my religion. And then my mind started to broaden."

"Sunset Limited" describes the less than joyous reunion of a group of former campus radicals from the sixties—all having grown in different ways and directions—who twenty years later reunite to help one member of the group escape from a Mexican prison. Harrison considers it the least successful story in the book. "It came from an attempt to write a screenplay. I wanted to see it in prose first. Those are the kind of people that I used to know. It's about how a woman—or a man—can love someone so totally unworthy, and not love someone who is totally worthy. That's the pervasive theme," he says.

When I mention that I think it would make a *great* screenplay, he scoffs at the idea of Hollywood liking the story. "Ya, well they're not sure of anything that's that heartfelt out there. They think there's gotta be an angle."

The title story of *Woman Lit by Fireflies* is told through the voice of a woman who, after too many years of a less than satisfactory marriage and social life, breaks away from the constraints of the status quo in a surprising way. It is a poetic and sensitive story that describes an entire lifetime in the mind of a troubled woman within a span of about twenty-four hours. "We subconsciously know we're going to quit a long time before we do," he says, "and then it's there. It's what we used to think of as walking off the porch, you know? *Sayonara,* I'm outta here."

Harrison does not enjoy book tours or interviews, though he gives them his best shot. He is well known for his voracious appetite for literature, and not surprisingly, our conversation is dominated by talk of books and publishing and his favorite writers, among them Peter Matthiessen, Douglas Peacock ("what a piece of work"), James Welch, Louise Erdrich and Michael Dorris, Linda Hogan, and his friends, writers Tom McGuane ("I think in some respects, in terms of pure, jewel-like prose, he's about as good as we have.") and Dan Gerber, painter Russell Chatham, and actor Jack Nicholson.

Jim Harrison began to take writing semiseriously at the age of nineteen when he was traveling around the country, working odd jobs, and finding plenty of time during mindless, physical work to think about the world around him and fantasize about his place in it. "What else can you write when you're nineteen?" he asks. "Poems about yourself," he answers. "That's when you dream the most brilliant dreams. Rimbaud and Dostoyevsky and Yeats, those were the people I was obsessed with at that age. Keats. And all of them at the same time, so you can see I was headed for trouble. . . . But now I'm more intrigued by the idea that the Chinese have, that you disappear into your work totally and not leave any trace of yourself anywhere. I like that idea." And then he laughs.

His first published poetry was generally well received by critics, but as is the case with most poetry, it didn't sell well enough to support the poet. Then, after a hunting accident that was to lay him up for several months, his friend Tom McGuane suggested that he try writing a novel. He did—*Wolf: A False Memoir* (Simon & Schuster, 1971)—followed by two more: *A Good Day to Die* (Simon & Schuster, 1973) and *Farmer* (Viking, 1975). Although they were also generally well received, they were also criticized for being "men's books"—they were too macho (a description he despises), with hollow female characters who were easily dominated by the men in their lives.

Legends of the Fall (Delacorte, 1979), his first collection of novellas, was the book that received the most positive reception from critics up to that point. The novella is a form he prefers and one that perhaps best exhibits his tremendous talent for storytelling. "I enjoy the form because it isn't such an exhaustive one. I can't write short stories at all. I've tried. It's not my form. About a hundred pages is as low as I can get anything out. . . . I got the form from the Germans and the French, and the longer stories of Kafka, Isak Dinesen—whom I've always revered—and then Katherine Anne Porter. The form is just suitable, I guess, for whatever voice I have."

Legends of the Fall was followed by two novels, *Warlock* (Delacorte, 1981) and *Sundog* (Delacorte, 1986), and later another book of poetry, *The Theory and Practice of Rivers* (Winn, 1986; Clark City Press, 1989) and perhaps his best known novel, *Dalva* (Dutton, 1988). It was his first novel to receive wide critical acclaim, which was somewhat surprising because most of the story is told in the voice of a woman.

To hear him describe it, he develops the characters of his fictions over long periods of time, and from every conceivable source. People he meets during his wanderings may turn into characters later on, memories might develop into plots, dreams may turn into magical sequences of poetry or dialogue. But these musings generally don't turn into stories until much later. After years of fermentation, they will end up on the page in a blaze of manic writing that will become a carefully crafted novella in the span of a few weeks to a month. The novels take a little longer. He worked fast, he says, "until *Dalva,* which was a one-page-a-day shot, because I was assuming a woman's voice. I didn't even get to drink much at all when I was writing that or else I'd lose the voice."

Often, in the process of completing whatever manuscript he is working on, he has come close to driving himself mad from sheer exhaustion. At that point, literary mission completed, his habit has been to hop in the car, and head out on the highway to destinations unknown, returning months later in some cases, to work on the next project. "I've driven up to 10,000 miles sometimes," he says, "mostly to empty places. Utah, Montana, Arizona, southern and western Colorado. Any place where there aren't many people." He stays in cheap motels some of the time, and sometimes he camps out "Peacock-style"—when he's tired he "just throws himself on the ground."

Along with other provisions, he stocks the car with audiotapes of his favorite writers reading from their work. On one recent trip he listened to *Tracks* (read by Louise Erdrich and Michael Dorris), Stephen Mitchell's *Tao te Ching,* and Evan Connell's *Son of Morning Star.* He enjoys listening to readings while driving the long, barren highways, because "that way you're bathed in lovely prose and images."

Our conversation drifts back to Peter Matthiessen and contemporary writing. "Peter has always been somewhat of a model for me. I had lunch with him the day after he got back from Tibet, when he was working on *Snow Leopard.* His work is astounding. Not to fall into the goofy glistenings of the New Agers, but he seemed to have sort of an aura that day, if you get what I mean.

"He has such range. That's the thing you don't get in what I think of as the Red Guard of the MFAs. You don't get the range. You get a concentration on perimeters, never the Dickensian part of the way we live, just fragile, attractive perimeters."

Does it bother him that some young, highly promoted writers receive so much attention in the press, while better writers often get considerably less ink? "It doesn't matter," he says, "because it [the writing] disappears very fast, anyway. Most of them are not resourceful enough to keep going."

How has *he* managed to keep going? "You know, all a writer wants is for his books to be in print. There are nine of mine in print. . . . And I haven't read *The New York Times Book Review* for twenty years, anyway, because it innervates me. I haven't read it since my year at Stony Brook." In fact, he prefers to keep his distance from most literary criticism. "But then Dan Gerber made me read this book," he said, "and I didn't really want to read it. It's by Fred Turner—*Spirit of Place* [Sierra Club, 1990]. What a great book that is. It's one of the best books about American literature I've ever read. I can't read any of the deconstructionists, at all. It's just another way academics have devised to make themselves more important than the source."

Book reviewing doesn't fare much better in Harrison's mind—"That's an art that's really sunken in the last twenty years, to be able to find reviewers who are broadly read who have a frame of reference. You read a lot of very earnest people who are not good reviewers."

Although Harrison's books have been widely reviewed, he is even better known in Europe, which delights and puzzles him. "You know, the French are very peculiar," he tells me. "When *Dalva* came out in French last year, three French critics came to my home in northern Michigan from Paris to talk to me. You never have such a thing like that in America—nothing quite of that order. Luckily I had a lot left in my collection of Bordeaux from years ago, compliments of Warner Brothers, and I put a lot of that out, along with grouse and venison and woodcock—everything that's difficult to find here—and they looked at the Bordeaux and one critic said 'only the Japanese can drink such wine.' "

"They are so intense. They were asking me about their favorite American authors. They liked me, which I was pleased with, and they liked this man they called 'Mc-Goo-ane.' But another one of the hottest writers in France is really going to shock you: James Crumley. Me, McGuane, and Crumley, boy, that's a far reach. Crumley thinks of himself as just a mystery writer, basically, but they don't see it that way. I don't either. I've always liked his writing. But the idea of what's hot in 'gay Paree' is really something.

"The French have brought out all my books except the *Selected Poems,* so that's reassuring—lovely editions, beautifully designed, too, and that's sort of flattering.

"That's one thing that keeps you going. They can neglect the shit out of you in New York, but if you're doing well in London and Paris, then you feel better."

As it is with most writers, the experience of publishing a book can also be troublesome to Harrison. "Every time you write a book, it's like giving a kid up for adoption or something, and that's a terrifying feeling," he says.

When Harrison turns in a manuscript it is not to be tampered with. "I don't allow any editing," he says. "When I turn in a manuscript, it's really clean copy, and it's what I want." Which is not to say that no one else has looked at it carefully. "The first one who reads my book is my daughter in Montana, she's my best editor, and then my wife. My daughter particularly can tell when I'm backing away. In *Dalva*, she [Dalva] was going to make love after drinking some plum wine, and I chickened out in the scene. And both my wife and my daughter said 'You can't chicken out here.' But it was too emotional for me at the time, I couldn't do it, you know. It took me days to think it through. But it's usually a matter of backing away, never structural things."

Inevitably, our conversation turns to what's coming up for Jim Harrison. I had read about a sequel to *Dalva*. "Well, the book I intended to write was about the grandfather that raised Dalva, but I got her voice in a dream, of all things, and I saw her sitting on a balcony in Santa Monica thinking about her Nebraska girlhood, and then she took over. But the grandfather was the one I was ready to write about, and there are five boxes of material I didn't use writing *Dalva*, because I got thunderstruck."

But next we should look for a collection of criticism and other prose writings and a new set of novellas—"they just came to me when I was writing these novellas," he says. "Now that my youngest daughter's nineteen, I feel I'm going to write a tremendously sexy story. I haven't for years."

As we walk back to his hotel, I'm reminded of lines from one of his poems, "Looking Forward to Age":

> In a one-room cabin at night I'll consign
> photos, all tentative memories to the fire.
>
> And you my loves, few as there have been, let's lie
> and say it could not have been otherwise.

Siren Song: Will Success Lure Poet/ Novelist Jim Harrison Out of His Midwestern Lair?
Robert Cross / 1992

From *Chicago Tribune Magazine* (30 August 1992), 14–18, 24. Copyrighted 1992, Chicago Tribune Company. All rights reserved. Used with permission.

The poet and the movie star dine at Gibsons Steak House in Chicago while a cordon of waiters flicks away autograph loonies as if they were so many black flies. The movie star, Jack Nicholson, naturally draws most of the attention. His close friend, the poet Jim Harrison, is sometimes mistaken for Nicholson's bodyguard, but in a certain metaphorical sense, just the opposite might be true.

In New York, screenwriter Jim Harrison offers hospitality to a Columbia Pictures producer by dabbing a pound of beluga caviar over their shirred room-service eggs at the Hotel Carlyle. "Hell, let's have some vodka too," the producer suggests. And they do.

Novelist Jim Harrison, late at night, leaves his cabin in the Michigan woods, strips off his clothes and jumps in the river. He plans to make one of his characters do likewise, and Harrison wants to know how it feels (brutally cold and deliciously scary).

Tracking all the movements of Jim Harrison would take the vigilance and sensitivity of a timber wolf. He lives on a farm in Lake Leelanau, Mich., about fifteen miles north of Traverse City, and retreats often to an isolated cabin near Grand Marais, on the Lake Superior shore of the Upper Peninsula, almost as if he needs to remind himself and everyone else that too much celebrity could poison the well of imagination. Show business frequently calls him to the "dream coasts," where he still insists that the hyphenated career described in photo captions—"novelist-screenwriter-poet"—is appallingly incomplete.

Harrison tends to juggle the lineup so that "screenwriter" falls somewhere near the bottom of the batting order (although studios do buy most of the caviar), and he certainly could add several other occupations, past and present: journalist, columnist, essayist, book critic, lecturer, farmer, carpenter, salesman, teacher, hunter, fisherman and, as he put it one time, "professional pig, gourmand and trencherman."

A steadily growing public knows Jim Harrison best for his powerful novella "Legends of the Fall"; the poignant *Dalva,* written in a woman's voice; and "Revenge," a tragic love story set in Mexico and adapted for the screen with Kevin Costner and Anthony Quinn heading the cast.

"Legends," too, may become a motion picture (Ed Zwick, director of *Glory* and creator of *thirtysomething* bought the rights to it), and this summer Harrison completed the sixth and final draft of an original screenplay, *Wolf,* in which Jack Nicholson is set to star under the direction of Mike Nichols.

Harrison's works invoke concise images of woods, water, plains, desert, mountains and the serio/comic twists of the human psyche. Some speak of solitude and the sort of life he has treasured since his boyhood on a Michigan farm—grouse hunting, trout fishing, tramping through thickets, watching birds and tracking wildlife.

He labored at writing and odd jobs in relative obscurity for most of his life, but now, in his fifty-fourth year, the old anonymity is beginning to elude him. Scholars find intellectual meat in his work, they press upon him invitations to do readings and they plead for literary-journal interviews.

Filmmakers admire Harrison's ability to spin yarns, so a lot of his product gets into play as potential material for the screen, making him, at last, quite rich. His novels and novellas have been published in nine languages. The French, in particular, adore Jim Harrison, and his books sell better there than they do here.

His output appeals to a highly eclectic audience, or several audiences, and as a result, nearly everything Harrison has ever done remains in print: *Wolf* (no relation to the movie script), *Farmer, A Good Day To Die, Warlock, Sundog, The Woman Lit by Fireflies,* seven volumes of poetry and a collection of essays, poetry and journalism called *Just Before Dark* that appeared in paperback (Houghton Mifflin/Seymour Lawrence) just before July.

Harrison's column, "The Raw and the Cooked," runs in *Esquire.* Sometimes it deals with food. Mostly it serves up whatever happens to be stewing in his brain: "Once I prepared quail for an actress of some note who doubled as a vegetarian. She was appalled after dinner to discover she had eaten a living thing. 'Not after it was shot and plucked and roasted at 400 degrees for 23 minutes,' I offered, suspecting Quaaludes."

Harrison swings with no apparent effort from poetry to puckishness. In his introduction to *Just Before Dark,* for instance, he explains, movingly, his affinity to dusk, which during summer in the northern latitudes last almost till 10 p.m.:

"Walking at twilight owns the same eeriness of dawn. The world belongs again to its former prime tenants, the creatures, and within the dimming light and crisp shadows, you return to your own creature life that is so easily and ordinarily discarded. I have always loved best this time just before dark when the antennae stretch far and caressingly from the body."

"Brown Dog," a novella in *The Woman Lit by Fireflies* collection, begins: "Just before dark at the bottom of the sea, I found the Indian. It was the inland sea called Lake Superior."

Thus, as an American Lit student might observe, Harrison's favorite time of day shades a long, pensive walk or splashes hilariously on the opening sentence of a tale involving a confused salvage diver who finds a well-preserved Native American corpse in the freezer compartment of the Great Lakes.

Harrison's books ring with something indefinable that often leaves reader sensing that his words will resonate through literary history. Maybe they will, and maybe they won't. But another Digby Diehl proclaims, "Somewhere in that big literary acreage staked out by Thoreau, Hemingway and Hunter Thompson is a chunk of space for Jim Harrison." And Bernard Levin in the Sunday *Times* of London submits, "Jim Harrison is a writer with immortality in him."

At one point this summer, just before dark, in his Grand Marais log cabin, one could be certain of this: Harrison had in him a pound and a half of Lake Superior whitefish and about six ounces of red wine. A fisherman in town had given him the entrée that morning, and Harrison broiled it with a sauté of tarragon butter on the grill out back. That project consumed a good part of late afternoon, seasoned all the way with conversations about dear friends and literary giants.

Harrison's voice creaks and snaps like an old harness strap at a volume sufficient to make himself heard over the noise in Elaine's of Manhattan or the Dunes Saloon of Grand Marais (both of which he frequents). The writer does much of his talking in places like those or with packs of boisterous pals. He discusses the authors he likes with the enthusiasm a Michigan lumberjack might use talking about the great Detroit Tigers baseball teams of years past.

That day, like most days, Harrison's forty-eight-inch chest often shook with laughter against the faded blue cotton of a collarless shirt, and his teeth gapped merrily beneath a scraggly black mustache. His left eye, which is made of glass, tends to stray. It can lull people with its aspect of bored inattention, while the right eye, small and brown, fixes on everything with the unshakable scrutiny of a marsh hawk.

Although Harrison's ancestors lived in Sweden, they apparently came from a dark-skinned line, not the light blond usually associated with "that dour land without sunshine and garlic." As a result, some Western bartenders have refused him service on the grounds that they don't pour for Indians.

Will Jim Harrison some day walk among the literary legends himself? "Only black holes have real immortality," he scoffed, relighting an American Spirit cigarette that he had stubbed out only minutes before. "I think it's a young man's game to worry about it all the time.

"Years ago, when I was just still a poet, I thought I would be better off if ignored. My publisher, Seymour Lawrence, told me, 'You're the only one of my novelists who doesn't think he should be more famous than he is.' I'm actually more educated than most novelists in terms of literary history, and I've learned that what's good this week smells next week—or next year.

"Last year, a publisher asked me to write a blurb for a reissue of the Sherwood Anderson books. I said, 'Don't you have this ass-backwards? You mean Sherwood Anderson has to be plugged by an upstart?' "

Yet Harrison does concede occasionally that he just might be remembered. He recently published his Michigan State University master's thesis, "A Natural History of Some Poems," although with obvious reluctance. "I view this as juvenilia, of interest only to assistant professors, should my work prove durable," he remarked.

On one of the 10,000-plus-mile drives he occasionally takes to cure "bad brain," Harrison almost lost control near the edge of Arivaca Canyon in Arizona. "As the car slid toward the precipice on the frost-slick dirt," he later wrote, "I undid my seat belt and opened the door, under the assumption that a car is easier to replace than a novelist."

Such subtle intimations aside, Harrison generally regards the future as the collection of mysteries that life trots out every day. His character Brown Dog, the one who found the Indian sitting on the bottom of Lake Superior, simply notes:

"I have my own theories about what people think of as the future. Imagine yourself lying in bed sleeping and dreaming of things people dream of—say, fish, death, being attacked, diving to the bottom of the ocean. . . . It makes the world seem blurred and huge. Then you wake up, and you're just B.D. in a ten-dollar war-surplus sleeping bag in a cold cabin. The first step is to pee and make coffee, which I can deal with, and after that, what happens is not in firm hands."

Harrison is one of the few literary personages in the United States who has managed not to get stuck in one stifling category. He seems to relish the glamor that brushes his life—dinners with Nicholson, meetings with the late John Belushi, fishing with novelist and old classmate Tom McGuane and actor Michael Keaton, hunting grouse with painter Russell Chatham and the Count Guy de la Valdene, schmoozing with Bill Murray, Orson Welles, John Houston, Jeanne Moreau, Federico Fellini, Kevin Costner and Harrison Ford. Yet he flees all that for his farm or his cabin and seems equally taken with the sight of a bear rolling in the river mud as he is with the menu at Lutèce.

At his cabin this summer, Harrison was shaking off the aftereffects of a professional ordeal. He had just finished adding the final touches to, and attending the last (he hopes) meetings about, *Wolf*, the motion picture. "The main thing I've been trying to get ever since I fell apart in New York a month ago is what I think of as the time disease," he said, "the overwhelming sense that one slices one's life too thinly in too many directions. And I've been doing that for four years.

"Up here, I've always adapted quite well to so-called Indian time, measuring it by moons. I've learned from a Sioux friend how you can do everything backwards to feel better, to reverse your boredom. You get up and cook a big meal, eat it, have two shots of whiskey, take a nap, have a little lunch, eat breakfast and go to bed at nine. Or you go for walks where you've never been before, which is easy up here."

Harrison often turns to Native Americans for wisdom and solace, just as he has dabbled in Zen, alcohol and cocaine over the years, although he has long since abandoned the last of those measures as largely useless. "My interest in Native Americans comes from the idea that I think I've seen the best that the white culture offers, and now I'd like to look into other stuff," he explained.

The *Wolf* script paid handsomely but evidently took slices of time that Harrison would rather have spent on some novellas he has in the works. "There was a sort of argument back and forth between me and Mike Nichols, the director," he said, "but now it's all healed up and I'm up here.

"It's about a guy who in a period of thirty days becomes a wolf. It starts in New York City and ends in Labrador. It's not a genre movie, not a werewolf picture, although that's where part of the disagreement came. It's more from an Inuit, an Eskimo, belief that if you're very ill physically or mentally—which they look at as the same—the only way you can have a chance of getting better is to go into the body of an animal. And you either come out the other side or you don't. Both are good things to them. They don't differentiate—'bad' animal, 'good' person. You do drop your rosary along the way, I suppose."

Jim Harrison in his solitude seldom needs to live his days backwards. During a steady rain one afternoon, he showed me a little of his territory: winding dirt roads and two-tracks through deep timber, pristine little lakes and the spectacular dunes lining the one big lake, Superior, that looms over some of his themes like a cold, wet sky. He expertly steered a massive Chevrolet van with four-wheel drive, a loaner he had agreed to test for *Automobile* magazine.

Harrison parked, got out, scanned the misty horizon and croaked expertly at some ravens. They glanced his way out of curiosity and flapped a retreat toward distant trees. On one such excursion, Harrison said, a wolf crossed his path, almost as if to validate all the hours he spends in the wild looking for creatures, rare plants and himself.

"I first heard the wolf four years ago, then I saw him three days later out on a two-track," he recalled. "Rangers theorize that they come over from Batchawana Peninsula in Canada and cross the ice at Paradise Point, north of the Soo [Sault St. Marie]. When you hear them cry out, it's overwhelming. My old Labrador would go up in the loft and hide under the bed. You feel blessed if you ever get to see one, because they're so hyperalert."

Harrison himself habitually sniffs the air for intruders. A sign near his barn yard in Lake Leelanau says, "Do not enter this driveway unless you have called first. This means you." At his cabin, a gentler sign cautions: "Please do not arrive unannounced. I may be working."

"Of course, nobody can announce, because I don't have a phone," Harrison said, obviously relishing the joke. Work: He may be putting words on paper with his pen, or he may be hiking thirteen miles into the wilderness. He may be casting flies or following his English Setter bird dog, Tess. He may be preparing elaborate meals for sportsman buddies from all over the world. Any of it could be classified as honest toil; the interesting parts of his life eventually find their way into poems or novellas, novels, columns, screenplays or bar talk at the Dunes Saloon.

If a U.P. local suggests, in a particularly nasty way, that Harrison has been sleeping late, he might say, "OK, if you think I'm so lazy, let's compare tax returns." If a grizzled U.P. fishing guide or deerstalker implies that Harrison has tender feet, equally grizzled friends jump to Harrison's defense.

"He's an original character," says Mike Ballard, owner of the Dunes Saloon and a friend of Harrison's for the past decade. "When it comes to hunting and fishing, he knows what he's doing. There's no bull—— about it. One day we were looking for brook trout, and we had to cross seventeen beaver dams. It took us seven hours to get where we were going. That didn't bother Jim."

Harrison's Los Angeles-based agent, Bob Datilla, also attests to Harrison's tough nature. A Michigan State classmate, Datilla remembers Harrison and novelist McGuane as kids who devoured literature the way most young people immerse themselves in movies or pop music.

"I was from kind of a blue-collar family, and he and some of the other writers that were there just made reading books so attractive that they made me a lifelong reader," Datilla told me.

"I think the great thing about Jim and Hollywood and writing in general is that he's done what very few other writers—classic American writers, or anybody for that matter—has been able to do. He's not been ruined by Hollywood. In fact, he's using Hollywood as a kind of cross-training regimen. He still keeps writing his novels. He has a novel out every couple of years. He still keeps writing his poetry books, and he still keeps writing screenplays."

It sounds rather easy now, but much of Harrison's life in letters was darkened by clouds of poverty. He and Linda King, his wife of thirty-two years and college sweetheart, often struggled to clothe and feed themselves and the first of their two daughters, Jamie Louise. Harrison published volumes of poetry during his two years of teaching at the State University of New York at Stony Brook, a job he loathed. He quit and fled back to Michigan with his family in 1968 and soon after wrote his first novel, *Wolf: A False Memoir*. That one and *A Good Day To Die* (1973) were mildly successful, but *Farmer* (1975) was a financial flop.

His work did receive some nibbles and modest option payments by movie producers, thanks to Datilla's persistence, and grants from the National Foundation for the Arts and the Guggenheim Foundation helped, but Harrison in the mid-'70s despaired of ever fulfilling his dream of supporting himself and his family entirely with his writing. He and Linda had produced a second daughter, Anna Severin, and Jamie was ready for college, which Harrison couldn't afford.

Often, when authors find themselves in such straits, they fall back on teaching, try their hand at writing dog-food ads or make a desperate grab for movie cash. Some illustrious novelists have followed the cinematic route, including William Faulkner and F. Scott Fitzgerald, although the literati would tend to look upon those episodes as pacts with the devil. Harrison often says he regards film work as a legitimate outlet for a serious author and supporting one's family as a crucial responsibility.

From the time he was twelve, Harrison had fantasized leading a writer's life, hoping it would serve as an antidote to "middle-class boredom." He was born in Grayling, Mich., a small town some fifty miles east of Traverse City, on Dec. 11, 1937. His father, Winfield Sprague Harrison, was a farmer and a county agricultural agent. His mother, Norma Walgren Harrison, was the sort of strong, composed woman who appears from time to time in Harrison's fiction.

Harrison's recollections of the past tend to collect in pools of images rather than hard data. Many of those pools are dark and troubled. In a remarkable essay written last year for *Psychoanalytic Review* and reprinted in *Just Before Dark,* Harrison charts the depths.

At the age of 7, a playmate poked out his left eye when he tried to play "doctor" with her. ("I sometimes tell people I lost it in the Tet Offensive, but that's a lie.") When he was twelve, the seven Harrisons moved away from wide fields and pure rivers to East Lansing, so the children could attend college. That led to Harrison's first bout with acute melancholy, not only because he would miss the flora and fauna: A new set of classmates would have to get used to his artificial eye. For a long time, he has said, his left side carried a number of bruises, because he was always running into things.

At nineteen, Harrison ran off to New York, pursuing a "bohemian life." "I admired Hart Crane and Arthur Rimbaud," he told me, mentioning two of literature's more notorious rakehells. "I met Jack Kerouac at a party—a truly nice man—and one day I followed Aldous Huxley down the street for blocks."

He returned to Michigan and completed his schooling, still periodically engaged in bouts of depression. "My instability was further compounded by the deaths of my father and nineteen-year-old sister in an accident when I was twenty-one," he writes in the *Psychoanalytical Review* essay.

"These were the two people closest to me, and in the legal entanglements of the aftermath, I was witless enough to look at the accident photos left on an absent lawyer's desk. Those were the main events along with a number of other violent deaths of friends and relatives including seven suicides."

His response was to lash out with a fairly large body of work, a difficult task for any writer unwilling to compromise high literary standards. In 1975 a chance meeting with Jack Nicholson on a *Missouri Breaks* movie location eventually helped Harrison overcome his chronic shorts. His friend Tom McGuane had written the *Missouri Breaks* script and invited Harrison to visit Montana and watch the filming. Nicholson read and enjoyed Harrison's books, so the two of them had a great deal to discuss.

"Jack really liked his work," Datilla said, "but he didn't see anything he could do [as a film] and asked Jim, 'What are you doing next? Jim said he had some novellas in mind, and Jack said 'When can I see them?' being an anxious guy. Jim told him, 'Well, in a couple of years.'

"Jack said, 'A couple of years is an eternity.' And Jim told him, 'Hey, I gotta make a living. I have to do poetry readings and things like that.' "

"Jack gave him a check for $30,000 and said: 'Consider this an informal option so you don't have to do all these little things, so you can do it faster.' Jim agreed that if he didn't have to lecture or do all his columns and articles, he probably could get the novellas out in a year. And he did."

"I paid him back," Harrison said, "but he wasn't counting on it, let's say. But now he doesn't have to worry too much, what with those gross figures from *Batman*.

The novellas, helped along by the Nicholson grant—"Legends of the Fall," "The Man Who Gave Up His Name" and "Revenge"—sold briskly and stirred up Hollywood interest not only in those stories but in previous ones as well. Harrison's life as an obscure, tattered poet changed radically.

"I averaged twelve grand a year for ten years, and then I got a little more, up to thirty-five grand," Harrison said. "Then *Legends of the Fall* came out, and I was looking in the paper one day and realized I was making more that year, out of the movie sales and everything, than the CEO of General Motors—about 600 grand.

"I became a lunatic. That only lasted a couple years, year and a half, and then I settled down. I learned that with cocaine, you feel like you can——the world, but you can't at all. I was always a complete failure at marijuana because I'd feel horny for about twenty minutes, and then I'd want to go to sleep."

Harrison sipped some red table wine as he stirred fried potatoes in his tiny kitchen. "This is the time of day when normally I used to have my belts," he said, "but I found that belts don't work anymore at my age. After dinner, I lie down an hour. Then I go to the bar at 9:30, quarter to ten, and make my phone calls. Then I get to have a couple of highballs. I don't know how many nondrinking experiments you've made, but the No. 1 thing is you don't get to sleep if you don't have anything."

The log cabin, built in 1935 and superbly maintained ever since, is a weapon against indulgence and the demands of success overload. His wife, Linda, and aide-de-camp, Joyce Bahle, picked it out thirteen years ago, and Harrison signed the check for it without even stepping inside. The surroundings sold him, he said. The five-hour drive between the cabin and his home in Lake Leelanau prevents a case of cultural bends, and no one is likely to visit Grand Marais on the way to somewhere else, which forestalls plagues of transients.

"I like the drive," Harrison said, "because it cools me down on the way up, and on the way home, I gradually get to adjust to the mudbath that is my life. My favorite walking area is about thirteen miles from any human being. It's just nondescript wilderness, but I love it. In thirteen years of walking out there, I've yet to run into another human being, which makes it pleasant, right? That seems to be the whole point."

According to friends, the leap in financial fortune did not change him all that much, outwardly, even in his lunatic period. "If you've never had any money and suddenly you make a lot, strange things happen," said Dan Gerber, a poet, Leelanau County neighbor and another Michigan State classmate. "Jim got into a little trouble with the IRS. His telephone was ringing off the wall. He rented a house in Palm Beach, against my advice. He probably loaned a lot of money to people who never gave it back. It's that old thing about the bitch-goddess Success. Fame is the stupidest thing to desire, and Jim knows that. That's why he has the place in Grand Marais."

Seymour Lawrence publishes under his own imprint at Houghton Mifflin, and Harrison has entrusted his books to him almost exclusively since they first worked together in the '70s. "He's loyal. He's a sweetheart. I love to publish his works," Lawrence said. "His audience is growing with each book. We were able to get *Dalva* up to over 20,000 copies. *The Woman Lit by Fireflies* sold 25,000, and the next book should reach 30,000 to 35,000."

Rather inadvertently, perhaps, Harrison may have widened his readership by writing with a female perspective in *Dalva* and "Fireflies." The first is a wrenching saga concerning a mother searching for her lost son. In "Fireflies," a wife deserts her investment-analyst husband at a highway rest stop and flees into a cornfield. "He has settled once and for all the question of whether a great male writer can write in a woman's voice," says *Chicago*

Tribune paperback critic Clarence Petersen. Some women in the literary world, of course, maintain that a male cannot possibly inhabit their lives.

"Why do I have to be limited to a man's point of view?" Harrison murmured over dinner in his cabin. "Why do I have to leave out half the world, both socio- and economical? People are always trying to put territorial limits on you."

Later that night at the Dunes Saloon, lumberjacks, fishermen and farmers filled the place. An ornate mirror framed by stuffed fish, birds and furry mammals reflected the customers' nodding tractor caps and glinting beer bottles.

A marquee-style sign on the wall said, "DUNE$ $ALOON WELCOME$ ALL THE SUMMER FUN PEOPLE," which I admired as a pragmatic demand for tourist bucks, subtle enough that a tourist might mistakenly interpret the message as a friendly gesture. But waitress Nancy Abbott quickly let the air out of that theory. "We just ran out of plastic S's, and so we had to use the dollar signs," she said.

Harrison went through his phone calls in the Dunes kitchen—wife and daughter back home downstate, a call back for a Columbia Pictures VP, a long conversation with a neighbor having marital problems.

Then he returned to his spot near the back door ("Where I can make a quick getaway if I see somebody I don't like"), sipped a Canadian whiskey and chatted with people until his personal and strict midnight witching hour. "It's important to a writer to have non-writer friends," he had mentioned earlier in the day. And clearly it was important to live like them too, when he could.

Harrison evidently worked hard to regain equilibrium after the initial shock of wealth. Spending most of it right away didn't work. Buying the cabin proved to be a partial solution. And extensive psychological counseling, he swears, did wonders for him.

"I've been seeing my guy fourteen years, when I get to New York four or five times a year," Harrison said over the noise of the jukebox and a crowded pool table. "And we have a 1,000-letter correspondence. Those guys are great if you can get the good one. It's like going to see the medicine man. Some people warned me against it, said that sort of thing might untie my psychic knots and take away my imagination. But I don't think a person's knots are part of his energy.

"There are some profoundly ill but functional writers who have given us a lot of beauty, but I don't want to ——in' die in the process. I want to live. It's better. We don't write out of sickness, we write out of health."

An Interview with Jim Harrison
Thierry Jousse and Vincent Ostria / 1993

From *Cahiers du Cinema*, No. 470 (July–August 1993), pp. 24–30. © *Cahiers du Cinema*. Translated into English by Dominique Duvert. Reprinted by permission of *Cahiers du Cinema*.

The writer Jim Harrison is a sturdily built man in his fifties, the writer of a handful of novellas and novels rooted in the great American tradition, among them *Legends of the Fall, Dalva* and *The Woman Lit by Fireflies*. A wild man who is not unaccustomed to the sophistication of European culture. A heavy drinker, a big eater, also a gourmet, he evokes some of his passions in his latest book, *Just Before Dark,* a collection of articles published in various American magazines. But Jim Harrison's greatest affair remains nature in its purest form, the nature of the unspoiled territories of the American continent. A trout fisherman and game hunter, he spends a great part of his time deep in the state of Michigan in his cabin and in the forest. If he celebrates a virile universe, Jim Harrison is not a macho man à la Hemingway as some have described him. He is more of a sensualist, an epicurean at heart. But he is also the great champion of Indians and a former professor of literature who flirted with the beatnik and hippy spirit of the '60s and '70s. He is great friends with the writer Tom McGuane and Jack Nicholson, and is also a regular in Hollywood, where he hangs out just long enough to bail himself out financially. At the time when the Institut Lumière in Lyon was paying homage to him, he talked to us about this difficult relationship between an authentic man and the jungle of the entertainment world that fascinates us (and him) so much. It was also an opportunity to take stock of the tumultuous relationship between the film industry and American writers among whom Faulkner, John Fante, Fitzgerald and Rudy Wurlitzer stand in the frontline.

Int: Could you enlighten us about some of the choices you made for your Carte Blanche at the Institut Lumière in Lyon? Why *Wild Strawberries* by Bergman or *8 ½* by Fellini, for example?

JH: At first, I thought they had asked me to choose films mostly from a sentimental point of view. My family is half Swedish, so the people in Bergman's films remind me of crazy relatives who would not utter a word for days on end. They just sat. But my favorite film by Bergman is not *Wild Strawberries,* it's *Persona.* As for Fellini, I had dinner with him a few times in New York and that's a good memory. They put *8 ½* in the program but I prefer *La Strada.* I think that's his best film, before he added all this bric-a-brac. As he went on, his films became increasingly rococo. Did I also put Orson Welles' *Othello* on the list? I adore that film, but nobody likes it. It's like the films by Renoir that Jack Nicholson loves—for example, *Rules of the Game.* When I see them, I tear up. Technically *Chinatown* is better than *Five Easy Pieces,* but I feel closer to *Five Easy Pieces.*

Int: In your works, you mention a lot of Hollywood movie actors. How did you discover films?

JH: I lived in a small town where there was a movie theater. At the time, I seem to remember that the ticket was only a dime. Almost everybody went to the movie. So, as I was growing up, I saw hundreds and hundreds of films. Films are part of my reference system. Everybody knows Gary Cooper. He is one of the embodiments of American mythology. Although he is not responsible for it, his character became a cliché. The same goes for Robert Mitchum and Jack Palance, for those who saw all the films between 1945 and 1960.

Int: In *Wolf* you write: "Thousands of films poisoned my mind."

JH: When I talk about poison when referring to movies, it's because you can never get rid of them. All these different versions of reality—I'm writing a long novella about this right now—come floating in your mind. It happens just the same with novels as it does with films. I remember some scenes in novels just like some scenes in a film. Take *The Possessed* by Dostoevsky. The lights go off. Stavrogin and Kirilov are in the room. Kirilov gets up and bites Stavrogin's ear. It's utter terror, one of the most terrifying scenes that I know. The type of scene you can never get rid of. It becomes part of your imaginary heritage. A poet, Wallace Stevens, said: "There are image reservoirs in our minds." It's as though images were thousands of fish in the water.

Int: You also say in *Wolf* that you are hostile to television.

JH: Television is like an art book: it reduces images. In an art book, a work becomes very small. It's completely absurd. Television is formidable thing. It reduces images that were not intended for the small screen. But I'm lucky, my secretary's husband has a movie theatre in the small town where I live. So I can get any film and see it in ideal conditions. You cannot compress the history of the West, pioneer films like those of John Ford, in a small Japanese box. It's impossible.

Int: You are talking about John Ford. Do you feel particularly close to western films?

JH: I'm trying to write one now. Westerns are part of my personal mythology. We all grew up with John Ford and westerns. He is the best. Nobody, by far, can hold a candle to him. And I went to Monument Valley. I took a long hike, at night, right before dawn. It was very cold, it was during winter. And I waited for daybreak. But could you show what I saw on a two hundred dollar Sony television?

Int: What kind of a western are you writing?

JH: It's a western that takes place during the '20s, at the time when the spirit of the West was fading away. In America, the '20s look like the '80s: people were rapacious. The country was almost destroyed because of greed. The film is called *The Last Posse*. A group of people gets together to go in pursuit of very bad outlaws. A number of the people who are part of the escapade come from the East and never rode a horse, but they believe in the myth of the West. But most of the people in this group die from exhaustion. It's the explosion of the myth. I wrote the script for Harrison Ford because he needs to do stronger things. They continue to make big budget films, but his last truly good film was *Witness*. He is an excellent actor, but he makes films that are too big.

Int: Did you see Clint Eastwood's *Unforgiven*?

JH: No. I will not see it until I'm done with *The Last Posse*. It's the same with novels, I cannot read any when I'm writing, otherwise it turns into mush. But Eastwood is extraordinary.

Int: Don't you think that the great film about Indians still has to be made?

JH: Yes, but the director would have to be an Indian. There have been a few attempts in this direction. But we are very paternalistic with them. We always tell them what they have to do. It's a very difficult problem because they have a culture which is completely different from ours. In fact, it's a complicated question. Indians are not ambitious enough to become movie directors. It would also be necessary to make a movie on Indians before the Europeans arrived in America.

Int: You worked on a script about the life of the photographer Edward Curtis, who took many photographs of Indians at the turn of the century.

JH: It was a nightmare. I had written the script for Taylor Hackford, but we did not get along at all. Hackford wanted Curtis to kill someone, or something like that, to make the story more interesting. He can go to hell! (Laughter) When you are telling a director that you feel like killing him with your own hands, you know the project is over. When you want to tear his heart out, it's bad. It means you are too upset to work. I doubt the film will ever be made, but it's possible. We did not abandon the project. I talked to Nicholson about it and he thinks he'll be able to play Curtis until he is sixty-five and the producer Douglas Wick is still interested. He bought Curtis's originals for 100,000 dollars. The collection fills up a very large room. I did a great deal of research and I was very interested. Moreover, I'm going to return to it and try to write a script. What's troubling is that after he spent thirty-five years with Indians, Curtis became an Indian to an extent nobody ever reached. He was committed to an insane asylum—to pretend that you are crazy is sometimes a way to settle your problems. He was seen for the last time in 1932 in a Cheyenne reservation during a specific ceremony, quite a dadaist ceremony. Only absolutely extreme things happen in it. At the beginning, somebody comes toward you, from afar, about a thousand yards away; he is painted half and half in black and in bright yellow. The ceremony goes on for a week. It's never been celebrated since. It's an incredible story. Curtis also danced with the Hopis with rattlesnakes in his mouth.

Int: In what context did you see European films for the first time?

JH: At eighteen or nineteen, when I was in college. At that time, for several years, I saw only foreign films. Later, I met Jeanne Moreau many times in New York, but we only had dinner together. We saw each other in restaurants and we talked about great films like *Jules and Jim, Shoot the Pianist, La Strada* and Antonioni's first films, which were fascinating because they had a completely different way of looking at reality.

Int: Your novel *A Good Day to Die* stages a woman and two men. Were you influenced by *Jules and Jim,* a film you even quote in the novel?

JH: Maybe. At the time it was a very shocking film. In our culture, we don't often see two men openly sharing a woman. But one prefers to share a woman than to lose her, so of course, one gets used to it. It's the same thing in *A Good Day to Die*. By the way, would you know who the people are who have an option on my novel? They are French people who have had it for three years.

Int: No, but what do you think of American filmmakers of the '60s or '70s like Bob Rafelson, Arthur Penn or Sidney Pollack, who made films when you were beginning to write?

JH: The best film by Sidney Pollack remains, by far, *They Shoot Horses, Don't They?* I had written a script for him because I wanted him to go back to the simplicity of this film, and to stop making syrup. One believes that more is more, but more is often less. We dump loads of nonsense. Rafelson was a very good director during a time, and then he and his wife got separated and he lost it.

Int: Pollack was supposed to film another one of your long novellas, titled "The Man Who Gave Up His Name."

JH: Yes. Another failure. Jack Nicholson was supposed to play Nordstrom, but at the last minute, they gave him the green light to direct *Two Jakes* and the project fell through. This kind of thing happens all the time. As soon as you have found the perfect people for a project, somebody comes to tell you (deep voice): "John Huston will never work for Warner Brothers." But who are these damn Warner Brothers? It drives you nuts. It's the same for nineteenth century authors: we don't care who Apollinaire's publisher was.

Int: You met Jack Nicholson on the set of *Missouri Breaks* by Arthur Penn.

JH: Toby Rafelson (Bob Rafelson's wife) gave him my first novel, *Wolf.* After that, he wanted to talk to me. It was a very strange meeting. We talked a little and he told me to call him if I had a topic for him. But I never called him. I saw him again a year later and he asked me why I had never called him. I told him I had not found anything for him. I'm not a very good businessman.

Int: And now, you follow his career, you see his films?

JH: Oh, yes, we've been friends since then. When I'm in Los Angeles, I stay at his place. I think he is by far our best actor. He has an extraordinary range. He does not always choose the best projects, but he is the American actor with the broadest range. He can play anything.

Int: In your last book, *Just Before Dark,* you talk about the dinners you had with Orson Welles. What kind of relationship did you have with him? Did you only talk about gastronomy?

JH: No, he talked about everything. Warner did not want John Huston to direct *Revenge* (an adaptation of the novella "Revenge," filmed in the end by

Tony Scott with Kevin Costner). So Jack Nicholson, under torture, said that if they did not want Huston, he only wanted Orson Welles to do it. We then had extraordinary meetings with him. He loved to eat sumptuously and we put our meals on the expense account of Warner Brothers. Our meetings were meals. But we practically did not talk about the project for the film. He said he was going to film the book directly. You know that Welles was in Brazil when he saw a picture of Rita Hayworth in *Life* magazine and, ten days later, he married her. He took the first plane and brmmmmm (he imitates the sound of an engine). Astonishing.

Int: What happened finally with *Revenge*?

JH: Everybody disappeared. It broke my heart. I had seen John Huston and Jack Nicholson in London at the time he was doing *The Shining*. Huston said (Harrison imitates the director's voice to perfection), "Let's make the movie." It was marvelous. And then, they go back to L.A. and Warner says: "No John Huston!" It was sad, mostly because at the time Warner said no to David Lean who wanted to adapt my novella "Legends of the Fall." That's the studio people for you!

Int: You did not participate in the last stages of the script?

JH: No, because the Screenwriters Guild was on strike and legally I did not even have the right to call production. Jack Nicholson made fun of them. He told Ray Stark (the producer of *Revenge*) that I had found a new brilliant ending for *Revenge,* but that I wanted 50,000 dollars cash for it. He is an adept at this kind of joke. But Stark was ready to pay because Hollywood producers are always happy when they find a solution so a heroine does not die. Huston's point of view, on the contrary, was that the girl had to die (as in the novel). There were dozens of different endings for that story. But I could not contact them because the Screenwriters Guild inflicted severe fines if you contacted the producers (during the strike). In that case, you have to hide and call them from public phones. But I'm not that kind. And in any case, at that time, I was fed up with these people.

Int: Have you seen the film *Revenge*?

JH: Yes. They added some stupidities. The director (Tony Scott) makes fashion images: to have an Englishman film that was the worst idea. He did not know what to do. Kevin Costner was so furious that he did his own editing of the film for his private collection. I have not seen this editing but I was told that it's much better.

Int: About Kevin Costner, have you seen *Dances with Wolves*?

JH: Yes. I liked this movie because all my life, I studied the Indians and I find that they have never been treated in such an honest way in an American film. It is very true. There is a sentimental dimension that is a bit conventional, but it was an interesting film.

Int: Is Mike Nichols's film, *Wolf*, completely different from your novel by the same name?

JH: Yes, but the idea did not come from the book. During this bad period in Hollywood, at the time when they refused to allow John Huston to direct *Revenge,* I was at my cabin and I suffered a true lycanthropy attack, which is terrifying. In the middle of the night, I thought that someone was coming to the cabin, but it was like a flash. I jumped out of bed and I hit a chandelier, which is logically impossible. Then I tore the doors and I started to scream. I became completely crazy. My dogs were afraid of me and ran away. That's how the idea for the script came. It's a Jungian concept. During times of stress, of mental tension, people have sometimes modifications of consciousness. Of course, at the bottom of all this, there is the Indian tradition. When an Indian is very sick, either mentally or physically, he enters the body of an animal, a bear, a wolf, or a seal, to heal himself. And then, when he comes out, he changes his name. Sometimes he does not come out of it but it's good too. It's the same thing with the Chippewa Indians near my home (in northern Michigan). People disappear and become bears. Nothing can be done about it. But *Wolf* is not a werewolf film, although everybody insists it is. It's the story of a man who becomes a wolf in thirty days.

Int: You don't like werewolf stories?

JH: Yes, but it's a European theme. I wrote the American version of the same legend. But they would not stop mixing the two things because they knew shit about it. I had many difficulties with Mike Nichols, although from a personal point of view, we got along fine. But we had a different approach of the subject.

Int: Do you see independent films in the United States?

JH: Yes, of course.

Int: Is there one you particularly liked recently?

JH: I liked *The Indian Runner* by Sean Penn. You have to see it. It is interesting because it shows this aspect of modification of reality I was talking about. The brother who is bad does not improve. He is bad, crazy . . . it's very strange. The film does not have this childish side we see in films today. You know that Nicholson is going to play soon in a film directed by Sean Penn, which is ideal.

Int: Do you write many scripts for Hollywood?

JH: About one every other year. It's simple. I think about it for a long time in my cabin and then I write very fast. I wrote the novella "Revenge" (on which the film *Revenge* is based) in a week. In America, most novelists are professors. I was a professor too, but it did not suit me. The other option is to work for the film industry. Now, I could live off my novels, but I also like to write films. What I don't like is to make five versions of the same story. I've decided that from now on, I would write only two versions of a script and after that they could get lost. I think I'm mostly good at inventing stories.

Int: Do you have many contacts in the world of production?

JH: No. I have a Sicilian agent. He is my sole contact. There is also the producer Douglas Wick with whom I just worked. He is very cultivated. I like him. He will be a great producer. He is only in his thirties. He is not very interested in business, he likes films above all. I like to work with him.

Int: Then, you are not like Faulkner, who despised Hollywood and called it the salt mine?

JH: Faulkner was a bit dishonest. They have his scripts at Warner. I read them: they were a disaster. He was cheating on them. In America, during the Depression, everybody was broke and he was making three to four thousand dollars a week. He wrote nineteen scripts, and practically none was ever shot (at least not in its original state.)

Int: When you write your novels, do you feel influenced by the cinema, or is it completely different?

JH: It's completely different, but when you are influenced by films, you visualize the novel as you write. The novel takes on a visual dimension. To write *Dalva*, I went to the Historical Society in Nebraska which has great iconographic resources. I looked at pictures of Nebraska at the beginning of the century, in the '20s. I had a visual reality in mind. Images make me feel the period. So, when I write a novel, I don't consider it to be prose—there are writers who are like that, like William Styron, for whom style is the most important. I see what I describe. But it's not the same as a film. Here, I write for myself.

Int: Did working on scripts change your writing?

JH: I don't see things like that. It forced me to write better dialogue because you write more dialogue in scripts. And also, you think more about movements, moves. A few days before I came to France, some women took an option to adapt my novel *Dalva* for the screen. I did not want to give up the rights for six years because I didn't like the people who were asking for them. Therefore I said I was going to read the book again, which I had not done since I had written it, to make small red marks to indicate the scenes that were important to me. But it was terrible, I could not do it. I gave up. It was too moving.

Int: Do you think that an American writer can live outside Hollywood?

JH: Of course. It's the case for many writers. They are professors. But the professorial milieu is steeped in that horrible political correctness, which is fascist, repressive and humorless. People do not flirt any more because it's not "politically correct." I'm writing a long novella on a theme that's quite similar. It's a professor who is beginning to have problems. He enters the classroom, it's in the spring. He greets the girls who are present and says: "Good morning, girls, you look charming today!" And he is immediately rejected for having said such a sexist thing. It's like the Inquisition.

Int: Talking about sexism, in your Carte Blanche in Lyon, you had planned a film with Marilyn Chambers, the X-rated film star of the '70s.

JH: Yes, it was a joke! (Laughter) They had asked me to submit a list of fifteen movies and I was stuck for the fifteenth so I wrote *Insatiable* with Marilyn Chambers. It's the most extraordinary porn film ever made. You have to see it right away! At the same time, it was a bit of a joke.

Int: And about violence? You said that violence was not filmed well in Hollywood.

JH: No, not at all. I explained it one day to Bob Rafelson in a club in New York. We did not agree about it. All of a sudden, I grabbed him and threw him on the other side of the bar, screaming. I told him that that was never done that way in films. Another time, I saw something with McGuane very late at night, in Key West. We were walking in the street and all of a sudden a man comes stumbling out of a bar. He makes some kind of gurgling sound. He falls backwards: his throat was slit to the neck. The slit looked like the tentacles of a calamari. Blood started seeping through. That's true violence. When I was young, in New York, in a bad neighborhood, I saw a man come out of a bar looking like he was scratching his check: he had an ice pick in it. In films, you don't have that immediacy of violence. It's very rare that it's a success. The best at filming violence is Scorsese because he knows what it is. He knows his subject. I had problems in Sweden, where they criticized me for the violence in my novella "Revenge." But there are only two dead in the story! In a made-for-TV film, there are often thirty-five. The scene they could not stand is the scene where a giant is disemboweled by the hero. I think you have to look at things the way they are because it's therapeutic. In films, people who are killed put their hand on their chest in a comical way. But when you shoot a deer with a rifle, he is thrown into the air and he falls spitting blood. When you are shot at, you don't say "Oh!" (Laughter.)

Int: Why don't you direct a film yourself?

JH: Because years ago I told my wife at a time when I was going crazy: "Today I give up all supremacy on the world and its inhabitants." My wife put that sentence on my desk. It means that I'm trying to fight this tendency I have which is precisely the one a director needs. Once, at Warner's they asked me if I wanted to direct a film. I said I found it too difficult. And it eats away two years of your life. There is another sign on my desk that reads: "I'm just a writer."

A Conversation with Jim Harrison
Joseph Bednarik / 1994

From *Northwest Review,* 33, No. 2 (1995), 106–18. Reprinted with permission of John Witte and *Northwest Review.*

Depending on whom you ask, Jim Harrison is a poet writing novels, a novelist writing screenplays, a gourmand writing passionate articles about red wine and garlic, or an amateur naturalist practicing Zen.

In late April, 1994, Harrison set foot in San Francisco as part of a reading tour for *Julip,* his latest trilogy of novellas. The morning after his "fandango" (as he called it) we were due to meet in his hotel room. A *privacy please* sign was hanging from the doorknob, but since we had an appointment I knocked. Harrison opened to a room accented by American Spirit cigarette smoke, a tray of dirty breakfast dishes, and the metallic rumble of trolley cars. "The trolley's a little noisy but I got to like the trolley."

When we talked earlier that week, I suggested he visit the San Francisco Public Library to see the permanent murals painted by Gottardo Piazzoni, the grandfather of Russell Chatham—the landscape painter who provides the cover art for all of Harrison's books.

Bednarik: Did you get a chance to see the Piazzoni murals?
Harrison: No I didn't. I visited with Barry Gifford and he took me out to the track. He's a racetrack tout. He knows everybody there so we went way up on the roof on this sunny afternoon. He's good friends with the official timer for California racetracks so we sat in the timer's shack. It was just beautiful. The whole bay, the whole world is out there. We stayed for five races. It's what I used to think of as a "Brautigan afternoon." You know, you wake up with a hangover and Richard says, "We must start today with a meatloaf." So we go to a cafeteria and have meatloaf. Well Barry is such a track sophisticate he says stuff like "Jesus, I'm going to baseball this bet." It's all that racetrack slang. And I of course just sit there listening to it because I like the sound of it, but I hadn't the foggiest fucking notion what was going on. But people traditionally have always been that way about horses. I know several people whose lives were literally saved by horses. McGuane,

for example, raising and training cutting horses. He does it all himself. It's very moving to watch—like I train bird dogs.

B: Is that where the dog training information for *Julip* comes?

H: Yes. I didn't really mean that when I wrote it, not consciously. It seems Julip survives these men and survives everything because she has this *very* specific skill in relationship with animals. It's a tremendous focus for her life, like in our darkest times we always have our poetry.

B: The line in *Julip* that stands out is that the three rounders, as you called them, were "still flipping books of poems open at random, hoping for secrets."

H: I had to speak at Sam Lawrence's memorial service in New York and I was flipping through books again. Stephen Mitchell's translation of the *Duino Elegies*. At the end there are what show business calls "out takes," intended lines that Rilke didn't use. I said one at the memorial service: "Beware, o wanderer, the road is walking too."

B: Last night at the reading you mentioned that you were writing poetry again.

H: Yes, I wrote two long poems this winter. One I had started earlier, and then one called "Sonoran Radio." Where I live part of the year in the southwest there's no contact, you can't get television. We don't have anything there except a VCR to watch movies. The only radio I can get to play at night is from Mexico. I don't really know Spanish but I was amalgamating all of my feelings about Mexico. It's a long suite. I am getting closer to having another book but I'm going slow. Also, I just feel tremendously overexposed now and I don't want to publish any more books for a while. It's flattering in an odd way because I never expected to have the range of audience I do.

B: Do you have a sense that there's an audience interested in your poetry, and another in your fiction, and more readers who discovered you through your *Esquire* food column?

H: Or the movie business. Although it was odd in Mississippi—where for some reason I have a lot of readers—and they really are *readers* in Mississippi. But down there they usually have the poems and the novels and they never ask about the movie business. It's a living, certainly, but it's a relief not to have to deal with the torpidity that comes with being in the business. Because Hollywood was just an option instead of teaching, which I simply couldn't do temperamentally. All your energy being sucked out. You're a walking blood bank for students, which you understand and respect, but for writing you have to save up for yourself and silence until the right time to release it.

B: Torpidity aside, you've been noted as saying that you desperately want to write a good screenplay.

H: I do because I love movies.

B: Do you feel that you've done it?

H: I had a good start on *Wolf* before I was interfered with, but that's the luck of the draw in showbiz. For a while when I was writing that screenplay—this is how we don't know what's really going on—I had a hard time because naturally I was re-living the experience that I had of lycanthropy and then my hair—my eyebrows—kept growing faster and faster and I was having to clip my nails every day, if you can believe this. I thought: "I can't deal with this craziness that I have anymore." And there were dreams I'd be sitting with the producer and director in New York and suddenly the hair started growing through my shirt and I'd throw them out the window. I thought: "Slow down boy."

B: Did you write the screenplay for *Legends of the Fall*?

H: I wrote the first couple versions, but I didn't claim credit on that one. The man who did the *real* work was Bill Wittliff. He's a marvelous Western writer and his screenplay was so much better than mine it was humiliating. I said that to him. "*God,* how long did you take? I spent a whole month on mine." He had spent a year on his, naturally. I was trying to rip them off for some quick bucks to buy cocaine at the time. Pack up my nose, you know. Should've stayed back on the farm like Bob Frost.

B: When you were back on the farm you helped co-edit *Sumac* with Dan Gerber. Did you enjoy the work?

H: Well, Dan worked harder on it. When you start an appreciable literary magazine you're absolutely deluged with manuscripts. We didn't realize it at the time but the problems in those magazines is that every MFA in the United States is trying to get credits, and they keep track. Of course the nightmare in editing *Just Before Dark* was I never kept track of anything. I just simply forgot about a lot of the stuff. That's when I began to think that maybe I was writing too much.

B: In "The Seven-Ounce Man," Brown Dog has his "best nature day" when he finds a bear's blow hole. That's a beautiful image.

H: He says: "What luck." It's a miniaturization of the Delphic oracle. That's a god sleeping down there and you smell the breath and hear the snoring.

B: In your *TriCycle* piece, "Sitting Around," you called bears your "dharma gate."

H: I never associated that at the time. Everything can be a dharma gate but there's this enormous specificity in bears. And you know, one's animal changes. When I finally got to see a wolf where I lived, that meant an enormous amount to me. To hear her three nights and to see her. And then there are bears up there and bears are mostly nocturnal but to see them occasionally, to follow them and to sense them—I wrote a poem about one—he fed on the sweet pea and the wild strawberries. He was a huge, gaunt male. I watched him for about an hour. Probably too close. They can get a little irritable in the spring when they're hungry.

B: I was interested to hear that black bears actually attacked more humans than grizzlies, and grizzlies have the bad reputation.

H: Well, of course there are more of them. We've had a couple deaths up in the Porcupine Mountains. But generally you just have to exercise the same caution you do in New York and Los Angeles.

B: Maybe less so, actually. In terms of your writing do you consider anything out of bounds?

H: What's out of bounds for me is somebody else's religious rituals. The most disgusting thing you see now is the "new age" appropriation of what's Native American. That just terrifies me. How could they do that? Just like that old Chippewa shaman seeing his first picture of a white man who shot a deer with his foot on the deer—Oh, God—you don't fool with that. Oddly enough, that's just like if a Catholic went into a teepee and saw all these priest vestments hanging there as wall decoration. I mean there's something tremendously inappropriate about one writer fooling with another person's secret religion or public religion, or using it for his own purposes. That would be the only bar, nothing else. You know, Terry Tempest Williams said something very odd the other day. She and her husband went down to Mexico and went to about 10,000 feet in this forest, where all the Monarch butterflies in North America go. As she said, "I don't know how they count them." There were twenty-five *million*. She could hear the twenty-five million. You can't typify the sound but she says: "It was just like being in God's brain." And I says, "That's it!"

B: What an unforgettable sound that must be. When I first heard Terry Tempest Williams read aloud I was utterly intoxicated by her voice.

H: There's a woman with a lot of mojo. She's dealing in an area now that's quite scary, or strange—calls it the "panerotics of nature." We're lucky that there are wonders.

B: And that the natural world is teeming with sound.

H: I had in this one part of a poem: "The cat drinking water was insufferably loud." [Harrison rummages for, then reads from a typescript]:

> At first the sound
> of the cat drinking water
> was unendurable,
> then it was broken by a fly
> heading north,
> a curve-billed thrasher
> swallowing a red berry,
> a dead sycamore leaf
> suspended on its way to earth
> by a breeze so slight
> it went otherwise unnoticed.

If you want to read this one you can take it and send it back to me. I don't know if I have another copy. [Harrison hands over a six-page suite.]

B: I'm sure we can get it copied here in the hotel.

H: It doesn't matter, just send it to me.

B: Thanks. I look forward to reading this. In regards to some of your earlier work George Quasha, in *Stony Brook,* wrote about your second book, *Locations.* He claimed there was a story afoot about the poem "After the Anonymous Swedish": That you woke from a dream having been a pond and recited the poem in Swedish, a language you don't speak, then translated it to your wife at 3 A.M. Is that bullshit?

H: That's bullshit. I was so envious at the time that I didn't know any languages, so I wanted to translate a poem too. So I just made one up. It sounds like a Swedish poem. I've been thinking about writing more of them. Drummond Hadley, who's an extraordinary poet and an old friend of Gary Snyder's, is a cowboy poet. He lives on this vast, strange fiefdom out in the southwest. We were walking down the road and he quoted the entirety of the "Tenth Duino Elegy" in German. Then he told me a funny story. He's from a wealthy family and he'd run off to be a cowboy down in the Sierra Madres. He wanted to be a Mexican cowboy, so he camped for months with this group of Mexican cowboys. Locating cattle is hard work, but they always told stories at night. And he didn't have any stories. He *does* have this gifted memory, and he loves Lorca, so he thought "Well . . ." So he stands by the fireside and recites a poem: "La luna, la luna, la luna," about the moon spilling like milk over the mountain onto this young girl in her torment. So every night: "Drum, we want to hear the luna poem," and they'd sit there and listen to it. They couldn't read, any of them. The beauty of that.

B: Do you memorize any of your own poems?

H: Never. Sometimes I surprise myself, I remember whole parts of them. I remember other people's lines. That is odd, I never have—I suppose I don't want any knots between the next one.

B: Do certain parts of your suites emerge at different times and in different places?

H: Oh, absolutely. The suite form I like is when all these little wedges are intended to *suggest*; then, finally, a whole—almost topographically. It's a *map,* the sacred, though they were written before I read that book by Bruce Chatwin, *Songlines.* That's a monster of a book because he determined—which was known only by anthropologists for a long while—that the Aborigines navigate by singing, knowing the songs of an area. So this guy's walking twenty-two hundred miles to see this girl he had dreamed about. Twenty-two hundred *miles,* and he's trotting along with his stick and he's singing the songs of the area that tell him how to go, where to go. It's just an unbelievable, utterly transcendent idea.

B: In your essay "Going Places" you talk about your seduction with maps. The first map being wooden puzzle pieces shaped like the states in different colors—

H: Iowa is yellow. It's the corn, you know.

B: —and the last map, to a remote, secret place, is drawn on thin buckskin which is slowly cut up for stew.

H: Eating your map. It seems certain things are ineffable and that's the barrier, back to writing what you can't quite reach. I was thinking that the whole notion of zazen is to be able to speak the language you spoke before you were born and the language you speak after you die, that's part of it. Writing is a lifetime pursuit. You never come up with anything.

B: Well, there's the old stories of the Zen poets writing on leaves and tossing the poems into the river.

H: Well, that's old Li Po. The river, in you go. Do you read Stephen Mitchell's translations?

B: I've read his *Tao Te Ching*.

H: *The Gospel According to Jesus* is a tremendous book because he's reduced the entirety of the whole thing to what Jesus actually said, separated from church history and all the gloss and accumulation, so the actual text is quite slender. It's very similar to what both Gandhi and Thomas Jefferson did with the *New Testament*.

B: In "Sitting Around" you wrote that you were creating your own religion called Bobo. Are there any holy books in Bobo?

H: Snyder's *The Practice of the Wild* probably comes closest. It's an incredible book. But Bobo. "Bobo knows all modernity is just a flaky paint job." That kind of thing. It goes on and on from there.

B: From Bobo back to the silver screen: Have any of your books ever been made into a foreign film?

H: No, although the French have owned *A Good Day to Die* for years now and the guy claims he's going to make it. I was ignoring him and then I was appalled—I saw this film I love, I've watched it three or four times now called *The Hairdresser's Husband*. Just a transcendent film about this little French boy. He likes to dance to Egyptian music. And he likes to get his hair cut by this sexy sort of woman, so he's always waiting for his to grow. His dad asks him at dinner what he wants to do when he grows up and he says "I want to get my hair cut." So his dad of course slugs him. He meets this beautiful hairdresser, gets his hair cut, and keeps coming back. Then they get married and he just sits around in the barber shop, talking, as other people get hair cuts. It's just a beautiful film. So then I found out the people that own *A Good Day to Die* are the ones who did this. And then I feel stupid. Because I couldn't see how they would make *A Good Day to Die*. Or why, but then I thought this is the kind of thing the French are interested in—and the Spanish. The Spanish liked the book too, for obvious reasons: a good day to die.

B: Do you think *A Good Day to Die* sealed your fate in the feminist world?

H: Oh, everyone forgets everything. Nobody reads very much. That did at the time, but I don't care. I mean, nobody knows how to locate *anybody,* and then I published *Dalva* and *The Woman Lit by Fireflies.*

B: Was there an equal and opposite reaction?

H: Oh, tremendously, to both those books. It was very overwhelming to me, in the pleasant sense. I must've received a couple hundred letters from women on *Dalva* and only one didn't like it, or was upset at my temerity. But we can't have abridgements of our freedom. I mean I don't even accept the abridgements that I mentioned to you, other than implicitly, it's just that I would fear to fool with somebody else's medicine. I know people do, and then the Native Americans justly get pissed off. There's some wonderful poems in Elizabeth Woody. She's an Indian poet up in Washington. Her book's coming out with University of Arizona Press. Some of her first poems are quite formal and not too interesting to me and then she hits some kind of really strange, powerful stride in a long poem about her sister. Crazy. It's like Louise Erdrich's poem to her sister who got beaten up by a drunk white guy. Overpowering poem. Elizabeth told this story when we all met in Wyoming. Matthiessen and Lopez and everybody was there—writers and nature. It was intriguing because I never met Lopez though we corresponded. We never met in what we call "real life." I like that, don't you? Anyway, Elizabeth got up—everybody's making very elaborate speeches, except Sam Hamill who's just sitting back there as Sam Hamill, which is quite wonderful—and she says: "I come out of the store." She lived way up in the reservation at the time. "I get in my car and then these two ravens come down that like to fool around, and they sit on the hood of my car and they grab my windshield wipers and snap them, looking at me," and so there we get the relation of writers and nature. It doesn't need many big adjectives.

B: Have you read Gerald Vizenor's *Dead Voices*?

H: I just ordered it. He's just a marvelous author. Nicholson's a great fan of his. I gave him *Griever: An American Monkey King in China* and *The Trickster of Liberty* because he's a real coyote figure.

B: In the magazine *Caliban* you dedicated the poem "Counting Birds" to Vizenor.

H: Because of that line in there about all those swallow holes. I was thinking that these are the eyes of the Anasazi bringing me the Manitou, because they look at the Manitou Islands. Sometimes when you look the Manitou are sleeping bears. I wrote the introduction, a couple years ago, for the local

Ottawa–Chippewa tribal history and went to the dedication of their new motel and casino. It was wonderful. They had a drum group and the smoking of the pipe. It was just gorgeous. I went to the ghost supper with all these very loud and very old Chippewa, and the one turns to me and says: "We were really something once, weren't we." [Harrison excuses himself and finishes packing.] I used to get terrified of missing planes, but then oddly enough I would think that everything will be OK if I get home. In recent years, I suppose because of my practice and what I've been doing, it doesn't come out anymore. It's Dogen's whole idea: Practice is finding yourself where you already are. So consequently sometimes when I'm in airports now I think maybe I'll go someplace else. You look at the tote boards and think—

B: "Well, there's a four o'clock flight to Rio."

H: *Yeah.* Or there are all these different Fayettevilles and Charlottevilles in the southeast, so you think "maybe I'll just check 'em all out." I think it first happened when I was writing "Brown Dog," the illusion that there is a home if you're not at home everywhere. I forgot that I could only write at home so then in this motel in Livingston, Montana, I started writing "Brown Dog." I just completely forgot that I could only write at home, which is like some sort of idiot savant bullshit.

B: There's the argument to be made, though, that Brown Dog's voice is very familiar, much easier to access for you than Dalva.

H: Oh, infinitely. He's sort of my survival mechanism. In an odd sense he's a true Zennist while I'm only a student.

B: Right. He's the one who's *there.*

H: *Always.* He says: "This gravy is not pork gravy." She says: "Of course not, it's generic. You wanna make something of it?" "I was just saying it isn't pork gravy." And he says: "She was beautiful. Her one leg was too short but it looked just like the other leg only shorter." You know, that kind of thing. It was just his immediate contact with life. And he can always get out of being cornered. "You don't have a social security card? How do you pay your taxes?" He only gets one letter every couple years and that's to renew his driver's license. He has no other official contact with anything. And he's always lived in unoccupied deer cabins. Well, Brown Dog's the emotional equivalent of what keeps me alive. In France I think I did thirteen interviews and nine photo ops, two lectures, three book signings, a couple talk shows in five days. I get a little walk in the Luxembourg Gardens and for some reason there's a lovely girl in a pink rabbit suit flouncing around in some promotion of some product. And the Luxembourg Gardens are overwhelming because I know Rilke walked through them. Every day, starting the next day, on French TV there's going to be this film about me on Cinéma 3, and they repeat it every day in the afternoon. I says: "I gotta get out of this fucking place before they blow my cover." I think: "Ah, pink rabbit suit." Weird. And then walking up: "Where's the zipper?" You know, reverting to Brown Dog emotions.

B: You didn't pack your green janitor's suit from *The Theory & Practice of Rivers*?

H: No, although that's from the same lineage, the green janitor's suit. I think that's partly the spirit of my father who was immediate like that. He said to me when I went off to New York: "Well James, maybe you should just stay there 'til the pissants carry you out through the keyhole." This is wonderful and I'm lucky I don't spend my adult life fighting against my dead father, because he was very pleased that I wanted to be a writer. I wasn't even sure I should bother that much with college because Hemingway and Faulkner didn't bother with it, and Sherwood Anderson. All these people he liked. That's not where you learn how to write. His roots were real Brown Dogian. He went to college to study agriculture. He and his brother worked for two years digging pipeline and living in tents in Michigan during the winter.

B: To pay for school?

H: Yeah. Living in tents during the winter in Michigan and hand digging up pipeline. Well, give me a break. Now everybody wants a fucking grant before they read a book.

B: Was Clare in "The Woman Lit by Fireflies" named after John Clare?

H: I wondered about that later. Maybe a little subconsciously. I was always obsessed with Clare and Christopher Smart. Like Clare I've had periods of mental instability, as it were, and one always fears being locked up because there's no food. I couldn't deal with institutional food.

B: One final question with an eye toward the future. *Dalva* was originally going to be the story of Dalva's grandfather. What's the status of Northridge's novel?

H: That's what I'm working on now. How I originally planned the book was to write about her grandfather, her son, and her. But then Dalva just completely took over the whole thing. So I have nine cartons of unused notes and I can't afford to let them just go away. They're in the attic of my granary if they haven't been chewed by mice. I found three galleys of *Dalva* the other day, but they'd been chewed up by mice. That kind of thing really disturbs my librarian brother.

Season of the Wolf
Anthony Brandt / 1994

From *Men's Journal*, 3 (June–July 1994), 96–98, 137. Copyright by Men's Journal Company, L.P. 1994. All rights reserved. Reprinted by permission.

Jim Harrison spends his winters in the little town of Patagonia in a plain but comfortable casita on Sonoita Creek, the only stream in southern Arizona that never dries up. Last winter a Mexican blue mockingbird, rarely seen in the U.S., wandered north and settled in a patch of bamboolike growth in Harrison's backyard. Word spread on the life-list hot line, and birders descended in force.

Harrison, a *very* private person, was desperate to get rid of them. He tried a sign: THE FUCKING MOCKINGBIRD IS DEAD. But the birders stayed put. Harrison got out his .357 Magnum and fired it into the air. That didn't work, either. Finally he put a tape of Mexican ranchero music on his car stereo and cranked up the volume.

That worked. The crowd began to disperse. One birder approached Harrison and asked him what it would take to get permission to come on his property to see the bird. Harrison considered this. "I told him it would take a million dollars," he says, still half-affronted at the insult to his privacy. "In cash.

"The guy looked at me as if I had just gone over the edge."

Well, yeah. Peering over it, at least. This is the man, after all, who some have regarded as the Dennis Hopper of American letters. Who is reputed to have lived in a whorehouse while researching his classic novella, "Legends of the Fall." Who has gone on toots so extraordinary they have become underground legends themselves. Who blew his final gram of cocaine out a New York hotel window. This is a man who, for that matter, actually *likes* ranchero music. But if Harrison has ventured quite a long way down the road of excess in his life, it hasn't stopped him from becoming one of the most serious and productive writers in America.

In April, at age fifty-six, he published his ninth book of fiction, *Julip,* a collection of three new short novels. He has also published seven volumes of poetry (more than many full-time poets produce in a lifetime); a collection of nonfiction; a raft of occasional journalism, including a cooking column in *Esquire* for three years; and in between all that written some twenty screenplays. He has not lacked for widespread critical acclaim. Or—ever since *Legends of the Fall* appeared in 1979 and two of its three novellas were sold to the movies—for Montrachet to go with his lobster. All he has lacked in fact is bestseller status, and the wider fame that goes with it. Harrison is a literary but not a household name.

Now that may be about to change. This year will see not only the publication of *Julip* but also the release of two large-budget movies based on Harrison's work. In late June, Columbia Pictures will release *Wolf,* starring Jack Nicholson and Michelle Pfeiffer, about a book editor who is transformed into a wolf. It is based on an idea by Harrison, and he wrote most of the screenplay. The studio thinks enough of it to schedule its opening in the heart of the summer-blockbuster season. The second film, the long-anticipated movie version of *Legends of the Fall,* stars Anthony Hopkins and Brad Pitt and will be released in October. Harrison has seen pieces of it—although he did not write the script—and to his own surprise liked it "enormously."

"I was overwhelmed by it," he says with some wonder, "and if *I* am, for Christ's sake . . ." So this may be it, Harrison's big year, his year of living famously.

If so, Harrison will have more than birdwatchers to fend off. And this is a man who is almost obsessively private. When the movie people asked him to do interviews with major newspapers to promote *Wolf,* he refused. "What shall we tell them?" the publicists asked. "Tell them," he replied, "I want them to be better people."

For his own reasons—I have known him casually and corresponded with him for a number of years—he has made an exception in my case. He picks me up at Patagonia's one hotel, the slightly seedy Stage Stop Inn, in his navy blue Toyota Land Cruiser. Even physically he is prepossessing. He has a great round head mounted on a body best described as burly; the overall effect is a bit like a full moon just cresting a hill. He sports a mustache to balance a lower lip that pushes out in a permanent pout. His left eye was blinded when he was seven years old by an "unkind" little girl with a broken bottle; they were playing doctor at the time. The eye wanders, but most often it looks down and to the left.

The eye is disconcerting until you get used to it. Not surprisingly, it made Harrison a terribly self-conscious child, but there's little sign of that now. He's warm and friendly. There is little evidence of the wildness he is known for, either. He laughs a lot. He's thoughtful. He listens with full attention. Except that most of the time he's driving.

Driving is what you do when you want a long conversation with Jim Harrison. He is compulsive about driving. When he's blocked or when he's depressed, he gets in the Land Cruiser and drives, sometimes for thousands of miles around the country. On this day, he drives me first through the Nature Conservancy preserve adjacent to where he lives and then down a back road to his house.

This is Apache country, high, dry, open, rugged. An old settlement about 100 yards from Harrison's house is where the Apache wars started. That is fitting, for Harrison has studied Native American cultures most of his life. The house, a single-story brick-and-tile structure that he rents with his wife of thirty-three years, Linda, is at the edge of a large ranch belonging to a friend from northern Michigan. After a brief stop, we drive on another mile or so to his studio, a small room with an unused bed and a round table in a ramshackle house up by the barns. The tiny room is spartan, unlike the studio at his farm in Lake Leelanau, Michigan, which is full of what can only be called totem objects a coyote skull painted in traditional Native designs by a Sioux friend; a dried grizzly bear turd given to him by another friend; a blue heron's wing; a crow's wing; odd stones picked up from here and there; a wild turkey's foot; a bone from a sea lion.

And then we're back in the car heading for the mountains. Harrison wants to take me to the San Rafael Valley, and there is only one way to go, on a gravel road over a jagged range called the Patagonias that rises perhaps 2,000 feet above the valley floor. We start talking about *Wolf,* and it emerges that there is a wildness in Jim Harrison all right, running very deep, and that his partying, his history of alcohol and drug use, his long wilderness walks and drives, the animal totems in his Michigan studio, have only been the merest expressions of it. For no one who was not profoundly wild could have dreamed up *Wolf.*

Literally. "I was having a bad time mentally," he explains as we drive into the mountains and the country gets even emptier and more beautiful. "And about 2 a.m., I thought somebody was coming into the yard in Grand Marais [also in Michigan, where Harrison has a cabin], which is isolated. I saw car lights—it was really just lightning, it was in summer—and I woke instantly and threw myself out of my bed. I was obviously in the middle of a dream, because I shot up in the air so high that I caught my head on a deer-antler chandelier. If you see it, you know that this is totally impossible, it can't be done; and I ran to the door of the cabin, and I tore off both doors, and I ran out into the yard screaming and howling. I stopped, and I don't know which part is dream, which is real, though I have the scar on my head from the chandelier, but my face was covered with hair, my arms, everything. It scared the living shit out of me."

He laughs a bit. He has told this story before, though seldom in quite as much detail, and it clearly still has power for him. This dream was the seed of *Wolf*, although the story in the movies is a little different. The character played by Jack Nicholson in the film hits a wolf with his car on a remote country road, and when he gets out and follows the trail of blood, he finds the wolf still alive, and it bites him on the wrist and runs off; it is the bite that transforms him over a period of a month into a wolf.

Wolves are important to Harrison. He refers to them frequently, and they recur in his work. Later in our drive, he will be at pains to show me the spot where he had once seen a Mexican wolf cross the road. He has written about waiting twenty years to see a wolf in the wild. His first novel, published in 1971, was entitled *Wolf*, although it is unrelated to his screenplay and was written long before his dreams of transmogrification. In the novel, his narrator fails to see the wolf he knows is in the area, and he experiences this as a loss, as a gift not given because he isn't ready for it.

Harrison says now he wishes he had written the film's story as a novella first rather than as a screenplay. That way, he says, he wouldn't have lost control of it. Nicholson, a close and longtime friend of Harrison's, took to the script after only one reading. But Harrison would eventually write five drafts before resigning from the project. "Mike Nichols and I—we became friends, you know, but we couldn't see eye-to-eye on the script," Harrison says in a tone that is less resentful than rueful. "The producer insists that it's still 70 percent mine, but I'll believe it when I see it."

It is the source of the movie in his remarkable dreams, however, rather than his frustrations with Hollywood that is so revealing about Harrison. Although he is a cultivated and even cerebral man who laces his conversation with quotes from Rilke and loves Bach even more than ranchero music, he is also deeper into the woods than Thoreau ever was. For all his sophistication, Harrison is probably closer, inside, to true wildness and more at home in it than any American writer since Melville took up with cannibals.

Harrison was born, in 1937, to a northern Michigan farm family. His father was a county agricultural agent. "I grew up hunting and fishing, and this," he says, waving at the pine and black-oak forest surrounding us at the top of the Patagonia range, "is the kind of landscape I respond to."

That response to wilderness grew as much out of emotional need as out of geographical familiarity. The physical and mental pain he suffered because of the accident that blinded his left eye when he was seven sent him regularly into the woods around his family's house, looking for solace and solitude. He says he remembers being constantly bruised on his left side from walking into trees and rocks that his blind left eye couldn't see. When he was twelve, the family moved to urban East Lansing in search of better schools, a move that devastated him. A year or so later, he entered the first of a series of deep depressions; he has had seven such episodes during his life.

When he was twenty-one, his father and his sister were killed in a car crash. He happened to look at photos of their bodies in a lawyer's office. They died, according to the official report, from "macerated skulls." His father and sister still appear to him in his dreams, he says, in the form of mourning doves. He has described his "memory knots" as "tiny claymores that blow up on contact."

It was his poetry as much as his long wilderness retreats, he says, that kept him sane during some of those years. He published two books of poetry in the late 1960s that earned him a fine critical reputation but not much of a living. Then in 1970, Harrison hurt his back while hunting in Michigan. The injury put him in traction for a month, and a reaction to penicillin laid him up even longer. It was his friend Tom McGuane who suggested that he try writing a novel. The result was *Wolf: A False Memoir.*

Two more novels followed in the next five years; none of them earned much money, and the third one in particular sold miserably. Years later Harrison told an interviewer for the *Paris Review,* "That was something I couldn't handle . . . I couldn't maintain my sanity. I had a series of crackups. I was at the point where I couldn't pay my taxes, which were a feeble amount."

Jack Nicholson saved his career, if not his life. They had met in 1975 on the set of *The Missouri Breaks,* for which McGuane had written the screenplay. Harrison subsequently sent Nicholson his novels as they came out, and Nicholson read them all. "Then he heard that I was broke and wanted to help out," says Harrison now, "so he spotted me for the time to write *Legends of the Fall.* He spotted me for a year of grace to write the book." To the tune of $30,000. And the book transformed Harrison into a major literary figure.

Legends follows three sons of a Montana family who cross into Canada to fight in the Great War in a Canadian unit. The center of the story is the volatile Tristan, who is as wild and reckless as a Cheyenne brave. When his younger brother, Samuel, is killed in battle in France, it is Tristan who finds him and cuts his heart out of his body to be preserved in paraffin for burial in Montana and then goes on a rampage of revenge. It is part of Harrison's achievement that he makes these Byronic gestures totally believable.

The novella is only eighty-two pages long, yet it has the feel of an epic, something truly grand, achieved with an astonishing economy of means. It is perhaps the purest example of what Peter Matthiessen has said of Harrison's work: "He's a writer who writes from plenty; he's sort of overflowing."

Legends was acclaimed as a modern classic. With the sale of film rights, Harrison had money for the first time in his life, and he went on to blow a fair amount of it up his nose. This was the period, in the mid-1970s, that solidified his reputation for partying, what Harrison describes as "my Leon Spinks behavior." He gave up cocaine in 1982 after returning from a singular binge in Brazil.

Since then, Harrison has settled down. As we descend on the other side of the Patagonias, the air is cool and the landscape is lovely, green in the pine trees but otherwise sheathed in shades of black and brown. Harrison stops here and there to point out sites that figure in "The Beige Dolorosa," one of the novellas in his new book. Psychological healing is often a theme in his work now. The lead character in that story is a college professor whose life falls apart and who winds up on a ranch near Patagonia, learning to ride and do physical work and take walks in the mountains and change his life.

We pause where the San Rafael Valley comes into view, a vast level spread of dry grass that extends into Mexico. "All the driving I like is like today," Harrison says, "where there's no particular destination." He speaks quite slowly, with a midwestern drawl to his words and a voice that, after years of sporadic cigarette smoking, sounds as if it is being sifted through ashes.

There is hardly a time anymore when he doesn't work. When finishing a novella exhausts him for fiction, he turns to poetry or a screenplay. "I'm not what they call a real screenwriter," Harrison says, not disagreeing with the point. "Stanley Jaffe once told me he didn't hire me because I was a good screenwriter. He hired me because I could make up people. Isn't that an odd thing to say?"

Hardly. It is in fact one of the strengths of his fiction as well. Harrison makes no apology for the almost operatic passion, or some would say the sentimentality, of many of his stories. "Writers err on the side of making people either smaller than life or larger," he says, as he points the car toward the Mexican border in the middle of the valley. "I'd rather err on the side of making them larger."

# Jim Harrison: "What I'm Thinking About for Two Hours"

Casey Walker / 1997

From *Wild Duck Review*, 3 (April 1997), 3–6. Reprinted with permission of Casey Walker, Editor and Publisher, *Wild Duck Review*.

The following two-hour conversation between Jim Harrison and Casey Walker took place in Patagonia, Arizona on 8 March 1997.

Casey Walker: What do you think of "nature writing" per se?

Jim Harrison: I don't care much for the term, "nature writing." In the hands of a naturalist like Ann Zwinger, I suppose the category makes sense. But, as far as what everybody else is doing—to act as if nature writing is something relatively new when it isn't—says a lot more about this American culture of ours. Nature writing has been around since the 1870s and right up to Loren Eisley, who wrote more magnificently than any of us, frankly, and whose books—all but two—are currently out of print. Sporting magazines around the turn of the century, like *Field & Stream* and *Outdoor Life,* were predominantly and very strongly environmentalist and Bernard DeVoto wrote vociferously from "The Easy Chair" position at *Harper's* right up through the 1930s–40s. Nature writing is nothing quite new or new at all.

At a recent talk I gave in Seattle, I spoke in part about a kind of schizophrenia in the environmental movement and in nature writing. To consider nature in any way as a separate entity that one looks down upon as subject:object is a problem because there is no split at all. Even Shakespeare said we are nature too. It's in the splitting that environmentalists get their egos, their self-dramas, their self-congratulations, problems I just don't see in the natives I know real well. The Anishinabe in the Upper Peninsula in Northern Michigan are wonderful at maintaining their humility in the natural setting. I think, though, it's because there's a religious base for them. It's also in the way people grow up. Some have been hunting since they were seven. Even for my friend, Nick, who falls into the loathsome category of "outdoorsman," it's nothing for him to cover 5–10 miles a day everyday of his life and what he notices are details, the particulars. There's no replacement for experience.

I remember when I first saw a wolf in the Upper Peninsula it was doubted by a professor. I didn't mind in the least because he sat in an office and I sat in my cabin in a forest on the river and had seen things from my window that were astonishing—male and female loons taking turns on the nest, each going crazy waiting for relief, making all kinds of noise, responding to coyotes and whippoorwills, back and forth. I think our sense of fieldwork can best be approached through what Thoreau called "sauntering."

Because the motive to sauntering is so different than the motive of entering an experience in order to write about it?

Yes. As Dogen said, "The study of the self is to forget the self. And to forget the self is to become one with ten thousand things." Okay, what he then adds and what people forget is that you (the ego) don't become one with ten thousand things, but ten thousand things become one with you. If you go out with expectations of any sort, you don't get what the outside has to give. In one novel, I parodied the mountain biker who told me he did thirty-five miles on a muddy road. I asked, Geez, what did you see? Hey, he said, I keep my eye on the road!

If every adventure in the outdoors is one of personal accomplishment and we keep attacking the natural world with equipment—our problems with 'self' in 'nature' will be just spectacular. Every extermination of any species has always been accompanied by mechanization. I once wrote a note of complaint to *Outside* magazine because they had a fabulous photo of a natural landbridge formation in Utah, but across the top they showed this geek running in his spandex. It all reminds me of the Nazi youth when certain forms of nature loving were at a height in Germany in the 1920s–30s, and it was all tied to a particular moral force, the purification of a genetic strain, vegetarianism and ego.

You don't get these cultural attitudes with native people and that's what is so wonderful about Richard Nelson's phenomenal books, *Make Prayers to the Raven; A Koyukon View of the Northern Forest,* about the Koyukon people; and *The Island Within,* about living on an island off Sitka. The trouble comes with a full elitism, the kind Robinson Jeffers was guilty of, the view, "I alone overlook the rock and the Pacific." It's the "I alone" that is on a family allowance for 35 years, surveys nature, and then loathes human beings. We cannot ignore humans or human habitat anymore than we can ignore animals, plants, or natural habitat. They all have to go together or you have, as in the case of Jeffers, a tremendous lacunae. I knew Ed Abbey and, as wonderful as he was, he had holes in his worldview vis à vis Native Americans and Mexicans.

Because of the exclusiveness of a singular point of view?

Yes. You have to think of reality in terms as an aggregate of the perceptions of all creatures. You look at the bear but the bear is looking at you, and you better consider the bear looking at you. He isn't something to just put a fucking collar on, you know? They've done this absurd thing in Michigan. I have an enormous wolf bibliography at home and we now have a couple hundred wolves on the Upper Peninsula that came back by themselves over the ice and around, 35 miles. No one had to help them, it's a matter of habitat, period. Now people are saying they have to radio collar all of these wolves. Well, there's immense, immense knowledge on Eastern Timber wolves already—what more do we need!?

The seduction of hard data, of funding more projects!

That's true. Everybody wants to get a grant, get funded for something. Now we've even got miniature telemetric devices for implants in quail, when you can tell an enormous amount about quail by simply watching. There's just an enormous self-dramatization going on—a missionary zeal—especially when we say we're going to help nature but then forget how to let natural processes proceed. That's what I liked so much about David Quammen's book, *The Song of the Dodo,* about island biogeography and the remarkable processes at work.

Environmental zeal also reminds me of the problems of feminism in the 1960s. If feminists had stayed unified as a political force, the ERA would have passed in the 1970s–80s; but they got bifurcated just like the environmental movement and splintered into hundreds of groups. Or, if feminists had stayed focussed on issues such as the ERA and equal pay for equal work, they might have changed the dominant social and economic injustices right there. When movements split into many little self-dramatizing groups, they lose force. With so many agendas, there's also a failure to understand the nature of Washington. You have to know you're dealing with a septic tank full of greed and you must go into it with power. If all the groups could agree on three things they wanted and could amass voters, they'd have results.

Do you see legal battles as the place to start?

If you can concentrate the legal solution, it's the place to start. It's also remarkable though how the minds of the young can change things. I appeared at the first Earth Day as one of the literati and I happened to say, in the talk I gave, that there were too many billboards. Right away, students went out and began cutting billboards down with chainsaws. Besides my embarrassment, I rather liked the idea. Today, the minds of the young are so much more aware, generally speaking, of what the consequences are of our behavior.

What fascinates me about the Nature Conservancy and what I adore about them as opposed to some groups, is that they do understand that the cogs and wheels turn so slowly in Washington we had better buy habitat now and take it out of harm's way. Things with enormous moral force are often completely ignored in Washington. You can't be like a big muffin going to Washington, you have to unify and go in there like a big axe. It's the only way things are perceived there and I don't care if the head of our groups have to spend a lot of money, it's a Machiavellian world and there's no sense going in there like Ghandi.

It's a challenge to think of extending our language, creating the language to change discourse and take the lead on issues in ways not co-opted at the semantic level, the power level, of politics.

Maybe that's the good of so-called, quasi-nature writing. It has a great deal more public appeal now. But, you're going to get co-opted all the time by data. It doesn't matter if you say, for instance, that only 3 percent of our beef by weight is grown on public land and how can you destroy this much public land for that 3 percent? That's about as far as you can go with data because of the digestive system for fresh knowledge out there. One way that works is money. When the ranches were sucking up all the water of certain trout rivers in Montana, a lot of somewhat monied trout fishermen pushed and pushed and now the ranches can't do it anymore. This is the nature of the world. When we approach adversaries innocently, with goodwill, it's fatuous. You don't get your best-intentioned, $50/hour lawyer, you get your savvy, $500/hour lawyer.

The other thing that speaks loudly next to money and legality, is just sheer votes. There's no question that the anti-environmental forces and Gingrich's "Contract for America" had to back up because they crossed the line with a lot of people, including Republican women birdwatchers. People don't want to hear that kind of rhetoric anymore, it's bullshit. What counts is a broad base of money, legality, and votes. You can frighten anybody with votes. I come from an agricultural background and have absolutely nothing against cows, but I have everything against improper use of public land for grazing. I can say to a rancher that we're carrying the load too, this is an entitlement, and some of my best quail habitat has been turned to leather since last year. Who's the landlord? As Rene Char said, "Who stands on the gangplank directing operations, the captain or the rats?" That's always a good point. So, in other words, in this incredible swapmeet that is Washington, we can't be so nice about it. We don't want to be simpleminded. I don't think it's cynicism, it's a recognition of how it works in America.

Beyond the politicians and the theologians, as you say in your essays, there are the writers and poets and artists out at the margins working away at consciousness.

Sure. But, you can't ever think, and, as I've said, you shouldn't ever have the illusion of coming to an artist for coherence. It's feeble-minded to think of being right as an artist. Being right is about as fragile a thing possible in the world. The duty of the poet is not to shit out of his mouth like a politician. Poets should be out there on the borderland saying this kind of thing. Truly, some of the nature writing being done today is masturbatory, what I call the pornography of nature, and can be as obtuse and disturbing as the ignorance of nature. It goes so far as the poor woman in the *Harper's* article who wanted to be kind to the sick hyena and got half eaten alive. I think there is a failure to internalize what we're saying, and to realize we know what to do when we're in peril but we don't know what to do when something else is in peril. Sentimentality forgets what it is to be wild.

And fails to see the appropriateness of backing away, backing off.

Sure. The function of adventure travel, which is somewhat debilitating in some respects, is not to count coup on everything, but to comprehend it all. We're not getting rid of the ego when we write to ask, aren't my observations elegant and astounding? The largest nature metaphor I ever heard, which is wonderful, came from Lorca who said, "The enormous night straining her waist against the Milky Way."

Part of the problem comes because America, with the disintegration of the Soviet Union, is at the peak of her empire now. We have to think of what happened with England in Victorian times when there was a great deal of rigidification, moral rigidification, and scrutiny of everyone else, all of which is, of course, what we have in our New Puritanism. With America's fear of losing world power and money, politicians are writing thousands of rules everyday to solidify their positions, to solidify the position of America. It's absurd. It's gotten so out of hand that you can't have your own personal, moral structure without thinking everyone should have your particular moral structure.

What do you think of the role played by the processes of modernity and increasing abstractions in our lives?

I think our problems are partly modernity, but as Paul Shepard said somewhat inadvertently, and which also goes well with Bruce Chatwin's last, posthumous book of essays on nomadism, this kind of rigidification came at the height of the agricultural cycle (post-hunter and gatherer), and now we're at the absolute apex of this rigidification. The power of the priestly class is being assumed by national and state congresses who are relentlessly trying to make moral rules. Bernard DeVoto, according to Lewis Lapham at *Harper's,* said the worst thing that happened during the McCarthy period, and what he found inconceivable, was all the constant snooping. Now the modern university, with all its political correctness, is closer to the cellular structure of Cuban communism than anything else. It's absurd.

Sometimes our political correctness nonsense is funny. A couple of years ago, my Italian editor went to a dinner party in Marin County. She was outside looking at the Pacific, standing by a buffet table. A wind had come up, the tablecloth was flapping, and she was asked not to smoke. She did what all good, strong Italian women do, she said, "Fuuck you" and was out of there. This kind of falling into line, whether it's academic or not, is part of the monstrous response you had to Jack Turner in the last issue of *Wild Duck Review.* How dare he question it all? It's amusing to hear all of these well-intentioned people chastening Jack. It sounds like something in the 1920s, with Lenin from the Finland station, "You're failing to follow the platform."

And, if you question you must have an alternative plan. Where's our desire for saying the unsayable?

It's absurd. It's just like the border problem here in Arizona and Mexico. Some suggest a moat should be built, but then you see these 12,000 foot peaks and you can see that a 1,900 mile moat is ridiculous. No one wants you to say the reason the Mexicans are crossing the border is because they earn $5/day at most in a factory in Mexico and they're earning $50/day working here. What do we expect? Unless you get a patrolman every 50 feet, a la Berlin Wall, you're not going to stop anything. It's fatuous—as fatuous as stopping marijuana from coming across. It doesn't mean I have any solutions, but you can certainly say, as does Jack Turner, that when the emperor is naked, the emperor is naked. You don't have to have any clothes ready for the emperor to see that he is naked.

Then there's the preposterous effects of social engineering. For instance, you know how hard it is to help friends. Now add millions and millions of friends. These programs are like cosigning a loan and you don't see them again for a year. It's essentially funny. There's no sense in saying, get all the cows out of the Rockies. That's not the way you do it. There are ample methods. One simply treats the property as any tenant should any landlord's property. Solutions are just not that obscure.

What obligations do writers carry and to what, to whom?

Ed Abbey was magnificent to me, and we were always quarreling about one thing or another, but the wonderful thing was that you'd never mistake him for anyone else anymore than you would Jack Turner or Doug Peacock. There's no point in pretending an artist is going to be a junior scientist. His obligation is to note the discrepancies in our environmental efforts as poignantly as Ginsberg did the world order as it stands.

It's hard to get up in the morning and look in the mirror and say, I am part of nature too. But you are, what the fuck do you think you are? We're just the most dangerous form of nature and we better be aware of it with all our brilliant little ideas. Some of the most powerful "nature poetry" you'll find is in people like Snyder and so on where it's not obtrusively didactic, or in the Chan poets of China. I don't think Wordsworth is read enough anymore.

There's been a terrible suffering of literacy in the last twenty years in particular, partly because the teaching profession is so sure there is a short cut to be had. Now with the invention of computers and the Internet, it's as if there is a new substitute for reading, writing, and thinking. There's not. A mass movement is being created that is even more susceptible to different forms of Nazism, you know? It's an implicit moral fascism. Look at the Savings and Loan debacle, and they're right back again. What regulations have there been on greed?

It's messianic to think greed is self-checking. I've never met a developer who wouldn't spit in the face of his grandchild for a buck—that's the nature of the beast and we better know it. I wonder at what's going on. I was in Burgundy, France, a big cattle raising area that is peerlessly beautiful. I remarked it was extraordinarily well taken care of, given all the cattle, and the fellow I was talking with said, well we didn't have any place else to go. We Americans have realized too late how limited we are. Here in America we've had a theological basis for land rape too, with the Christian assumption that we're going to die and go to heaven and, meanwhile, it's our duty to do anything we want to the land to prosper. We can't forget that wilderness has always had people living in it and that you don't have to notice people. In terms of wildness, I always thought it was comic that I knew of more forty-acre woodlots in Michigan that are wilder than Yosemite.

Of course the be-all, end-all problem is overpopulation, as we all know. I haven't heard any intelligent solutions to this problem. I've heard intelligence but not functional intelligence. In the case of China, where you consciously limit your birth rate to two children per family, there's amniocentesis and suddenly everyone wants sons. We can't keep up with the technology. Then, here we are with cloning. Newt Gingrich will want 900 versions of himself. The stew we're in is enormous. A movie mogul told me you have to play hardball twenty-four hours a day to get ahead in that business. I want my leaders in the environmental movement to play hard ball twenty-four hours a day. Maybe they can file their teeth.

And writers?

Oh, filing their teeth comes with their nature. It's unthinkable for me to have any hesitation about what I say in a poem. I suppose that's always been true for a particular kind of a writer. Once you receive your calling you can't back off at all. Writing isn't something for people who don't want to spend their entire lives at it, and most people figure out that commitment early, by age eighteen. You see you don't get to be a lot of things, that writing will take a full commitment.

You've quoted Rene Char as saying, "Lucidity is the wound closest to the sun." Will you speak to what it means for you in your work?

Yes. Your obligation as a writer is to be utterly vulnerable moment by moment by moment. It's the regrettable trap. It's like Dostoyevsky questioning whether at some point to be too conscious is to be diseased. Or, as Nietzsche said, if you stare into the abyss long enough, it'll stare back into you. Without question it is not a process that frees you from your common humanity, because writers are as susceptible to greed as anyone I know. The seductions are countless in this world to make the least important come first—vis à vis putting the lucrative screenplay before a book of poems. But, it can't bother you too much because that's the nature, too, of writing. Like Faulkner said, if you've got to take it raw, take it raw. That's what writing is.

As a writer do you consciously protect your vulnerability?

Yes. It's a great part of it. There's something very troublesome that D. H. Lawrence said and I came upon it in my twenties, "The only aristocracy is that of consciousness." Consciousness is a moment-by-moment obligation, and if you have it then I suppose you're finally entitled to say something. It's the same thing as what is meant by "tentativeness" in Zen, or meant by Dogen when he said, "No changing reality to suit the self." There's no sense in marching or having a meeting when the world is being destroyed, as in the case of the bison, right outside. There is always the new wound or the new corruption right here, the moral corruption, that is absolutely profound and opens us to international ridicule. When the consciousness of Americans catches up to what they're doing, the shit is going to hit the fan.

What do you think of psychotherapy?
I've been to a mind doctor off and on for twenty years and it's made a profound change in my life. All they are are contemporary shamans—there is no other way to look at them—but, the trouble is, as many will admit, only one therapist out of a thousand is any good. I don't object to therapeutics, but I object to therapeutics becoming a giant machine as it has in this culture. Now we have human imperfection numbered in the thousands so therapists can bill insurance. He drinks coffee: #582.6. He washes his hands too often: #584.7. He turns off the light too often: #631.2. If such therapeutics free people from the responsibility of being human, we have a real problem. And, this great, great embracing of victimization that took place a decade or so ago has created real problems.

Yes, and the emphasis on the confessional in public as therapeutic, or in poetics as art, has real limits to it.
I never could read Anne Sexton for that reason. It's not very interesting. When I say, oh woe is me in extremis, I'm just another coal miner, what's the point in thinking it's unique? Our cures are interesting. Our infirmities aren't. Everyone knows about infirmities. Our occasional luminescences are what contribute to the human condition. The idea that somebody can say, for instance, that I get up and work hard—well, try saying that to the Chicanos. Give me a break! I grew up in a rather poor family of dirt farmers in northern Michigan. Can you imagine the idea of a professor teaching six hours a week and whining about it? But, the confessional movement is rubbish and will go away fast. People will tire of lifting the Band-Aids. Even Rush Limbaugh is fading. People will look for something else, something new, as we do all the time and have throughout our history. Dozens of women I know have grown tired of thinking of themselves as victims. Now they're on to kicking ass and taking names, which is infinitely healthier than saying, oh poor me. I have a

profound Jungian therapist who points out that he has patients in their late sixties still whining about their parents. It is all very comic. It's that illusion that parents are always dominant, that big brutes are always dominant, in our lives.

In one of your essays, I liked your statement on the necessity of grandiosity for survival. Will you speak to what you meant by grandiosity and by survival?

Yes. There is a realization that to live your life you have to write your own songlines. Your own songlines and the degree to which you want your life to be an independent project is up to you. It's harder for people, of course, whose parents or whose society has crushed them, and that has happened over and over again. In the 1940s there was a craze in America for tying kids' hands so that they wouldn't pick their noses or misbehave. The elegant thing is to transcend being a victim.

I just wrote a children's book called *The Boy Who Ran to the Woods*, which is what I did at seven years old when I was blinded by a little girl. I think it was Edith Cobb's *The Ecology of Imagination in Childhood* that made it clear to me I had gone to the natural world to survive, to do my time alone. In *Dalva* I wrote about having to withstand implacable blows. When my father and sister were killed in an auto accident, I thought, isn't this strange, any possibility of agreeing with the world has just left me.

However, we Americans have been relatively spoiled. Look at Europeans and their suffering—millions of people dead. Our country is now seething with generalized resentment. There's more whining in the upper middle class than amongst the black population or natives by far. Certain people know through their consciousness as primates when they've painted themselves into the corner, and if they've painted themselves into the spoiled kind of corner, there's nothing more depressing than a Rolex and BMW. I know you have to keep one ear for your friends and one ear to the conversations in the world around you. I see it, hear it out there, this malaise. It's because there's no spiritual life, of course, and that makes for an enormous vacuum because we're spiritual creatures.

In your own work, whether from day to day or in its general arc, what does it look like to you? Where is your curiosity?

Well, you can go through it to the point you see not just what is in front of you, but can look at yourself walking away. I see more of the same work I've done before, I don't change gears in quantum leaps. I do find myself reading more and more about botany and anthropology, which reminds me of Erik Erikson saying reality is mankind's greatest illusion. We are overwhelmed by the perception of how short life is, as in the old Don Juan thing about the whining man who is always whining and whining about hoeing corn and then you hear a dog barking in the distance and the screen door slams and suddenly it's evening. You have to be very aware of that sensation. Time is one of our great illusions too. In "The Beige Dolorosa" there's a man who wants to rename the birds of North America, and he's created a calendar in which there are only three days a month, which gives him these great open spaces. Three 200-hour days. Natives know this kind of thing—how to renew oneself. The interesting thing about being in a rut is that the only thing you see are the sides of the rut. You don't see out. The frogs who fell into the well now think that's the universe. It's the perfect metaphor for people rich or poor.

I'm working on a second chapter of a novel where I've moved from a seventy-one-year-old man to a thirty-year-old grandson. He's questioning how, if we primates are mapped for anything that moves, do we discriminate between the spiritual caffeine of TV or movies and what lies mostly still outside the window? Occasionally a bird goes by, the sun goes down and then comes up. But people crave movement and forget that the movement seen on TV and in movies is not part of a living process, that it's coming out of a tube. Life is subtle and complex. There are no easy, fast answers. There aren't even any easy questions, let alone answers. In America this affects us in the environmental movement—the idea, the illusion, that every question has an answer. It's our Calvinist upbringing to believe that everything is solvable. It's sheer hubris.

How do you describe the core, the spirit, of your work?

This consciousness, I would say. Otherness. Otherness to remind ourselves of the bedrock of life, and death, and love, and suffering. Back to Lorca, what is poetry but love, suffering, and death? Or, the idea of making a heap of all that you have met. I haven't been nearly as unflinching as I'd hoped to be, no. But, that's part of my makeup. Early on, my inability to face certain horrors as directly as I should have contributed to that. But, then I'm always looking for the song I could make out of it, too. I can't quarrel with the limitations which are part of me—everybody has the severest of limitations. You are ultimately what you collectively wish to be. When someone says they could be so much more, I say well, you better get started right now, who's stopping you? Face it, there's an anchor tied to your ass.

Are you writing poetry—is it the writing closest to your heart?

I'm always writing poetry. I don't differentiate, though, between poetry and novels at all. Short things are short all over and long things are long. I've never been able to write short stories. The shortest I ever get is a novella, about 100 pages. Certainly it's too late to become a fireman or a cowboy. Early in my environmental activities it was always requested that I not speak a lot because, as my daughter would say, I could make an audience weep in five minutes through one means or another and the environmental movement is one area in which we need a lot of rationality. The poet has to be off to the side giving his two cents, but two cents isn't the whole dollar. One isn't really good without the other, but I see how brutally hard some people have worked and it's paid off for the movement by just being out there plugging away day in and day out.

How might the proliferation of creative writing programs and workshops affect literature?

You can't ever have enough of what's good. I think sometimes the bad or mediocre obfuscates the good—that's what Ezra Pound thought—and I think there's a problem if one thousand literary novels are published every year and they are all recommended with sincerity. Certainly sincerity is not then a very high virtue. Give me back the art. I can't read prose unless it's interesting prose. I don't give a shit about anybody's good intentions, you know? Juice can't be taught in a creative writing program.

I created an ideal creative writing program once. I taught it for one semester and I gave students 148 books of poetry for the main part of the modernist tradition, from the French Symbolists onward. I lost some students there. But, I think an ideal MFA writing program would require one year of manual labor in the country; one year of life in the city; one year spent along reading; and only then would anyone return and begin writing. How else would anyone know anything?

Sorrowfully, success in writing is not a democratic process. No matter how hard you work and study, it either comes or doesn't, the door opening or closing on good prose. I'm just stunned how a man like Gabriel Garcia Marquez, in his novella last year, can write as he does. As I've said before, most people look in the mirror and say, "I'm getting old." But Shakespeare looked in the mirror and said, "Devouring time, blunt thou thy lion's paws." There is a difference. No one can teach you to make a metaphor. Or Lorca's, "Your belly is a battle of roots,/ your lips a blurred dawn./ Under the tepid roses of the bed/ the dead moan, waiting their turn." That's a different way of saying, gee, you're nifty. So much of our current fiction sounds like the contents of white guys at loose ends. Our own history has been sanitized to leave things out like women, Indians, Mexicans . . . more examples of white guys at loose ends. Instead, good art smells like life.

Lord Jim: A Sense of Place
Terry W. Phipps / 1997

From *Grand Rapids Magazine,* (May 1998), 19–25. Reprinted by permission of the publisher, *Grand Rapids Magazine* © May 1998.

"Late in October 1914, three brothers rode from Choteau, Montana, to Calgary, Alberta, to enlist in the Great War (the United States did not enter until 1917). An old Cheyenne named One Stab rode with them to return with the horses in tow, because the horses were blooded, and their father did not think it was fitting for his sons to ride off on nags. One Stab knew all of the shortcuts in the northern Rockies, so their ride traversed wild county, much of it far from roads and settlements. They left before dawn, with their father holding an oil lamp, dressed in his buffalo robe, all of them silent, and the farewell breath he embraced them with rose in a small white cloud to the rafters."

And so began two legends, one in an epic film and one a living legend: Jim Harrison, author of "Legends of the Fall."

Tucked in rural Leelanau County, Harrison's granary, a vine-covered building behind his refurbished farmhouse and right of the gray barn next to the garden, provides the solace that generates novels and books of poetry that slip through our hands like gold dust. Recent Harrison films like *Revenge, Cold Feet, Dalva, Wolf,* and *Carried Away* may ring familiar, but literature-entrenched readers realize this writer has emerged from his chrysalis and only now dries his wings in full sun. From the stuff that made Steinbeck, Hemingway, and Faulkner, Harrison convincingly carved his niche, not by formula writing, but by his formidable literary depth, his sheer intelligence and experimental tenacity with the literature itself. His critics, like a spring wind, embrace and bash his work but uniformly agree that "Harrison is a consummate storyteller" (Judith Freeman, *LA Times Book Review,* 1990) and "an exceptional writer."

"Harrison offers the challenges for those professional devotees of high art who wish to examine his poems and fictions, but he also offers interesting characters and good stories for those who do not." (Robert E. Burkholder, Pennsylvania State University).

Haunts around the Leelanau valleys spark Harrison's visual seed. From his character-reaping in local pubs like Dick's Pour House in Lake Leelanau, Art's Tavern in Glen Arbor or the Blue Bird in Leland, Harris occasionally settles himself unobtrusively into a bottle of Merault and grilled duck breast with tart-cherry barbecue sauce and garlic mashed potatoes at Hattie's, his favorite restaurant in Sutton's Bay. "I left the woods and made my way over to Hattie's Grille in Sutton's Bay, my favorite restaurant in the vast expanse of northern Michigan," Harrison wrote. "Naturally there are other good places, but they have largely neglected a responsibility of first-rate restaurants, which is to educate our palates. Jim Milliman is the owner and chef of Hattie's Grille, assisted by Alice Clayton, a birdlike young woman who is breathtakingly deft in the kitchen. . . . I poured a largish glass of Trefethen Cabernet, which is a steal, and was reminded again of the sheer speed that is demanded of the chef."

Over off M-22, the Jolli Lodge, across from the Good Harbor Winery and on Good Harbor Bay, once provided Harrison a nine-day refuge in late winter: he walked out with "Legends of the Fall." Although frequently seen, he guards his privacy trenchantly. Signs, reminiscent of those Wall Drug icons along South Dakota highways, still warn visitors who enter his driveway uninvited of their status; his Grand Marais two-lane has more signs than the population of the town itself.

James Thomas Harrison was born on December 11, 1937, in Grayling, Mich. His father, Winfield Sprague Harrison, a county soil conservation agent, influenced Harrison's awareness of the natural world. His mother, Olivia Wahlgren Harrison, introduced him to the vastness of classical literature, but both parents were unbridled readers who plunged Harrison into Dos Passos, Rimbaud, Joyce, Hemingway, Whitman, Melville, Steinbeck, and Faulkner. At seven, a run-in with a female playmate wielding a broken bottle gashed his left eye into darkness. From that point, Harrison said, "I'd turn for solace to rivers, rain, trees, birds, lakes, animals." At sixteen, he decided to drop his preacher notions and become a writer. "It was a combination of my romantic convictions and my profound boredom with the middle-class way of life which gave me the urge to become a writer," he said in an interview with *Le Monde* (October 27, 1991).

After a brief walkabout in New York and Boston, Harrison returned to Michigan and enrolled at Michigan State University. There he met and married Linda King and befriended Thomas McGuane, novelist and screenwriter, who would later introduced Harrison to Jack Nicholson during the filming of

Missouri Breaks, an encounter that was to be Harrison's break. Harrison graduated with a B.A. in English in 1960, followed by an M.A. in comparative literature. In 1965, while still a graduate student, he published his first book of poetry, *Plain Song.* Harrison was appointed as an assistant professor of English at the State University of New York at Stony Brook. After an agonizing year, he gave up his last steady employment and returned with Linda and daughter Jamie Louise to Michigan and an annual income of $10,000. The first light came with a NEA grant (1967–1969) and a Guggenheim Fellowship (1969–1970). Two books of poetry followed the grants.

After yet another life-altering accident—falling off a cliff while bird-hunting—Harrison accepted McGuane's suggestion of writing a novel: *Wolf* was the result. The birth of Harrison's second daughter, Anna Severin, made success more imperative. He wrote numerous articles for magazines like *Sports Illustrated* and *Esquire,* but it was the McGuane/Nicholson connection that networked Harrison with Hollywood. Nicholson loaned Harrison $15,000 to finish *Legends of the Fall,* his first real success. Film rights for all three novellas were sold, and Harrison eventuality became a screenwriter. Said Raymond Carver of the *Washington Post Book World* regarding *Legends.* "I can't begin to do justice to the nuances of character and honest complexities of plot in this work. The writing is precise and careful—and sings withal."

Robert Houston, in the *New York Times Book Review* went further, saying it "may well be the best set of novellas to appear in this country during the last quarter-century."

Harrison is often ill-compared to Hemingway. "It doesn't exist," he said. "You know what that is? It's just a convenience. I don't think average reviewers have read very much. There's no remote comparison." The comparison may have grown from his lifestyle, his love of the outdoors, hunting and fishing, or his past reputation for hard living. Gordon Chaplin of the *Washington Post* described Harrison as a kind of plundering Hemingway "fishing and carousing" and who loved "the edgy, seedy existential sharpness of hangovers."

Last fall I was summoned to the granary for an interview. A slept-in single bed tucked in the northeast corner; a potbellied wood stove mid-room; his desk on the south wall; and a museum quality to his collectibles—snake skins, photographs of a groupie's bare breasts, paintings, Navajo blankets—sparked curiosity. Notably absent was a computer; he writes longhand, only once; he never rewrites.

GR Magazine: What project are you currently working on?

Harrison: I spent all summer on this. This is the second chapter of the novel . . . the big one; I hope to finish it . . . oh by March.

It's just the novel I intended to write when I wrote *Dalva*. Some of it takes place before, and some of it takes place after. The first chapter is sort of the grandfather that raised her, who lived in the other house. . . . I knew his character. Then the second section is her son that she gave up for adoption; then the third chapter is the rest, . . . so it's been a long haul.

GR Magazine: When did you begin working on this?

Harrison: Two years ago. I can do only about . . . the first chapter took me 200 pages; it took me about four or five months; the same way with the second chapter, and there's a year in between the two because I went broke and had to do a . . . I had to research the second chapter and had to write two versions of a screenplay, which I finished last May.

GR Magazine: What was the screenplay?

Harrison: Oh, it's this project I've had with Harrison Ford almost seven years now. I've been trying to come up with a . . . we're going against the tide because they're trying to come up with something that's Western but outside the genre. The screenplay is set in 1928 in Western Nebraska. Sort of a cusp thing, certainly not modern, certainly not Old West but sort of the area that isn't exhausted.

GR Magazine: Like "Legends"?

Harrison: Just about; that was 1914. It's the same sense of that kind of time frame. That's the only sort of empty period. . . . Politically, nobody seems to know much about what occurred before the second world war; there's some kind of cutoff.

I was fascinated through that, because in the first chapter I've got a kid who's gone to the Omaha Exhibition. Those world exhibitions at the time, like world's fairs now, were immense. There are promotional things to try to get investments in the Midwest, but he, when he's like thirteen, he goes to the French Pavilion which was there in Omaha, and he sees a woman, attractive—you know how you are when you're thirteen—and she's got art prints and she's talking about French art, so he decides that's what he wants to be. Now he ends up at the Chicago Art Institute in 1912. If you look at the history of American art, it was an inordinately lively scene in Chicago and in the Midwest. . . . Everybody has to use the reality they know.

GR Magazine: Will Harrison Ford act in this?

Harrison: I don't know, . . . that's always a crap shoot, the seventh version of it, you never know. But after you write it, it's no longer up to you, because you're thinking of a possible hundred million dollar investment which is not your money. It's again, who owns the bat and ball. My access is more on a friendship basis. I'm a godfather of his daughter. We've just known each other a long time.

I'm not thought of in Hollywood as a real screenwriter. I get my jobs partly through the fidelity of a certain actress or actor that requests me, Costner or Nicholson. Once, when I was broke, I got a job because Sean Connery had read "Revenge" in *Esquire* and wanted that writer. That's how I get work. I'm too arrogant to become a real screenwriter, that way you have to really kiss butts out there, and I've never perfected that. It's not necessarily my favorite because you're fired dozens of times. Everybody does get fired out there. It's one of the places that you get fired, and you feel quite wonderful.

Say I'm having a meeting at Columbia or TriStar and I'm pissed off, or I get fired or something, and twenty-four hours later. I'm at the Dunes Saloon; it's like a Voorhees story; is it a dream or is it not? I contributed an essay years ago, it's in *Just Before Dark*. It's an essay called "Dream as Metaphor for Survival." It was contributed to the *Psychoanalytic Review* in an issue on dislocation. Many artists are permanently dislocated. In this world, it probably makes them more functional.

Place anonymity—that's why I like interminable car trips. I think my longest one ever was eleven or twelve thousand miles around the United States. I like complete freedom, and you're not a target because you're moving, and nobody can get to you except by your permission; so it's like "Brown Dog" in a sense; he's free. He has no papers. His only mail is every four years; he gets a notice to renew his driver's license—that's all. But sometimes what they get in the bad sense is that old sense of army brats where they never had any home really to even long for. I dealt with that in "Julip," because she's permanently back and forth between the North and South.

I have remembered something; I looked at it again this year and realized how good a book it was—I've always been a Steinbeck fan. There was a Steinbeck scholar up here for a couple of days talking to me this year, and I had brought up that point that he had met many people in *Travels with Charley* and enjoyed this freedom of the road and freedom of movement. When somebody says, in the Thoreau sense, does he own the farm, or does the farm own him? Like a teacher-writer sometimes is, once he makes the down payment on the house and has a kid or two, then his mobility is permanently atrophied, and consequently it becomes easier to kiss ass because it's the only thing there is to do.

GR Magazine: Are you involved in other screenwriting projects?

Harrison: I'm either doing to do "Julip"—that's revived right now; they've got a bad script. I might do that, but I'm only going to do screenplays from now on with my older daughter, Jamie. Her third mystery novel's coming out. She had worked years ago for Michael Douglas. Her imagination and sense of plot is more immediate than mine; I'm just tired of doing it, but it makes her more solvent. It takes some of the load off me. Or I might do one for Nicholson and Juliette Binoche, whom I got to know in Paris. I like her. She's a darling. She's so intelligent and melancholy.

GR Magazine: Do you watch or deal with television?

Harrison: I don't watch anything. Somebody asked me if I watched this hideous bullshit thing they did on *Dalva* on television, and I said no. . . . There's how things can go wrong. When I sold that, it was under the understanding that Jessica Lange was going to be Dalva, which would have been sort of interesting. But it's a business, as they say as it filters down. She was interested in it if I would do the screenplay. There's no way I was going to do that screenplay because I didn't think it could be done. It's like way back when John Huston had asked me to do a screenplay of *A Hundred Years of Solitude*—and he's the man I least wanted to turn down because I really liked him because we spent time on "Revenge" together in its early stages. I said you can't make a movie out of that.

The same thing with Coppola. . . . For two years, he was pissed at me because I wouldn't do a screenplay of *On the Road*. And *Dalva* was way too sprawling. It's like the Yeats notion. "Are you going to cut off the legs of the horse to get it in the box stall?" There's just some properties that won't work.

GR Magazine: What did you think about the production of *Carried Away (Farmer)?*

Harrison: I thought that was really quite good. . . . I liked that of all the movies . . . four or five connected to my work. That was by far the best; extraordinary. Of course, it's not the kind of movie that was going to do well commercially but was widely admired in the film business.

GR Magazine: How did Dennis Hopper fit into the picture?

Harrison: When I talked to him in that, it's interesting, because he's from Fort Dodge, Kansas, and it's a farm area. I was just amazed he just had a, you know, the peculiar way they tilt up their head a little bit? Well, he had it. But of course, he grew up, as he pointed out, around hundreds of farmers out in the center of Kansas. No, he had it perfectly, the combination of farmer-teacher. I thought they did a lovely job on that.

That's odd. I knew from the beginning when I was talking to directors, a Brazilian director, but he has made a film I loved down there. He totally understood the property. Sometimes a foreigner can do that. Sometimes if they're a little distant they can understand that. It's like you get to see it freshly again through their eyes from their responses. I'm most concerned with consensual reality; it's what you get from photography and literature when it's somewhat visually oriented; painting is. You realize it back when Erik Erikson said "Reality is mankind's greatest illusion." So what you get from good photography or good painter is, you remove habitual and conditioned responses from reality, and then you get to see it again. Ordinary mortals, like nearly all of us, don't get to see it again except under special circumstances. The light, if they get up on first light in summer or last light, then something changes about it, and they see it again freshly.

GR Magazine: Tell me about your poetry.

Harrison: You know, I had that last book of poems out last October. It's totally uncontrollable. You don't have any idea when its going to emerge, and when it's not going to emerge. I've never stopped writing it. I know I was praised years ago. After (Jimmy) Buffet started making some money, he gave me, as a present, Faulkner's first book of poems, which my brother, who's the bibliophile, immediately put in his storage so I wouldn't lose it. That was true of Hemingway, too, he started writing poetry. Not too interesting. Faulkner's isn't either. It's sort of like Keats or Shelly imitations. It's an intensification of the image.

GR Magazine: When you start a book, do you start it with character or plot?

Harrison: Images, I have to see it. For instance this one, the second chapter, this guy [Nelse] has a high fever, and it's a sensation when you camp. He's logged 403 campsites in ten years in the United States. He's a real wanderer, a pickup truck kind of guy. He has the illusion, he has a high fever, that he's looking at the constellations up on a river in Nebraska, that the earth is moving beneath his back, which it is of course, but we usually don't have that sensation, so it's an image; I have to get that kind of thing. Like in "Legends," it was saddling the horses before dawn with the father holding the lantern and the breath rising up in the air: that kind of thing. So it's a combination of images that have a distinct emotional equivalent. I see the scene like a master. It starts filling out like in the "Man who Gave Up His Name," a man in his forties is dancing alone to music he borrowed from his daughter. You can imagine what he's doing, but he just never had danced. He thought he would try it; that kind of thing, or in "Revenge," it's the guy lying there with the hermatomas with the vultures, so the plot is secondary. Because, how many plots are there?

GR Magazine: What is the relationship of plots in film?
Harrison: It's enforced. What makes it interesting is characters. What they keep blowing is—they don't realize that, number one, you have to have a story that people care about then they keep creating, say, fascinating, violent stories that nobody gives a shit about. There's no one in the movie that you can respond to, so you have to have an engaging story. You have to have some sense of response to the characters. . . . There's a reason why B movies are called B movies when they're frequently supposed to be A movies. There's no "there" there. People think you have to read a whole screenplay. No, you have to read about two pages. If somebody sends me a manuscript, I have to read a few pages because of my interest in the art. If the prose isn't engaging, I can't continue; life's too short.

GR Magazine: Are any of your characters generated from real people?
Harrison: Several people wanted to meet Clare, the woman in "The Woman Lit by Fireflies" who leaves her husband, walks off in the corn field. Well they liked her. And I remember Thomas Berger wrote *Little Big Man* after I'd written *A Good Day to Die*. He wanted to meet Sylvia. I says, you're a novelist, you make these up! but there's sort of an accretion, a suggestion. I met three people since I wrote "Brown Dog" that rather reminded me of him but not any specifically beforehand. It was a complete anarchistic notion. What is freedom now? Who can be totally free?

GR Magazine: Do you get the kernel from someone?
Harrison: Always the kernel. Like "Legends" was the notebooks that Linda found in their family home up there. Part of Ludlow comes from her great grandfather who was on the expedition with Custer, and I think what set me off then is he did do things like they chased down the last of the grizzly bears, and as he says, "with considerable difficulty released the animal afterwards." Now those were the real cowboys. No kerchiefs, but they

can do it! You're always getting blamed for being the characters in your book, but if there's a couple hundred now, how can I be all these people?

GR Magazine: Do you then have to write about the place you experience more than you have to write about the people you experience?

Harrison: Exactly! Exactly! The location.

I think character so often arises out of location. You know the media keeps trying to tell us we're all the same; maybe we're all the same if you don't get off the freeway, but if you take . . . the time to talk to anybody, more than an hour, you're just convulsed again by the mystery of personality. That's what keeps you going. If you've got five billion people in the world, all with distinct personalities, this is obsessively fascinating. What's the sense of reducing people to a parody of what they are like on television? Anything that's even moderately good on television, people respond to it because they aren't those reductions. I said once, years ago, I said, why do you want dialogue that would bore a mechanic down at the Ford garage? I said, listen to these people. Even they speak much more interestingly than these movies. These people are trapped in Hollywood and don't have any exposure to the immense differences of people; it's monochromatic.

GR Magazine: Do writers' diverse lifestyles produce interesting literature?

Harrison: Sometimes you don't know if that's the cause or the result. I think of Rilke, a poet I revere up with a few others in the twentieth century. . . . I was appalled once to see that he had forty-two residences in three years. It's an emotional, spiritual restlessness.

GR Magazine: What is your favorite type of literature to write?

Harrison: Long novels are long all over, and short novels. . . . Somebody said that about poetry: A short poem is short all over. You know it at the point of conception. I remember when this editor turned down "Legends of the Fall" unless I would make it 400 pages; it's only eighty pages. I said no: that's probably its charm, its specific density. I'm stuck with this, and any other novel. I just know I can't do it in a hundred pages.

GR Magazine: Do you work on more than one project at a time?

Harrison: Well, it's fluid. I haven't been very good at it. I'm trying to. I just got a letter from Matthiessen the other day because I was pissed that I had to go write another screenplay this fall for the family larder. He says, well I've tried it several times, and it hasn't worked very well; at least use the first hour of the day to keep your hand in. That works best. My last book of poems came in the middle of a screenplay in its long sequence, and I had to drop the screenplay because if you refuse the poem, it won't go away. You can put off a novel for a while, but you can't not write a poem because that particular muse is not very cooperative.

GR Magazine: Would it kill your creativity?

Harrison: Well I think it does, and then you would, you would really feel that you had fucked up. The lid would close down, and you'd finally recognize that was a coffin lid because you would then be refusing your calling.

GR Magazine: How do you know when you're finished with a project?

Harrison: It's like a poem. Yeats says a poem ends like a clicking of a box. It's just what you've been doing, basically. It's the way you've been thinking since you were fourteen when you first started thinking about this stuff. It's the same sense; you know when you've got a great picture before you see the print. I'm a failed painter. I wanted to be a painter when I was eighteen or nineteen, but I always made framed reality. I read this English anthropologist from the '20s and '30s, and she says that's why we have ritual in our lives—because it frames reality. Maybe it's because I have one eye, and it's a camera. But I've always made squares out of reality I want in fiction. Which of course like any painter or photographer does. It's the way I would like to see it, and that's what I remember.

GR Magazine: Do you read your work after it's published?

Harrison: I never read my own work, except for this—when they wanted to know if I had a take on how they could make a movie out of it, and then I read it. There would be no reason to, because that would stop you in that place.

GR Magazine: What was your attraction for Leelanau County?

Harrison: We drove up here in '64 when we lived in Kingsley for a year and a half. We didn't think we wanted to live there. We liked the atmosphere. When I got those two years of grants, I only knew them one year at a time. We rented a house up here on Horn Road and finally bought this place after the next year.

GR Magazine: What about Grand Marais?

Harrison: It was partly my father because he was an agronomist county-agent-type person, and he used to have to go to Chatham all the time in the

U.P. in Alger County, and then he and some other men from Reed City were invited to join this little deer shack they had up there near Shingleton. When I wrote *Wolf,* I'd gone up there before with a friend from Kingsley, usually to fish and rambled all over the U.P. and saw Grand Marais and thought, if I ever turn a little coin I'm going to get me a little cabin up here. I'm basically surrounded by public land. I can wander I'd say ninety-nine out of a hundred hikes, I never see another person.

GR Magazine: And Patagonia, Arizona?

Harrison: I'd gone through that in the late '60s, and I thought it was an honor. I found out, it wasn't really. As a poet, they got me to visit a lot of Indian reservations to talk about poetry and also a lot of black high schools. I was supposed to be one of the last of the proletarian poets, so they figured out, Let's send Harrison; he'll do this! It was wonderful to stand before an assembly of 200 Papago children and talk about poetry; the alien.

GR Magazine: Is there a sense of having made it?

Harrison: I don't think one ever feels the difference. I used to think it's at least two percent better than being broke. It's like a baseball player improving his average late in the season; every little thing helps. Even some phenomenally successful people I've known like Nicholson or Ford, in their business, don't go around feeling successful, or I don't see that. I don't think it's natural to feel puffed up. The good reviews always make you feel good for about two hours and bad reviews make you feel bad about four hours. The basic one is that your books are in print.

The biggest barrier to writing well and doing anything well is self-importance; it's blinding. You know that's the problem you have with politicians. Self-importance blinds people to life. It was very awkward when I first became so-called successful. I was very uncomfortable with it for about three years or four. I didn't want to deal with it. No one in the history of my family had ever made any money, so I felt guilty, but then I thought, I don't have to change my life that much. This isn't a studio of a rich writer.

An Interview with Jim Harrison
Eleanor Wachtel / 1998

A conjoined version of two separate interviews Eleanor Wachtel conducted in Toronto on her syndicated Canadian Broadcasting Company radio show, *Writers & Company,* on 25 September 1994 and 15 November 1998, the latter when Harrison was attending the International Festival of Authors in Toronto. The composite interview of material (primarily drawn from 1998) was published in *Brick: A Literary Journal,* 63 (Fall 1999), 18–26. However, for this longer version edited selections from the original 1998 radio broadcast interview have been restored in their proper sequence. Additional transcription by Robert DeMott and Anne Langendorfer. Reprinted with permission of Eleanor Wachtel.

Jim Harrison is a surprising writer. He quotes Wallace Stevens in the epigraph to his collection of essays, "The worst of all things is not to live in a physical world." Harrison has always had a close connection to the natural world, but often through traditional male pursuits like hunting and fishing. His settings are frequently in those traditional "proving ground" landscapes—the north woods or a cattle ranch in the Midwest. Jim Harrison is a man's man; buddies with Jack Nicholson, he co-wrote the screenplay for *Wolf.* A slightly grizzled, Hemingway-esque character, Harrison says things like, "I like grit. I like love and death. I'm tired of irony."

Alongside that gruffness is a sophisticated, erudite writer, a man who frequently quotes Rilke or Creeley, whose favorite book as a teen, his religion, was Joyce's *Finnegan's Wake.* A man who loves to cook and eat, he wrote a food and wine column for *Esquire* magazine called "The Raw and the Cooked." Or he does a few travel pieces for *Sports Illustrated.*

He is a Zen Buddhist who knows a lot about Native American life, peopling his book with characters who are half Lakota or Oglala Sioux, writing with passion, but not presumption. For instance, when referring to tribal elders in his new novel, *The Road Home,* he says, "These were not Methodist Indians, warriors with a lineage that owed nothing to the white man. We did not live upon the same earth that they did. And we flatter ourselves when we think we understand them. To pity these men is to pity the gods."

When Jim Harrison writes from the perspective of women, as he does in his novel *Dalva* and in the novellas "The Woman Lit by Fireflies" and

"Julip," he's extraordinarily sensitive and subtle. In writing that is comic and redemptive, Jim Harrison subverts the myths of male initiation.

Harrison is sixty years old. He has published ten books of prose, nine of poetry, and a collection of essays. His latest novel, *The Road Home,* is a kind of sequel or companion novel to *Dalva,* which came out ten years ago. Set mostly in Nebraska, *The Road Home* takes up Dalva's story through her grandfather, mother, lost son, and finally, Dalva herself. Like virtually all of Harrison's writing, it is moving and utterly humane. An important but elusive character in *The Road Home* says, "Just do your art and be good to people. It's that simple and that difficult." [When I met Jim Harrison in Toronto last month at the International Festival of Authors, I felt that this must be his credo.]

EW: You write about how you like to surround yourself with special objects at your farm in northern Michigan, where you live and work, things like animal skins or a heron wing or a pine cone from the forest where Garcia Lorca was executed. Can you tell me about them? And what they mean?

JH: Well, I don't know. I think actually when I thought it over, it's a little similar to the kind of collection of stuff you have as a little boy, you know. I brooded so much. I kept calling my mother a couple years ago to find out what had happened to my marbles, for instance. And I know there's a particular house in Reed City, Michigan, where under the back porch I buried some marbles. So I called my mother. This sounds slightly daffy but now the house is owned by someone we no longer know, so I'd feel a little uncomfortable as sixty-year-old, going and trying to dig up my marbles. [Laughs.]

EW: This is literal, we're talking about? [Laughs.]

JH: Yes! [Laughs.] But, no, I have a lot of stuff. I even have a grizzly turd that Doug Peacock gave me and a walrus tusk that an Inuit gave me—you know, that kind of thing. I have a wonderful coyote skull that a man gave me for helping him put up his teepee at a powwow. And I said, "You're a little rusty, you know, putting up the teepee." And he said he had been in prison for seventeen years. And I'm trying to think, now why does someone go to prison for seventeen years? This is a tough customer. But he gave me this beautiful coyote skull with his medicine painted on it. Stuff like that, you know.

EW: Why are these objects totems for you? Or what consolation do they offer?

JH: Well, I don't know. I think it might have even come partly from Rilke, who said to surround yourself with beloved objects, you know, rather than gimcrack, junk, and lint that most often surrounds us and suffocates us. Some objects that you have a direct emotional response to, even in the kitchen, where like, my grandmother's hundred-year-old Wagner skillet, stuff like that. [Laughs.] You know. I suppose it's continuity and that battles against the dislocation that we ordinarily feel to have these kind of things close to us. I think it's partly as if objects could be fellow creatures, too, just like our dogs.

EW: In terms of continuity, or stability, or reminders of happier images, you have made a connection between collecting these beloved objects and images to the precariousness or the instability of when you lost your sight when you were seven, when you lost your sight in one eye.

JH: Well, I think there probably is an attachment there because you're in that kind of prolonged zone of recovery, you know. Actually, a French critic caught me up on this. My obsession with thickets.

EW: Your obsession with?

JH: With thickets. Certain thickets throughout the United States. I think I have fifty of them that I particularly like. You know, thickets being a place you can sit within and see out but nobody can see in, you know, that kind of thing. And so, I have quite a collection of those, too.

EW: Favorite thickets?

JH: Favorite thickets. Solace thickets, you know. [Laughs.] It is absurd. Mary Douglas, the English anthropologist, whom I read deeply because she wrote the best.

EW: *The Purity and Danger* and other books.

JH: Yes. Yeah. And she's an overwhelmingly good writer. But she was talking about ritual, how we use ritual to frame reality. And I think sometimes our little fetishes, I mean, in the good sense—I don't mean in some kind of absurd sexual sense—our little fetishes, our beloved objects also help us frame reality on our own terms, rather than on the terms of the predominant culture.

EW: And this thing about your favorite thickets being related to your losing your sight is so that you can see in a controlled way, or a hidden way, or what?

JH: I think that's partly that. Because you do collect, if you think about it. I was given a beautiful camera by a wealthy friend but then I found out how much it costs to develop the film after taking a lot of rolls. Then I gave it back to him. But I started to think, well, my good eye is an aperture and I blink it and I take pictures. Well, I have been doing this for years and years. If I really want to store something in my image bank, I stare at it very closely, blink my eye, and then I have that photo.

EW: That's free.

JH: Yeah, free! [Laughs.]

EW: You've talked about the effect of losing your eye, and you've said it left you feeling that, at any moment, you might "fall through the earth where the crust is thin."

JH: Yeah, well you can't seem to count on much. That's just a metaphor where people actually think the earth is solid, but not necessarily! At first it's the hellishness of having nothing to fall back on—or as I said, "Life had become so bitter that I had nothing to fall back on except the sun and the moon and the stars." Like Aristophanes said, "When there's nothing for you to count on."

EW: Was that something you sensed when you were seven?

JH: That's definitely true. Though severe. I don't want to make too much of it. So many have really violent traumas in their youths, but it's something you have to accommodate. You realize the shape-changing keeps going on. Life is a fundamentally unreliable experience. As you may have noticed!

EW: One of the things that comes out in *The Road Home*—the character in the middle section, Dalva's son Nelse, says that, "I can't see the virtue in studying the natural world. It's just that everybody should do it and it's the only world you're going to get, as far was we know."

JH: Well, that's true because there's a great deal of schizophrenia in the environmental efforts. It's not a true I-and-thou relationship, you know. It's a me-and-you. It's an almost implicit condescension because we can't forget were nature, too. You know, as much as a bear or any other natural creature is, we're nature. So you can't separate yourself. You're either intimate with the natural world, or you're not. And you can create the distances, all sorts of distances, by sort of philosophical condescension. I remember when somebody told me they went to Montana and they thought people would be far nobler there because of the beauty of the surroundings. I said, "That's not the way it works at all. Maybe less likely." [Laughs.] Because you assume you know, you can go to Shangri-La, if there is such a place, in Tibet, and you can make it banal in a day through your own self immersion. You know, it depends on you. You don't get anymore out of a place than you bring to it, I don't think.

EW: Schizophrenic in a sense of?

JH: Well, it's just this continuing sense of distance. I'm saving the Colorado Plateau from the people that live there, as an environmentalist said. Which is absurd. So, they're here. They don't even know that topography. They don't know the spirit of that landscape. It's self-dramatization rather than true absorption or obsession, which would be far healthier.

EW: In a way you're quite specific about the ways in which nature should or shouldn't be viewed, I think, as one of your characters says, "We always destroy wilderness when we represent something else."

JH: Yeah.

EW: The natural world in your fiction isn't an especially romantic place. You don't romanticize nature. It's harsh, but it's also enormously interesting.

JH: Yeah, well it's not very romantic. The local press in Michigan was discouraged recently when they saw two bucks run a doe into the lake and make love to her until she drowned. It's not always very pleasant in our human terms. But it's always obsessively fascinating to me, because we're nature too.

EW: You talk about speaking to the birds. In one of your novellas, "The Beige Dolorosa," the professor takes on as a project to rename the birds.

JH: He thinks some of their names are corny and banal, and it's time that we gave them some more interesting names.

EW: How do you forge that kind of intimate relationship with nature?

JH: Lifelong exposure. I suppose it's quite sophisticated, in an odd sense. What I use to detach myself from the public world is a lot of walking in remote areas. But I also use Mozart and Rilke. If you find yourself properly tuned and you spend a lot of time around these creatures, you have at least the illusion that you're communicating with them, on some fundamental level. I'm not going to get goofy about it, like those poor souls who think they're talking to dolphins and so on. The dolphins don't need to talk to them, they should know that.

EW: The professor in "The Beige Dolorosa" says, "the birds made me feel I understood nothing, nothing at all." And at the same time he feels watched and spoken to by the birds.

JH: That's true. Now we're back to Blake. What did Blake say? "How do you know but ev'ry bird that cuts the airy way is an immense world of delight, clos'd by your senses five"? That's the visionary experience.

EW: I think, as you yourself have written in an essay called, "Everyday Life: The Question of Zen": "The bird passes across the window is a reminder of the shortness of life." But it's mostly a bird flying past the window. [Laughs.]

JH: Yes, of course. There is that problem. You know, I love the way even on greeting cards, they misquote Thoreau. They keep saying, "In *wilderness* is the salvation of the world." But no, "in *wildness*" is the salvation. So it's an entirely different concept, which I love. The way people want it to be so, to make wilderness represent that which has to be saved because it's mostly itself.

EW: So, it's misguided to be projecting too much on to it?

JH: Well, yes. Even Jesus said "step aside into the wilderness for awhile." You know, he did a solid forty days, which is a long camping trip. I've never made it that long. By then I'd really crave a restaurant or a bar.

EW: [Laughs.] But you talk about the need to absorb the landscape, or better yet, become absorbed by the landscape, that you don't really become it, but it becomes you. How does that work?

JH: Well, it's just the idea, it's the old Dogen dictum or point—the fifteenth-century Japanese Zen master—who had said, "To study the self is to forget the self. To forget the self is to become one with ten thousand things." People usually stop there, but he goes on to say, "you don't become one with ten thousand things. Ten thousand things become one with you." Which is the whole point. That rather adds to one's range, I think. Hopefully, anyway.

EW: So if I ask you how it works, you'd have to explain the whole Zen . . . ?

JH: Well, you know, if you think about it, I read that in ancient India, they used to tie troubled people beside a river. Okay? Well, if you're willing to say try it sometime, sit down on a stone or a cushion or just on the bank of a river for two solid hours. And you find, if you're willing to give up everything, or open up a bit, the river does absorb rather nonchalantly your poisons and after awhile there's just nothing there but you and the river and you're not confusing your separateness at all. The river is the river. But it's really done a marvelous bit on you.

EW: The idea sometimes seems to be carried almost to an extreme by some of your characters. I was thinking of Nelse, in *The Road Home,* who says, "Once I spent the whole of a cool, blustery May afternoon being a goshawk. And I had difficulty finding my actual body and reentering it."

JH: Well, that's just what you would call—which he knows very well—he doesn't want to be didactic or scholarly. That's just very traditional medicine in some cultures, to become something else for awhile. And the main danger is to be able to return to yourself.

EW: Have you ever done that? Have you entered something like that?
JH: Oh, sure. Yeah. I don't do it very often, you know.

EW: Like what?
JH: Well, a bear, you know. And birds. It's actually relief, but it's not something you toy around with because that should be left basically for people who have given their life over to that discipline. An archaeologist I know and I like very much wrote *Rites of Conquest,* about what happened in the northern Midwest, including Canada. He was with the Cree people way up in northern Canada. This was thirty years ago. He went trapping on a long thirty-day trapping trip with an old Cree native and he kept saying to the older guy, "Are you sure you know where you're going?" And the guy says, "Yeah, I've flown over the area before." It made him feel better. But after he was up there for thirty days, it occurred to him, he didn't mean he really flew over it. He flew over in a different way. It was just quite amusing. But there's not really that much of it. I just notice that that's as valid a form of human behavior as anything that goes on in Washington, certainly.

EW: You've described a transformative experience as a "little attack of lycanthropy," you and a wolf.

JH: Oh, well, that was caused by anger. I was thinking that at my log cabin years ago I'd seen this female wolf in my driveway. But this is odd—they did a terrible job on the movie—I saw it and in general I didn't care for it at all, and I quit after I wrote a couple drafts about the subject of *Wolf* with [Jack] Nicholson and Michelle Pfeiffer. But what had happened in the middle of the night—I was just there with my dog at my cabin—I thought somebody was coming in my driveway, but it was really only lightning. Okay, so for some reason—it might have been a dream—I hurled myself off my cot there and I went so high in the air that I gashed my head on this iron deer horn chandelier, and I cut my head. And then I ripped off the doors to the house and went running around, and I came to myself and it was very unpleasant. I kept the generator going all night and everything. My dog was frightened for a couple days. I mean, that's historical that that can happen to people, you know.

EW: And what had you felt had happened?

JH: I don't know. Just that. I was howling and everything. I don't know if I came unnerved, but what I'm still amazed by—I can sit on this cot and look at that chandelier and I'm a heavy fellow—How did I get up there? To cut my forehead, you know. I'm an artist. I don't like to fool with stuff like that. Leave that to people that are absorbed in that. Because it's again just part of the whole, and it's not the overwhelming whole. How interesting though.

EW: Yes. [Laughs.]

JH: It's not an academic experience. [Laughs.]

EW: The idea of attentiveness to nature, which relates also to your practice of Zen, I think, could also be seen as having some connection to Native American ways of being or seeing. I mean, is there a connection for you between the two?

JH: Oh, I don't know if there is or not. I was thinking that way because I was talking to one of my favorite authors, Peter Matthiessen, and he had said once, to find a practice, or a discipline, or a coda that overwhelms the least pleasant aspects of the culture, is part of what the terms are. So I don't care where it comes from—you can't take out of another culture what doesn't already exist in yourself and you discover there. You see what I mean? So that's the preposterousness of that New Age nonsense, you know? It better be there.

EW: It better be there in you.

JH: In you and you discover it. And that's the same way with any, I don't want to become a nickel-plated Oriental student, you know, I mean a student of that culture. But I do know that for instance even in a northern Japanese Zen sect *yamabushi* or distinctly natural world people, many anthropologists think that *zazen* itself was an ancient, a very ancient hunting tactic, you know. If you sit very still for an hour, then the natural world assumes its total shape, that it temporarily dispersed to avoid its main predator, which of course is man. You know, they forget you're there, and they think that's where *zazen* probably started. It's an interesting point. But no, I don't think of myself as a Buddhist at all. I'm just an artist. I find these kinds of things absorbing, you know.

EW: But you have affinities to some?

JH: Yeah, well, of course. Empathies, affinities. I think that probably emerges also from the habitat, you know. If you spent fifty years in the woods as much as possible, of course you'd have some affinities for the people that always lived there, because you've seen their world, unmitigated by our own as much as possible.

EW: Your characters in your novels are unusually philosophical, and they come up with these neat ways of pondering the "big questions," I think as one of them puts it. The question is how you make your soul clap its hands and sing.

JH: Yeah, well, that's that Yeatsian overwhelming irony, you know, "an aged man is but a paltry thing, a tattered coat upon a stick, unless soul claps its hands and sings." Which is true. But how do you keep alive? It's a question for all of us, you know. Even kids have trouble trying to keep themselves alive. But I think that in that, oh God, in that question the question is always how I can live without cutting off my arms and legs to get along with the world? That's critical, how can I maintain? That's back again to that peculiar notion I read in my late teens, where D. H. Lawrence said, "The only aristocracy was that of consciousness." You know, to the degree that you're totally conscious, you're totally alive, and that can't be bought in any sense.

EW: So have you figured out what makes your soul clap its hands?

JH: Yes, I think so. But sometimes I don't have the resources for it. I think you can't rate everything. It's all been extricably intermixed, you know. Like I said the other day, a Hasidic scholar I know had said to me, "Don't you think that reality is an accretion of the perceptions of all creatures?" I said, "Yep!" [Laughs.] What a statement! My wife adopted an orphan crow this spring, which was a little sort of pink thing covered with sores, and now it's a nice, big crow. But when I have a chat with him and we look at each other, it's the twilight zone in a way. Because you know, he's really thinking things over. I'm not projecting that. He just is. Because suddenly he turns a little bit and way, way down the road a mile you see the dog trotting along. [Laughs.] That kind of thing. You know.

EW: When you say you don't always have the "resources"?

JH: Oh, I mean, we all just get tired. We drown. We drown on a daily basis and then we recover.

EW: And does it have to do with this attentiveness to the dailyness of life?

JH: Well, sure, sure. For me it's more likely to happen outside than inside. Inside it usually is music or a good book, you know, that will lift you out of your doldrums. Weather that you can't sail in.

EW: I'd like to talk about your characters. Sometimes they're not only a little off course, it's as if they've dropped through a hole in their own lives. Why does that interest you in particular?

JH: Because that's what I see people doing. All the time. You create a life sometimes out of very mediocre assumptions, and then suddenly the whole structure no longer works. The human being tends to suffocate within the structure. Of course that doesn't happen to a lot of people, but they don't make the most interesting fiction. So you pick your characters that evolve along these crisis lines: Whether their hearts are wounded or their physical or mental structures disappear under societal pressures, whether it's losing a job or a divorce or wondering what they actually are.

EW: "Wondering what they actually are" would describe the novella, "The Woman Lit by Fireflies," where you've got a middle-class, middle-aged housewife, who ends up literally naked in a cornfield.

JH: That's more isolatable, in that she has sort of an elegant mind. Clare loves to read and she loves good music. But she'd reached a point—at that rest stop on Interstate 80—where she could no longer bear the simple and brutal mediocrity of her husband. So she went over the fence. It's funny, after that was published [in *The New Yorker*] I got, oh, I think it was 150 letters mostly from women—I would say 90 percent—who had done the same thing. It's very liberating sometimes to just walk off the porch, climb the fence, disappear. Especially when your reality is that much smaller than your mind. Which hers was.

EW: The men in your books are broken, in a way. The professor says, "If ours was more directly a cannibal culture by now I would be so much more lunch meat." Julip—the young woman in the title novella—is much more vivid, much more immediate than the men. What gives her that vitality?

JH: You know it occurred to me—and feminists might not agree with it, but it was certainly true when I wrote *Dalva,* which was in the voice of a woman—in general I find women in our culture much less of a mess than men. I've met many more extraordinary women in those terms, in my life, than I have men. Really strong, full of grace, powerful people. The thing you're most likely to get from men is, "Nothing turned out like I thought it would!" That whining. If you think women whine too much, there's so much more from men! It's amazing. Victims of the economy or their parents or their culture, blah, blah, blah. Complete infantile paralysis, in the pure sense of the word. That's true of Clare, who assumes a greater dimension in "A Woman Lit by Fireflies" or Julip, or Dalva. For the men to do it, it's not even a question of picking up the pieces—there aren't even any pieces, there are just smears here and there.

EW: What kind of relationships can there be between men and women?

JH: I don't know. Whatever you can come up with. I think we've lost something when lovers don't even observe an ordinary etiquette. And then you lose something because you can't maintain stability without that kind of etiquette. If you have a psychodrama every day, you just burn each other out. The trouble is, everybody is talking about their ills, and the only thing that makes them unique is their cures. You get what I mean? If men and women bring the best of what they figured out to each other, rather than this perpetual keening about how life has screwed them, then you have very positive and lovely relationships.

EW: If there is a prescription for living in your books, or a way of keeping yourself going, it is a slightly surprising one in that you say much of life is not disappointing, much of life is really nothing at all, just sort of big, open spaces in one's history. And a character in *The Road Home* feels a "delicious and particular sense of nothing." What is that about?

JH: Well, you're not going to get an epiphany every day. But sometimes you never get the epiphany unless you have some open space where your mind embodies that moving rest. You ever notice very wealthy people—I observed this one time—fill up their lives with appointments—you know, everything is a meeting or an appointment or an itinerary. Some I knew were going around the world and they showed me their itinerary and there wasn't a free minute in ninety-two days. The tickets were five inches thick. You know, that kind of thing. But that's not what I mean. [Laughs.] The loveliness of nothing. Emptiness, of course, isn't empty. The loveliness of nothing—if you're walking along the shore of Lake Superior for a couple hours—that's what I mean by nothing.

EW: The epigraph to your three novellas called *Julip* is from Rilke: "When the wine is bitter, become the wine." Can you talk about that?

JH: The other translation is: "When the drinking becomes bitter, become the wine." It's the way people think they can take all the fervid psychologism that flood through American culture and the *Modern Living* pages. People are relentlessly taking this Band-Aid approach to these deep, psychic wounds they have. Rilke's meaning here is if you are ill, you have to go through the whole thing, you have to cure the whole body at once, even if it takes years. You can't continue just simply putting another patch on the tire.

EW: Is this something you've had to experience yourself?

JH: Oh, yes! [Laughs.] I've had some tough times mentally. Not any more than my heroes. You know, when you're a young writer and you have to read everybody's biography to see how it's panning out. If you've read Malcolm Lowry's you realize you've been lucky indeed [Laughs.] So you have these periods of mania, or prolonged depressive periods, when you can't quite function at all.

EW: How does becoming the wine get you through that?

JH: Because by force you explore the entire dimension, and when you come out, there isn't a lot of residue. You see what I mean? Can you remember—maybe you're not old enough—I had all these friends who went off to est and changed their lives in just two weekends. But this isn't how it happens.

EW: Thank god.

JH: That's very funny [Laughs.] It was okay. Doubtless it did some people good. If they hadn't spent it on that, they might have just bought another new Saab. No, a Volvo! And maybe white wine, when they should have been drinking red all along.

EW: One of the things that makes your writing so special is the distinctiveness of the voice, the persuasiveness and authenticity of the voice in each novella, whether it's Brown Dog, or a professor, or a young, attractive woman. Do you know how you get at that voice?

JH: I knew I had to quit as a novelist if all I was going to write about was nifty guys at loose ends, you know, that kind of crap. Then I started thinking about—that's even in Zen literature—to study the self is to forget the self and if you forget yourself you get to become ten thousand things. Other people became more accessible to me. While you're working you totally enter the other person. I suppose that's the oldest version of the artist—hocus pocus, mojo, whatever you want to call it—it depends on what culture. The primitive roots of artist as magician, where you might want to become a tree or a creek or an old woman. Children's stories are full of that kind of stuff— the old children's stories.

EW: You've created a striking character in Dalva, the heroine at the center of these two big novels written a decade apart. How would you describe her?

JH: Oh, I don't know if I could. You know, the last hundred pages of this novel *is* her. I don't know if I could. I think that's the entirety of the novel is to try to figure out—she's the sister I abandoned at birth in that Jungian sense. [Laughs.]

EW: What does that mean? Because you say that somewhere, that she is the twin that . . . .

JH: Well, no, Jung said that, why do men abandon—this is a fascinating idea—the culture makes you abandon your twin sister, you know? Because most cultures are not involved that consciously with a form of manliness that mostly exists because it's convenient for the economy of the culture in which we live: working hard at thrift, don't be late for work, be manly in all matters, that kind of thing. And the same way with the women, who I obviously have noted—since we went from hunting and gathering to farming and industry— the woman's society is less matriarchal. But what Dalva is, I say, I suppose is the kind of woman that takes all male prerogatives and more. She takes all prerogatives. It's unbearable to not be what she totally is.

EW: Well, she's terrific. She's beautiful and determined and sensuous and passionate, independent, financially secure, socially responsible, and an expert rider. So, is this your twin?

JH: No, I don't know, I don't know. I just brought that up. Because, like any intelligent person, I don't know if I would describe her that way, but she is a melancholiac, too. Because there's that character of longing in all our lives for something that doesn't quite get to be seizably there. You know, because of course, that's the nature of the human creature that life passes so quickly, you know. I only know one person, an interesting French count, who's a good writer, too—he says he thinks of life as really rather too long rather than too short, which is a nice point of view that we don't hear often. [Laughs.]

EW: When you talk about longing, there's a Portuguese expression that comes up several times.

JH: *Saudad.*

EW: What does that mean?

JH: Oh, I forget when I first heard it. I think I'd heard it in references years and years ago to Fado and I was in Brazil fifteen years ago for awhile on a movie project and then I heard this Cesaria Evora song, "Saudad." You know, she's a Cape Verde from Portugal. And defined the whole concept of longing for something that no longer can exist, say, a dead lover, a farm, a home.

EW: But it clearly strikes a chord in you?

JH: Oh, sure, oh, sure. Like good poetry, you know. Lorca saying, "I want to sleep to dream of apples far from the tumult of cemeteries." You know, that kind of thing. Those chords that are struck by either literature or music are why we are so intensely human, I think.

EW: At one point in your journal, "From the *Dalva* Notebooks," you worry that in creating this heroine you might be doing it because you're lonely and you want to have someone you can utterly love.

JH: Well, I don't know about that, because sometimes we tend to exhaust ourselves by questioning our motives. I once thought if the goose that lays the golden egg turned around and watched, it probably wouldn't happen any longer. No, there's that suspicion. I once said, in some little piece of journalism, that way, way back in a marsh on a hummock of hardwoods, there's an old farmhouse hidden within the trees, and in that farmhouse live all the heroines of my novels and all my beloved dead pets. And that's where I'm headed. [Laughs.] Isn't that funny? Not to males. No males. [Laughs.] Just me and all. . . .

EW: All the women characters. [Laughs.]

JH: From Sylvia on in *A Good Day to Die*. You know, step by step. It's an amusing idea, of course.

EW: Dalva is not only melancholic by nature. She has experienced a lot of loss.

JH: Oh, yeah, tremendously.

EW: Her father crashed in Korea, her lover committed suicide, her infant son was given up for adoption.

JH: Yes, truly. Yeah. So I don't care what your bank account is. We're all human by what happens. But the interesting thing is, I think, that we can concentrate on our own considerable wounds to the extent that we forget the only thing that can make us unique is our cures. Period. Not that we've been wounded. Not, as Hughes would call it, the nation of complaint. But how we resolve these kinds of things.

EW: In what ways are the cures unique?

JH: Well, the cure would be unique if you managed to through your ardor, through your day by day life, attain a specific victory over the humiliation of trauma, whether it's physical pain, murder, death, you know. I mean in my own case, my nineteen-year-old sister and my fifty-three-year-old father were killed, you know, so, that took awhile. And then I saw my brother read the Episcopalian grave service over his own thirteen-year-old daughter. That's bravery, I would think. A bravery that I wouldn't be capable of.

EW: So, your cures are through your writing?

JH: Through your art. That's the only form I have. I mean, it's quite enough, frankly, if you think about it. I mean, I said once, I can't give anybody advice except to say, "more red wine and garlic." Or, as I admitted in the *After Ikkyu* book of poems, I've now closely advised seven suicides, so I'm backing out of this. I mean it came to me to say, "What should I do?" Whatever I had to say wasn't enough, so . . .

EW: Well, that's because . . . ?

JH: The illusion of control and power and grace fly out the window. People that are good at that are people who give their entire lives to it, you know, and if I were wanting to survive, I certainly wouldn't get in touch with a writer who says "more red wine and garlic," you know. [Laughs.] Just because it worked for him.

EW: But you've seen a lot of death? There's been a lot of death around.

JH: Oh, sure. Sure. That's one thing we all have in common, isn't it? But I can't say it distresses me in the least bit. How could it be otherwise? I remember driving my dad crazy about that while we were fishing. He says, "Well we have time so everyone doesn't die at once," or something, and I'm asking him, "How come one day is longer than the other"? And he said, "What do you mean"? "Well, it just seems longer." You know, which of course, it is longer, despite clocks. Some days are enormously long and some are enormously short. All these devices we have for ordering our life sometimes just whisk themselves out the window. [Laughs.]

EW: In *The Road Home*, there are Biblical elements in Dalva's story, or maybe even a touch of Greek tragedy. She unwittingly falls in love with her half brother, and they produce a child who eventually comes back to her and finds out the truth. But you don't make much of this aspect of the story.

JH: Well, you shouldn't. Myths, as Ezra Pound said, myths are news that remain news, you know. That's the structure, the very structure of our life, you know, if you think of the fall of the House of Atreus, or the conscious Greek chorus that can sing out the history of what America did to the natives, or so on like that. It's just that the mythos of our lives follows a certain, specific structure. So many of the plays were lost, of course, I think Euripedes wrote eighty plays and Aeschlyus forty, and we only have a few left over. But the illusion that you get out of Hollywood—there are new, fresh stories, instead of there are master plots—and there's not a lot you can do about it. That's the very structure of our life.

EW: So what does it satisfy in you to tell the big stories? To tell the stories in this way?

JH: Well, I think I need to do that. I have to keep large stories to resolve my own demons, the so-called fear—whatever you call them now—in my own sense of consciousness. I have to resolve these issues. I have to resolve life herself, as I say. It's certainly not a boy, is it? [Laughs.]

EW: You also seem terrifically romantic. I mean virtually every character in *The Road Home* loves forever, even, or especially, if their beloved dies.

JH: Well, when people fall in love with somebody else, doesn't mean they stop loving the other person. That's another fiction we have in our life. How many people you know, after a couple drinks start talking about their first girlfriend. I mean it's idiotic but our hearts are such that it doesn't mean that our subconsciousness is Biblical or it obeys the rules because we even love to wallow in the memories of this. But life *is* sentimental. Why should I be cold and hard about it? That's the main content. The biggest thing in people's lives is their loves and dreams and visions, you know.

EW: Another dimension of existence that gives these novels such texture and gives your characters' lives, and evidently your own life, such texture, is the world of dreams. And you've talked about dreams as a metaphor for survival or even a path towards home. Tell me about it.

JH: Well, that's just the point, you know, it's almost an irritating point, when you talk to some people. Say if people placed immense, immense value on their dream lives for a hundred thousand years, and then ceased doing so a hundred years ago, then who is right? I'm not saying that if you dream, you should go swimming in the winter, that's not how it works. It's a very a sophisticated procedure. But the idea of ignoring your dream life is a perilous one, I think.

EW: Can you say what you've learned from yours?

JH: Oh, sure. I think I've learned more. Well, in that essay, "Dream as a Metaphor of Survival," I said you're considerably enriched as a human being if you know what your dreams are telling you. At times. If I dream that they're trying to kill me in New York City by pushing me off a waterfall— where they got the waterfall I'm not sure—but I fly away and I'm too heavy to fly and it's really hard to fly, but then I land in a tree and discover that I'm a half bear and half large bird, well, that's very consoling. That tells me, well, that's enough of New York for this year. I should be around bears and birds, where I belong.

EW: You probably didn't even need a dream to tell you that!

JH: No, but it helped. It was sort of interesting. God, he got out of that one alive, you know. I better quit this screenwriting job and go home. [Laughs.] I know how to get there. There's a road. That kind of thing.

EW: You talked about how there's a Native way of dealing with boredom, which is to do everything backwards. You say you want a lot of interesting things to occur before and it strikes you that, rather than wait around for them to occur, you're going to have to arrange most of them.

JH: My character probably said that, but I definitely agree. We all feel a bit dried up. I tell my wife that I have to take a car trip and collect new memories. I like to drive around absolutely randomly for weeks on end, around the United States and parts of Canada. Or I'll feel trapped—you know, like you do when your life is completely planned out months in advance, and you think you're not getting enough oxygen in your system. Something like that.

EW: At the same time, you say that "the hardest thing for me to accept was that my life was what it was every day."

JH: That's particularly Zennist, and that's hard for us that grew up as little, white Christians, where we have that Protestant notion—from that song "Jacob's Ladder"—every rung goes higher, higher in every way, every day, we're getting better and better. Then you realize, through study or meditation or getting older, that what you are is just what you are every day. It's a very non-romantic leap, but then it becomes quite pleasant.

EW: The notions are some way at odds. You either accept that this is what your life is, or if you want interesting things to happen you have to go after them.

JH: I think they go together very well, because once you accept the reality of your condition, you can better figure out what it is you need to do to change it. Even if it's taking the train over to Montreal and eating too much. I'm not thinking about vast, wonderful, global things all the time. Sometimes it's just an extension of your ordinary appetite.

EW: You've written a lot about your various demons and about your sources of strength. Do you feel that you've found some sort of balance in life? Or is it always a struggle?

JH: Well, I better have because I'm sixty now. But I don't know if that's true. I think balances are temporary and anytime you think you could fix yourself in one place, that's absurd. Properly, life lived properly, is a river. Or that Yeatsian concept that life is best viewed as a dance. You know, an interminable dance. So, if I thought I had reached some point, I would hit myself over the head because the path is the way. You have to keep reaching the point on the continuum, you know. It never stops, even for a moment. I would say there is a bit more consolation now, because what I had thought as a young writer was that I would never whine if my books stayed in print and so they have. So that's the only thing you have to hope for.

EW: Do you think that earlier instability served you as a writer?

JH: Oh, of course, of course, because it gives you range. Instability would really be euphemism. [Laughs.]

EW: Various tough times. Depressions. I mean, things you've given your characters, too.

JH: Yeah, true. Well, I haven't had an actual depression now for almost fifteen years. So that's quite nice, you know. I mean, there's all this whining about the poor artist, but I mean, really, what a grace note, you know, to have found a form that you can express yourself totally in, so we should think of ourselves as inordinately lucky that this happened.

EW: I'm really glad to have the chance to meet you. Thank you very much.

JH: Thank you.

Creating Habitat for the Soul: An Interview with Jim Harrison
Robert DeMott and Patrick Smith / 1998

Edited, streamlined version of a previously unpublished interview conducted by Robert DeMott and Patrick Smith on 30 and 31 July 1998, at Harrison's home in Lake Leelanau, Michigan, with additional supporting material from an unpublished interview by DeMott and Smith at the same venue on 28 and 29 August 1997. Transcription by Robert DeMott and Patrick Smith, with assistance of Chris Walker, Rae Greiner, and Anne Langendorfer. Clarifications and refinements added from follow-up interview by DeMott on 2 September 2000. Final transcript by Robert DeMott.

We arrived at Jim Harrison's home on the Lelanau Peninsula on a blessedly cool, dry late July evening. The Harrisons' remodeled farmhouse, their main residence since 1968, has a modest, subdued, orderly air to it and sits in a grove of mature hardwoods, the walkway to its front door accented by stately white birch trees. We were well met by Jim and his wife, Linda, who were in the middle of readying a backyard barbecue, no less elegant and inviting for its informality. We joined in the bustle, helping where we could, and trying to hold up our ends of the wide-ranging conversation that commenced the moment we entered. Mostly, however, we savored our Côtes-du-Rhône, scratched dogs' ears, admired Linda's magnificent flower garden, and watched evening come down over the pond behind their house.

At sixty-one, Harrison, despite gout, still does nearly everything—including writing and cooking, eating and talking—as if his life depended on it. Although it was doubtful he had reached that transcendent level of freedom from dread, alcohol, gluttony, money problems, and so on that he wished for in his 1984 essay, "Fording and Dread" (reprinted in *Just Before Dark: Collected Nonfiction*), we felt that he had at least reached a degree of nonchalance or indifference. He appeared to be unconcerned with what people thought about his opinions, his self-described "burly" physique, or his sometimes disheveled attire. "I don't have to pretend," he told us.

Harrison personalizes his experiences in ways that are both memorable and nearly untranslatable. Once you hear Harrison's voice, which seems to have been "sifted through ashes," as Anthony Brandt aptly claimed in *Men's Jour-*

nal in 1994, you know you have never heard anything quite like it. And yet it is Harrison's conversation that compels attention. Inquire about this or that issue, ask a question, mention the name of a book, or a writer, and he is off on such long and involved responses that he occasionally forgets the original query. Some answers are self-cancelling, as though talking itself is a means of thinking through an answer. Asked whether echoes of Quentin Compson's suicide exist in Dalva's preparations for her death in *The Road Home,* Harrison said, "Yeah, of course. No, I don't know." In the space of a few minutes his conversation can range from literary recollections of a visit to poet Charles Olson in Gloucester ("One of the first best readings I ever got of *Plain Song* was from Olson") or of poet Robert Duncan visiting Harrison's classroom at SUNY Stony Brook to discuss James Joyce and Modernism ("And by the time Robert's done, two walls of blackboards are filled with the structure of *Finnegan's Wake*"), to confessions about his own excessive past self-abuses, recurring depressions, and general malfeasances.

Interviewing Jim Harrison is an exuberant experience, but also a sobering exercise in keeping up. This was our second try (we conducted a preliminary and somewhat more exploratory conversation a year earlier). As with so many interviewers before us, he was almost always working the territory far ahead of us. But if Harrison is opinionated and boisterous, he is also reflective, sensitive and—once he realized we were not "the enemy" (his term for hostile or ill-prepared interviewers)—extremely generous. We knew he had better things to do with his time than be interrogated, and we wondered secretly what he really got out of it. We realized that he is one of those rare people who has the capacity to make your efforts appear better and more important than they probably really are. It's an illusion we were happy to accept, and it reminded us of John Wesley Northridge's avowal in *The Road Home:* "Bad is bad and you let it go. Good you cherish as it whizzes by."

And yet, despite Harrison's forthcomingness, we also sensed that much of him remains protected and set apart for his family and for his work: "There's nothing you can do about anything except to write the book," he claimed. On this occasion, Harrison was in good spirits. His youngest daughter, Anna, was visiting. Mail on the second day brought a copy of the French edition of *The Road Home,* with attendant pleasure. That evening Jim and Linda escorted us to the Eagle's Ridge Restaurant and the Leelanau Sands Casino in nearby Sutton's Bay. Later, he dug out a videocassette of *Tarpon,* a pioneering saltwater fly fishing documentary produced by his long-time crony, Guy de la Valdene (and featuring Richard Brautigan and Tom McGuane), and we sat up late that night over Calvados to view this rarity, while Harrison provided additional running commentary on a film he had acted in but had not viewed in many years.

He seemed pleased, too, that in the aftermath of having ended his lengthy and lucrative (and not always successful) screenwriting career in Hollywood fifteen months earlier, he had taken up some slack by becoming a contributing editor of *Men's Journal*, for which he would be writing occasional feature pieces of his own devising. He had recently completed proofreading the American galleys of *The Road Home* without mentally "delaminating" (a current favorite word); the day before we arrived he had begun proofing *The Shape of the Journey*, his 463-page collected poems, and while that task hung over our visit, it wasn't a killjoy. He had earlier provided us with copies of both bound page proofs and the typescript of a personal essay, "Why I Write, or Not," that was scheduled to appear in Will Blythe's edited collection, *Why I Write: Thoughts on the Craft of Fiction* (Boston: Little, Brown, 1998).

Though Jim Harrison was not relishing the multi-city book tour Grove/Atlantic planned for the fall, he was at a juncture in his career that seemed to promote reflection as well as anticipation: "Sometimes you write best about what's most distant from you, where you're really reaching, and you just don't even know where you are." Trying to locate that place, that habitation, became a recurring thread in this interview.

PS: Publishing *The Road Home* and *The Shape of the Journey* at the same moment is a remarkable feat. But this isn't the first time that you've brought out a novel and a collection of poems at the same time, is it?

JH: Oh, maybe it isn't. *Outlyer and Ghazals* and *Wolf* came out the same year, so did *Warlock* and *Selected and New Poems*. But this time it's the idea that it's two big books—the collected poems and a long novel—both at once. Sam Hamill at Copper Canyon Press wanted to take advantage of Grove/Atlantic's advertising budget for the novel so we could ride its coattails, so to speak.

RD: In the introduction to *The Shape of the Journey,* you say that poetry "is the portion of my life that means the most to me." Many people would consider the collected poems alone a suitable life's work, but you also have an impressive stack of prose books as well. Is your attitude toward the poems nostalgia?

JH: Well, I don't know. Nostalgia in the sense that you value the work that's closest to you. Like the "Geo-Bestiary" suite I showed you, which is a strange thing. That isn't exactly what I wanted to write. I started it the day I finished *The Road Home* last winter. I'd been thinking about this poem for five years. It didn't turn out to be the poem that I expected at all. It's like falling or something, as you get to that very strange place that penetrates to a level you don't often reach in a novel.

PS: What occasioned the change of the title from *Earth Diver* to *The Road Home*?

JH: Oh, its very simple. A writer I revere inordinately, Gerald Vizenor, had used *Earth Diver*, so I didn't want to copy it. And I thought, curiously, *The Road Home* isn't a bad title.

RD: The title resonates beautifully with *The Shape of the Journey*.

JH: Yeah, I didn't realize that. The terrifying thing in your life is when you see the repetitive nature of your obsessions. I woke up after the novel was finished and realized I'd been working for eleven years and not doing much else, and I was appalled. Part of that was caused by sheer money fear. I got to my early fifties and came to my senses and realized I had to save some money, you know, and I'm not very smart about financial matters. So I decided to do some extra screen work. But then of course all that working becomes specious, too. I worked way too hard for six or seven years to accumulate some dough for a defined benefit plan. It got to be a real crusher and I cracked up a year and a half ago and quit to write *The Road Home*. I can't say I didn't *not* write a book because of Hollywood, I was just too exhausted. I just became a human factory. One year I wrote six drafts of two screenplays and three novellas and, you know, I mean what do you have left? No time during that stretch did I have the real consciousness that I'd been overdoing it, though other people would tell me I was. It's the time disease. You have blinders on. I had a minor crack-up a year ago in May. Fifteen months ago I couldn't get close to that place until I got *The Road Home* done. For a while I didn't even think it was going to be possible, but now I see it's no big deal. But the barrier got pretty huge there for awhile because I was desperate to get my own work done. You got the point where you say, "What's money if it just makes you suffer?" But you finally crawl out of yourself and realize it is true. No person is equipped to work that hard and still be a human being, you know. It's midwestern *hubris,* that Calvinist *hubris* à la the Marines—"I can do it." But you really can't. You are always semi-enraged, or feeling self-pity or suffocating, feeling put upon. They can all destroy your work. Lawrence Sullivan, my New York mind doctor, has helped me see that you have to get to the point where you realize your primary obligation is to your art, your family, your friends.

PS: What are those repetitions in your work?

JH: Well, thickets keep appearing in my work. You know, Nelse and his lairs. It has always been an obsession with me, so much so that my oldest daughter, Jaimie, has on occasion bought a painting or a print of a thicket and sent it to me. But I'm just evidently obsessed, even in my dream life, with hiding places and thickets. Rilke said, "What is fate, but the density of childhood?" So I'm still informed by the same thickets I was looking for at age seven. [Laughs.] I hope it's not cheap psychologism, but I wrote a children's book that's coming out called *The Boy Who Ran to the Woods*. It's about being blinded at age seven, you know, when I ran to the woods for solace. And it's arguable that I never came back. [Laughs.] I'm trying to recreate the essence of the woods sanctuary in my granary studio here, or in my cabin in the UP [Michigan's Upper Peninsula], or at my *casita* in southern Arizona. And then that extrapolates from there. If you think of the Northridge farm, it's almost a maze, you know, a monster thicket, with all those lines of interlocking shelter belts back to the spring and the pond. It really becomes a mirror of the sub-basement in the Northridge house. The kind of thing when I was growing up I knew about in big lumbermen's houses in some northern towns. They always had secret rooms or hidden places to store money and stuff. In one house, this man had three of them—a whole other room and steps down. It's wonderful mythic stuff, you know.

PS: After Seymour Lawrence died, why did you switch publishers from Houghton Mifflin to Morgan Entrekin's Grove/Atlantic? You said once you could have gotten more money from other firms.

JH: Morgan Entrekin was Sam Lawrence's protegé. Grove/Atlantic and Norton are just about the only independently-owned publishers left. I didn't want to be lost in a big pond or suffer the level of self-importance you find in some of these huge literary combines. I could have gotten more from other firms, but I would rather work with somebody I like. There is nothing worse than being with the wrong publisher for years and not being able to get out of it. And now at my age I know I don't care to waste time with a publisher I don't like. If you don't have some fundamental respect for your publisher, it doesn't matter who your editor is or what your situation is. My editor has always been my eldest daughter, Jaimie, and whoever my publisher is knows that from the outset, so that is part of the deal. Like Sam Lawrence, Morgan is essentially a book person—he loves books, loves literature. He is also good at securing foreign rights. With Sam I went from two foreign publishers to twelve or fourteen in one year, and then finally, with Morgan, to I think twenty-three or so. There are aspects of the publishing business that are utterly disgusting and don't look promising, but at the same time now I see the complete rejuvenescence of academic publishing and smaller presses, such as Gray Wolf, Story Line, Copper Canyon. It changes the financial situation for any writer because small presses, even the good ones, aren't positioned to pay very much.

RD: Do you have any idea how many copies your novels sell?

JH: *Dalva* sold about eighty thousand hardback copies in France. I think *Legends of the Fall* has sold over three hundred thousand copies. I don't know about the others, but I could find out. They sell enough to keep them alive, you know, and put them into paperback—that Delta series from Dell, and now a Washington Square Press series from Pocket Books—so there's always been something. There's at least a modest continuity. The more important thing to me is that they're all in print. As far as I am concerned your only ambition should be that your work stays in print. So foreign editions mean a lot to me.

PS: You've said you are not a nationalist in terms of literature, and that there's no sense in arguing about who's best here when there are the likes of Gunter Grass and Gabriel Marquez on the landscape. Does that global perspective help put individual reputations and the vagaries of the "literary establishment" in proper perspective? You told Kay Bonetti you don't consider reputation a "horserace."

JH: Yeah. I don't think in terms of a literary establishment like some people do. If you think you only exist when the media is talking about you you're going to have a problem when they stop. I see how people get used up by over-exposing themselves. Or they get so tired by doing public appearances, so I've always tried to limit myself to two a year at most, and to strictly limit my book tours, because constant book touring or giving readings at colleges wears you and everyone else out. I have been willing to go to France because, even though I don't read French very well, I get my back patted there by a reading public and very serious literary journalists and critics, but then I can just come home and forget about it, so that distancing works well.

Anyway, in geological terms we all own the same measure of immortality. Since I'm making a living and my books are in print we'll let it go at that.

RD: You say in your essay, "Why I Write, or Not," you've left a trail of books, but you really mark the passage of time by the series of hunting dogs you've owned. Is that facetious or disingenuous?

JH: No. Sam Lawrence told me once I was the only author he had who didn't think he should be more famous than he was. But that comes from studying literary history so that you don't get lost in rages of jealousy like John O'Hara or Theodore Roethke, or starvation for reputation or fame, like James Dickey. If you look up eighty years of the Pulitzer Prize, you're going to be astounded. The arts are fabulously undemocratic. You either finally get a lot, or you don't get much at all. It's just appalling. And now, even the middle ground has been taken away. You know, like HarperCollins' canceling over a hundred contracts, so mid-market novelists can't even get published now. I know a lot of them who just can't even get a book. I remember when I was a senior in high school, learning that when Hemingway and Faulkner were publishing their first novels, the best novelists in the world were thought to be Arnold Bennett, Joseph Hergesheimer, Louis Bromfield, James Gould Cozzens, those kinds of people. The main chance is your work and your development of the work, and if you've read as much as I have about literary reputations you don't have to walk around like some novelists saying, "I don't get it, I don't get how any of this works." I do get it. I know how it works. Everything about the literary life is basically catty and trashy from the start, so my point of view, which gets better organized every year, is that you may as well ignore it all and just do your work. All of it moves too fast for any of that stuff to matter. All that reputation stuff dissipates so fast so you may as well do your own work and forget about it.

RD: I don't mean to keep pressing, but literary ambition was never something you were concerned about in your career?

JH: Only briefly. But, no, you know what I figured out a long time ago? I realized that early success can quite often be disastrous and create burn-out. I had a beautiful dream about ten years ago. I was up at my cabin in the UP and I was really affected by the evident failure of *Dalva* and then I had this weird dream where I put all my so-called literary ambition, which even at that time was a very occasional thing, into this crypt in an estuarine area and I shoved it out on the tide. When I looked out I could see a lot of other crypts floating on the water, and I said, "My God, there are a lot of people who have done that." You finally realize any literary ambition is an illusion. Tom McGuane had a brilliant little statement once in a comic interview we did in *Sumac:* "I would gladly create one thousand acts of capitulation to keep my dog in Alpo." I love that, because then you realize the deep fraudulence of it all. To write an accessible popular novel that would actually make you a living would shatter everything I believe in as an artist. Because I'm not that kind of writer. First of all, you can't get anything commensurate to your effort, so it's best if it is reduced to a decent check. Secondly, as long as you're still around, fame just seems so hopeless and haphazard. It's a club that's only organized in retrospect. I wanted to have my fiction writing totally on my own terms, and if I needed the money, then I went out to Hollywood and got a job and received what I like to think is an appropriate check for my work. A big studio head once said to me, "You're supposed to be a nice rural person but really you're a horse trader." And I said, "Well, that's part of the same thing!" [Laughs.]

RD: This takes me by surprise, because I remember the very enthusiastic reviews of *Dalva* by Jonathan Yardley and Louise Erdrich. What do you mean by the evident failure of *Dalva?*

JH: The general non-acceptance of *Dalva*. The feeling that *Dalva* was published unhappily because during that time Sam Lawrence had left Dutton and Dutton was pissed at me, and they didn't even have an ad budget because they knew I was going to go with Sam to Houghton Mifflin after *Dalva* was out, so they didn't want to have anything to do with me. So it was just a nightmare, that whole period of my life. The novel didn't do as well in sales and in reception as I'd hoped. Nobody could figure it out very much. What is this? What is this about? Most of my material's utterly alien to many reviewers, and so then whatever audience I now have, I've accreted over the years. Certain books, more accessible books, like *Legends of the Fall,* expand it, and then the following gets bigger. And the absorption and attention of some people helps too. I remember once about fifteen years ago, I got a phone call from PEN in New York. There were half a dozen French journalists that wanted to come out to Michigan to see me, and the PEN person says, "If you'll excuse me, why do they want to come out and see you?" I was in a bad mood, so I said, "Well, you'll have to ask them." That's New York as opposed to the rest of the country, you know. [Laughs.] The lesson is that we should leave off any notion of getting what we deserve because nobody can get what they think they are worth in a given time. You can only emerge in as much as your audience is ready to receive you. I always worry about people I know who have gotten enormously well-known for sociological or extra-literary reasons, because that's always a very brief portion of fame. If you're a little too easy on yourself and your books have a big sociological rage, there's nothing that wears out a writer faster. I don't care what that person writes, from now on he's not going to get a break. Action, then reaction, sets in when somebody gets caught up within sociological praise.

RD: You've produced screenplays, poetry, novels, nonfiction prose and literary journalism, and have referred to yourself as "quadra-schizoid" regarding these diverse genres. But I can't find any record that you have ever published a short story, though you told your sister-in-law, Rebecca Newth, in 1994 that you sold a collection of short stories to Houghton Mifflin.

JH: Well, I just can't write short fiction. I think I've written two stories in my entire life, both of which were unsuccessful. About fifteen or twenty years ago my wife, Linda, read one and thought it was about an indiscretion I had with an actress. So I thought, "Well that's not worth it." And I'd written an early one about a boy whose father was a county agent, you know, that kind of autobiographical thing. I tried to write short stories, but I just couldn't. It was a nightmare for years and years. In fact, I even sold a book of short stories. I sent Sam Lawrence, who was then my publisher, a list of nineteen titles. I loved the titles, but then I never got any stories out of them. One was "The Swimming Cows of South Dakota," so named from a time in a 105-degree heat wave when I saw cows in the stock ponds with just their noses sticking out. But I just never could write a short story. Part of the problem is that I don't have any good sense of beginnings, middles, and ends. And you need that if you're going to write a short story. I just don't see that kind of sharp delineation in my life or that of my friends. I've always had trouble with beginnings and middles and ends, anyway. [Laughs.] I really admire some short story writers, but I can't do it myself.

RD: Did any novellas spring from those incipient short stories? You told Ric Bohy in 1986 that you had started a short story about forgetting to go to Spain.

JH: Yeah, of course. I wanted to write this novella, which I've thought about for years, called "I Forgot to Go To Spain." All through my youth, I was obsessed with going to Spain. I'd saved up the money to go to France and Spain when I was nineteen but spent it all on an eye operation. And then when I got relatively successful I forgot to go to Spain, what with the nature of time and so-called success, you know. [Laughs.] I don't have the voice yet. I have a lot of the images in my notebooks.

PS: Do you feel the story form is too restrictive? Too limiting?

JH: Yes, because I don't get to do my divagations, my digressions, which are mostly what's interesting to me because they are the nature of reality.

PS: So you wouldn't consider yourself a plot-driven novelist?

JH: No, not at all, but occasionally it happens. The worst trouble I've gotten in, in fiction, is when I know too much where I have been. Dostoevsky said two plus two equals death, that kind of thing. The way we see isn't always plotted. I think that's what dragged us in so mightily to Cezanne's paintings—they look more like reality than reality does. [Laughs.] Even though it looks jumbled, that's just how you would see Mont Ste. Victoire when you turned that way out of the car.

RD: No one today has published more novellas than you have. It's a remarkable record. Henry James called it the "blest *nouvelle*." What's the attraction of the form to you?

JH: Well, I was so fascinated with that form. Now, quite a few people started after my first three novellas in *Legends of the Fall* came out. But the attraction was that of a mid-form, that half-way form between novel and poetry. I don't like looseness. I'd read Hugo Hofmannstahl, Isak Dinesen, and Katherine Anne Porter who were so adept at handling novellas, and I felt that some ideas just simply aren't long enough for a novel. You try to write the kind of prose that you admire and since I like density, compression, I felt attracted to the novella form.

RD: Do you just have an inspired premonition of how length, form, and structure will play out?

JH: Yeah. I know the minute I have the idea. I don't think form is an artificiality, every story has its form. I've published nine novellas, and maybe five of them could have been novels. When the first publisher saw "Legends of the Fall," I was advised to make it four hundred pages long, so that then we could have a bestseller and make a lot of money, as he said. I refused. Tristan wouldn't be Tristan if he were a babbler. *Legends* eventually paid off anyway, for other reasons. But I don't like marking time or fluff in prose, and I don't like claustraphobic or culturally encapsulated fiction. Maybe that comes from starting as a poet. I love that specific density and compression that I can get in the novella form. That's one reason why Isak Dinesen's such a powerful writer. She has that "once upon a time" sense when she starts off: "In 1857 in a small town in Denmark, Count ——— ———," like she's protecting his name, "said, 'I must go to Paris.' " And then you get immediately caught up in it. I generally prefer more of a voice novel, but once in a while, like in *Legends* obviously, I was doing what Rebecca West called "god-like omnipotence." Pretending I was the big guy just looking at these people. Which is admittedly sometimes too distant, like Knut Hamsun. Thomas Mann's earlier work when he's more personal is more interesting. But again, you can do this range of things with a novella.

RD: Then is it accurate to think of *Dalva* and *The Road Home* as each being made up of three novellas, rather than one long novel?

JH: Oddly enough I thought about that and can see your point. But I don't think so because in both works the sections are intimately cross-referential and connected to each other. In *The Road Home,* especially, the three sections are woven intimately together. So is *Dalva.* I went back and reread *Dalva* when I was writing *Road Home* so the voices, characters, actions would mesh as a totality. It was a fucking nightmare because I hate to reread my own work.

RD: You play fast and loose with traditional fictional unities and our expectations of form and technique. The two novellas devoted to Brown Dog— "Brown Dog" and "The Seven Ounce Man"—tease our sense of continuity and play with qualities of voice and point of view.

JH: Well, I like to experiment because, you know, rules are made to be broken. Those two are not strictly voice novels, because they're also within that picaresque tradition. Also, I like that Russian sense of the serial. Brown Dog will keep coming up when I need him because he is sort of an alter ego, a nonliterary Henry Miller. No numbers are attached to him. I love that kind of thing, that kind of consciousness that's quite unrelated in a basic way to the main culture. I'm planning at least one more Brown Dog novella. At the end of "The Seven-Ounce Man," Brown Dog and Lone Marten head west to get away from their problems. Brown Dog is abandoned in a gas station in Cucamonga and starts walking to Westwood where I pick him up in "Westward Ho." He's going to get his bear skin back in Hollywood.

PS: Does Brown Dog owe anything to Twain's Huck Finn?

JH: I don't know. I never thought of that. But that idea of influence, the way influence seeps in is just so indeterminant and mysterious. I like Twain, but I never thought of being influenced in that way by him. Certainly there was no conscious attempt at imitation. When I'm writing a novel I can't read fiction while I'm writing it because I am at a point where my brain is peeled, and I am utterly vulnerable, and everything can seep in. It's that mimicry that you get even when you aren't aware of it. So regarding Brown Dog the character, maybe an influence but then maybe not, because that kind of character still exists in pockets throughout the country.

PS: Do you put yourself on any kind of timetable when you're writing a novel?

JH: Not any more. I did for a long while, but now that I'm older I have to take a break between novellas or between sections of a long novel. Like after I wrote the first section of *The Road Home*. It was a nightmare for me because it's a voice novel, so the first two hundred pages are completely in the voice of the elderly John Wesley Northridge II, so I had to become seventy-one myself. Then I went broke and had to do screen work for a year and more research. The second section is narrated by Nelse, Dalva's son, and he is a good deal younger, so I had to adjust there. Then the third section is three other voices: Dalva's mother Naomi, and then Dalva's uncle, Paul, who is quite eccentric—I couldn't give him up—and then Dalva herself. It was quite a stretch. When I wrote the last two sections, they were more or less a blur. I almost don't remember how they occurred. They were written somewhat consecutively. But you become an absolute hyperthyroid geek and the only reason you finish is because you can't stop, not because you have to. Writing a long novel just about fucking kills you. You're disgusted with the process, but then you don't have any choice, I think. You've created characters of sense and there's no room for them in the world. There certainly isn't any room in this world for Dalva, none that I can think of, except home, wherever that is.

RD: Steinbeck thought about his fiction for years ahead of time. And when he wrote, he knew exactly where he wanted to go. The manuscript of *The Grapes of Wrath* shows very few deletions or corrections after one hundred days of steady writing. Is your process similar?

JH: Mine are pretty much that way too. I write my original drafts by hand—*The Road Home* was in pen on yellow, lined legal paper. Then Joyce Bahle types my manuscript and gives it to me and then I check it against the manuscript, go through it again and give it back to her. I don't revise substantively. I don't think I've ever written any fiction I haven't thought about for three or four years. I've even diagrammed some books. I cheat though by doodling around, but not with the basic story. I revise fiction much more than I used to because now with Joyce's computer I have an infinite shot at it without laborious retyping. But I know the story before I sit down. Even at that, with "Legends of the Fall" I only had to change one word, but that's the only time that ever happened.

PS: Is this a way of saying that "Legends" wrote itself?

JH: I wrote "Legends" in nine days at the Jolli Lodge, but that's the only time it ever happened like that, the only time anything like that's ever happened to me with fiction. I couldn't stop once I got started. It was truly like taking dictation. But I had been thinking about it for three years. Lawrence Durrell wrote *Mountolive* in two weeks, but the other *Alexandria Quartet* novels took him quite a long time. But that illusion of taking dictation from wherever always makes you wonder what's going on, what can this be? Part of yourself you've radically freed up. You don't quite understand just what's going on. You know, like when you get a relatively inspired passage that just writes itself. I can't account for that. Suddenly, the voice is in a perfectly energized marriage with the language and the sensibility. Like with "Geo-Bestiary" which came all at once virtually intact in that shape. Whereas with the novel those perceptions stretch themselves way out. It's more like a black hole; it sucks everything in. I don't know quite where those gifts come from. I've always felt that you shouldn't over-inquire about the goose that lays the golden egg. [Laughs.]

RD: You have a highly visual, even cinematic prose style. It's iconographic and painterly.

JH: I don't get this visual sense in my novels because I write screenplays. When I was fifteen I wanted to be a writer because Keats and Byron were writers and they got laid a lot and had a good time. And also because from the age of fifteen to eighteen I also wanted to be a painter—I admired Van Gogh, Gauguin, Modigliani—and then I majored in art history for a year, and I was just fascinated with art books. I think that's partly because I just had the one eye, so that concentrates you. So I think that's where it comes from. You know when you're a kid, you go around making squares in reality, or you use windows that way. And then you move around until you've got the scene just right. But you can't stop doing that. And since I have one eye, and it's always been sort of an aperture, I start more from my senses quite often than my mind and so I actually see what I'm going to do. For instance, my problem with the film version of "Legends" was that I'd already seen it in my mind, so there wasn't quite enough dirt and blood rubbed into it. It wasn't gritty enough. It got too pretty. Even when it's a philosophical novella like "The Beige Dolorosa," which is about having to literally reconstitute reality to survive, there is still that visual dimension that's very important to me.

RD: Is that a theme in your work, that your characters must reconstitute reality? You say in "Why I Write, Or Not" that by "creating an environment for certain of my characters I often find myself trying to create an environment for my own soul."

JH: Well of course, not only them, but me too. In order to survive, your only alternative as an artist is to create your own habitat for your soul. I figured out that my main obsession is freedom, and if I didn't have the freedom of close access to the natural world, I wasn't going to survive. I think that's basically why I feel like an alien in New York City. You have to create your own environment or you couldn't endure at all. A few years ago I wrote an essay on dislocation, "Dream as a Metaphor of Survival" for the *Psychoanalytic Review*. If you don't create your own habitat, dislocation becomes permanent. You know, let's say if you can't figure out depression in an interior sense, there are no pats on the back that will mean anything whatsoever. Like the Rilke line I used as epigraph to *Julip*, "When the wine is bitter become the wine." There's no way to get out of it by avoidance, and in Jungian terms it's really a need to regenerate your whole persona, a need to regenerate your life. It's your whole person saying "No!" Really quite debilitating, and you have to do something, though it may sometimes be very radical, or sometimes just very nominal.

PS: In old man Northridge's section in *The Road Home*, I get swept along by the accumulating account of his psychological life, his individual memories and yearning for home. How aware are you of creating that effect?

JH: Well, I did with him, and that was what was hardest, that's what took the longest, why this novel took so long for me. I knew I had to enter honestly into his individual voice and I couldn't betray it by showing off, by making it too consciously an act of literature, which would prevent being carried long. From line one, I don't want his section to be a literary act, but be more like Chekhov, who just carries you away, no matter how inane the situation might be. You're swept away by the story rather than the conscious literary aspects of the writing. Whereas, say, the first sentence of *Wolf*, which is a couple of pages long, is basically, nice but it's showing off. But since *The Road Home* is in Northridge's voice, he's not showing off so I can't show off. I have to depend, with him, on the meat and the bones and the terrible sense of longing he has about his life, and then his rapid failing, the surprise for all of us of our failing bodies. The last time he goes hunting, his dog, Tess, won't help him dispense the wounded sharp-tailed grouse, and he has to do it, he has to feel those little crinkling vertebrae himself, as he pinches them. And then of course he can't quite find the car.

PS: In that scene he seems disoriented, or as he says "unsettled."

JH: Yeah, and then seeing Smith in the potato field, at a point when Smith doesn't want to talk to him. Finally his little victory in a sense is when he starts growing again and he's seated in that old easy chair out in the pasture, sharing it with mice. Now that's as much as we get of his recovery.

RD: And that's a way of honoring the gift of that character?

JH: Yeah. I don't have the right, given that character, to show off, because who knows where he comes from in my psyche? So I don't have the right to show off. The gift of fiction is to make life live itself, just to live itself, so that's what you do. So you're not there. I don't want people to see my hand on the page. Northridge just has to give his story as directly as I am able to do it. Even down to Paul's inability as a son to accept all the facets of his father's personality. Like when the two little boys, John Wesley and Paul, are having hamburgers in the bar, and Northridge accuses that man of trespassing and blasts him in the guts and the man pukes all over the kids. That kind of thing used to be funny. It's not any more, but in a way it can be considered humorous. I'm not presenting Northridge as somebody to imitate, or as an admirable figure, but he is the kind of man who doesn't take anything from anyone. But see, that's the real world, and Paul can't quite accept that, though he's more similar in some ways than he thinks. But oddly enough, Nelse, the loner, understands that kind of situation, understands letting go into what I call "otherness," which he is already deeply involved in, even at Berkeley. In some ways Nelse is even a little bit like Tristan, if we knew what Tristan had been like when he was older. My daughter Jamie wanted me to shorten Nelse's section, but I refused. Obviously there's a lot of early me in that character too, that kind of relentless wandering, you know, logging hundreds of campsites in the U.S. Nelse is a loner and acute claustrophobe and he's addicted to the most profound of contemporary diseases, which is dislocation. He says he's read Bruce Chatwin dozens of times. Nobody belongs where they are, or nobody has the feeling of belonging where they are, so he thinks maybe he can belong everywhere. Which is a possibility. It is definitely true in a nomadic culture, as Chatwin knew, but you can't be a nomad all by yourself.

RD: So you know things about Nelse that he doesn't know. Are there things that you don't know about your characters?

JH: Oh, absolutely. I was talking once with Mike Nichols, who directed *Wolf*, about this odd thing in acting—that an actor or actress can't act smarter than they are. That's a limitation. And I don't think a writer can render a character larger than the dimensions of his head. It doesn't exist. On the other hand, I'm not all my characters. How could I be all two hundred or three hundred of them? These are people of their own. Because that sense of discovery is paramount. That's the hardest thing in reading galleys—it underscores how you have no idea how you made all that up. This outpouring is a cumulative process, and when it ends, as with *The Road Home,* and then with "Geo-Bestiary," you just don't always have any idea how it happened. You think maybe it was more like a seizure, a long seizure. A lot of the novel writing art is conscious, but it's the emergence of the characters that are sometimes like seizures, even coming out of a dream, like Dalva, which I've said many times. Because with Dalva, it didn't matter who wrote it, it was Dalva's personality that was compelling. In another sense, what keeps me writing is the mystery of human personality. You know, how did we come to be what we are? Along with the natural world, it's the great mystery that we have to deal with. Despite psychology, there's really no accounting for a great deal of it. It's like what Rupert Sheldrake calls "morphic resonance." It's not an "evolution," they just pop out here and there in different forms.

RD: You also use that phrase "mystery of personality" in your essay, "Why I Write, or Not," and I think with a similar twist in "Dream as a Metaphor of Survival." To put it another way, characters in *The Road Home* are obsessed with large categories of existence—what Melville called the "mysteries of iniquity."

JH: Sure. Why be timid about turning your head to larger issues? Naomi starts off thinking that Nelse, her grandson, might have been like Rex, that retarded student who still comes to visit her—both men are about the same age in 1986. Its all a mystery of human behavior, like when it occurs to her that every human voice on earth is different from every other human voice. All these kind of things utterly puzzle us. I think one reason why I'm an alien in New York is that certain of their concerns are too narrow for me. I'm not interested in claustrophobia or culturally encapsulated experience. I can't write a novel about somebody jacking off for two-hundred pages. I don't think that way anymore, or maybe I'm in a different phase. One of the main things you see in literature and politics, in every area of the United States, is acute xenophobia, a willing blindness to everything, which I deplore. Novels are generally notoriously stupid about history. When I started out on this road years ago, Bernard Fontana said to me, "You'd better watch out." The Indian obsession can be a kind of disease that doesn't let you alone. What really took place in this country is an extended holocaustic experience, you know?

RD: Some characters in *Dalva* and *The Road Home* keep journals. Is that part of exposing what Edward Reilly in his Twayne series book on you calls "layers" of human history and personality?

JH: Yeah, that's a literary device I like because it creates the sense of layering in fiction. It's another illusory step, to spring on the reader a journal entry. If you read a person's journal then maybe you're getting closer to the inmost leaf of the flower. Remember the Ken Burns film about the Civil War? I'd read a lot in that area before that film came out, and I knew that people in that tradition developed this epistolary style so even a relatively simple-minded person wrote beautiful stuff. And then in the case of my wife Linda's great-grandfather, Ludlow, a mining engineer, his journals were filled with beautiful writing. It's lovely to read, some of which I just extrapolated in "Legends" and in the Dalva novels. In fact, I'd eventually like to have the originals published at the University of Nebraska Press.

PS: Writing this all down is conscious, but you've also said many times that you imagine much of your novel fully before you even write it. Can you elaborate?

JH: Oh, sure. When I was a very young man, I read in Wallace Stevens's notebooks, "images collect in pools." So it's just like certain image banks or pools in our brain are filling up with these people, and frequently they're visual. They're real metaphors that you don't at first quite comprehend. Like seeing a sunset underneath a girl's bare foot in the apple tree. Nelse with a fever looking up at the stars in Nebraska, feeling the earth moving under him, that kind of thing. You know, Nordstrom dancing alone to music he got from his daughter. Or Adele in the opening section of *The Road Home* catching those little black snakes and putting them in her hair. Right at that moment you know she isn't the kind of girl that lasts. It's out of the question.

PS: Are some of these photographs above your desk part of that image pool?

JH: Sometimes a couple of images concentrate what you're thinking. I found these at the Nebraska Historical Society, which I love and have visited often. They have a huge photo collection. This one is William Jennings Bryan's daughter and her friend doing the hurdles. And you know they're really up there too, if you think about it. I found this old photograph there, years ago, of an incredibly elegant, great big man standing in front of this big house in Omaha. He has three coyotes on a leash and he's wearing a Homburg. And I thought, "Oh, that's it, that's that." [Laughs.] That's in *the Road Home* in a couple of places, but I changed it to my purposes.

PS: You told Jim Fergus in your *Paris Review* interview that you "over-prepared" *Dalva*. Do you still think you can do too much research?

JH: Well, I think the research is just obsessive behavior, and sometimes I over-prepare historically, because it's a nervous habit. But you never know where it will end up. I read for years. In *Dalva* it was a lot of work to know the nature of what really went on between the end of the Civil War and say 1890, just after the Dawes Act and up to the Wounded Knee massacre. Besides genocide, what I found was monstrous—we lost fifty million buffalo, for instance. You never saw such rapacity before or since, except for maybe in Africa. Anyway, nine years ago, the year after *Dalva* came out, I realized I hadn't used at least two-thirds of the material that I had accumulated. So I had about a thousand of those pull-tabs of written images and constructs. I resisted it a long time, then I recognized, well, I have to return to these people. Originally, Dalva was going to doom the grandfather, which didn't happen, but she just kept coming up in my mind and took over. The horrible thing, as everybody knows about being a writer, is sitting there all the time. My so-called research gives me an excuse to go do something, like months of aimless driving around to comprehend new landscapes. That's not only fun, it's tremendously oxygenizing. You keep wondering, "Where does that road go?" and you have to follow it. I had that old Subaru with cruise control, which I would set at about 30 mph, and I could, in Nebraska, steer standing up with my head out the sunroof and see the whole landscape. No one thinks that's extraordinary. They only see one car an hour anyway, and they could care less. [Laughs.] It was essential research for *Dalva*. I said once that I thought dreams emerged from the landscape and though I don't have any specific proof it seems that a landscape has its specific spirit. No matter where it is, the degree to which you get something out of an area is based on the degree of your accretion of preparation. You can't do it shopping-wise, it has to ooze into you. It's that idea that you can't get anything out of another culture unless it's already in you and you discover it for yourself. When you go into an area with somebody who knows the flora and the fauna and the geology and the Indian history of the place, having all the information and no ulterior financial motives changes infinitely the quality of the trip. The folklorists and anthropologists like Roger Welsch I know in Nebraska are extraordinary like that. So is Doug Peacock.

RD: Did you have to go back and drive around Nebraska between *Dalva* and *The Road Home?*

JH: I did a number of times. I love that landscape of the Nebraska Sandhills, the Niobrara River area, Cherry County—to me it is just utterly overwhelming. I am fascinated by that locale, right in the center of the country, because more than Oregon or Washington or California or any other place you can name, that was the scene of the last struggle of two cultures, ending in 1890 at Wounded Knee, between Native Americans and the interlopers. The other thing I valued is the freedom—that nobody knows much about Nebraska. Very few people have even the foggiest idea about its geography and history, and that's fascinating because it gives me a tremendous freedom. Like that screenplay for Harrison Ford I was involved with set in Nebraska in the late 1920s. Not a modern Western and not a cowboy version of the old West, but that area in western Nebraska that isn't really known. Not always appreciated by Nebraskans, but, you know, nobody sees themselves as a novel sees them. It's like talking to people around Oxford, Mississippi, about Faulkner, who was so alien to them.

PS: That reimmersion in the landscape is only part of the preparation, though, right? Last year you were reading in Roger Welsch's *Omaha Tribal Myths and Trickster Tales,* Pritchard's *The History of Anthropological Thought,* Geertz's *Works and Lives,* McIntosh's *The Practical Archaeologist,* Rockwell's *Giving Voice to Bear,* among others. So, when you talk about over-preparing, do you feel that you can expose too much of your intentions?

JH: No, I mean that basically, like with Nelse, I read about eighty anthropology texts. And then I got diverted, but it bore fruit in the long run because it's again the iceberg idea. You want to infer just in passing certain things about the character, and while you just itch to deliver the whole goods you really can't, because this is a novel not a tract. I mean, certain things in anthropological texts are just overwhelming, and show these amazing traceries of human behavior. But you can't be didactic about that because you know your character isn't didactic about it. The absurdity of Nelse as a young scholar thinking that he should go out and actually talk to Ponca and Pawnee Indians about coyote stories. Well, that University of Nebraska anthropology professor tells him he's not supposed to, he's supposed to use the "qualified" research at hand, you know. So what's Nelse supposed to do? He has an adoptive family and a biological one. This is again nurture versus nature. How much of which is not enough or too much? So, if you are given a hard time and you're Duane and Dalva's son, you aren't going to say, "I'm sorry, sir," you're going to tip over the desk on the cocksucker. You know, Nelse tried to be a good boy because of his adoptive father, and he has good manners in fact. And every time anything goes wrong in his life, he just says in passing, "I resist it somewhat." He's trying to put a nice light on it. But I've seen too much of my life to ignore the fact that blood is blood in some respects. Even Paul gets to the point where he wonders if his attraction to those thousands of different multicolored rocks didn't start with his father's art books. Some of the children that are most like their parents are the ones that have most thoroughly rejected them.

RD: That reminds me that Steinbeck was influenced by Tolstoy when he was writing *The Grapes of Wrath,* and said he wanted his characters to be the "over-essence of people." So he often created large impolite experiences for the Joads that risked sentimentality.

JH: Well, very good. Extraordinary. I didn't realize he'd said that, because I feel that way, I know. I was about thirteen when my dad had me read *The Grapes of Wrath.* He was an agriculture agent and something of a populist and that was one of his favorite novels. But, see, writers either err on the side of making people less than they are or more than they are. They're both errors, but I favor the latter. The content of what I call true sentimentality is everywhere in good novels. What are you supposed to do? Ignore what people do? Exclude? Dostoevsky or Tolstoy or Dickens certainly do not. Once you come down the food chain you get some pretty cold hearts. [Laughs.]

PS: It seems that many reviewers can't always see or accept the implications of your aesthetic. The most pointed critique was Peter Prescott's *Newsweek* review of *Legends of the Fall.* It makes you subject to misinterpretation.

JH: Yeah. Now even so-called literary people seem to want a mono-ethic. I got attacked more than once for bad taste earlier and I said to someone in New York that I've known seven people that have been murdered—people that I knew quite well—who were involved in the drug business. One had his arms and legs cut off to destroy the evidence, and his mother picked up on his appendix scar. And I said you're not going to know these people if you're just hitting the fucking fern bars in New York or L.A. [Laughs.] This is life. That's the reason that Charles Bukowski, a very good poet, never got his due in America, because he was always trying to rub their noses. He was a secret intellectual, but he was going to give them their full dose. Same way with Nelson Algren. Fantastic novelist. But he wouldn't cooperate. James Jones got attacked for not being more literary. He was sloppy, which was his real downfall. But he had some very, very good sections. Tremendous writer in that sense. So it's really a kind of cultural snobbism. There are monsters afoot on the earth who have to have their say. If I write a character I am accused of being sympathetic with that character just because I wrote him, and that's a very naive approach to literature. It's like Hillary Clinton saying that Julia Roberts shouldn't smoke in a movie. It's that mono-ethic. Some critics don't want any real nastiness to enter fiction. They think of it really as a polite game and that's what it usually is. It certainly isn't writing from the depths, you know. But I would rather, in Neruda's sense, have the sloppiness that can grab my gizzard than any kind of anal-compulsive fiction.

PS: Carol Bly reprinted "The Woman Lit by Fireflies" in her anthology, *Changing the Bully Who Rules the World*, which I am sure you can take as a vindication of sorts for having been accused by Prescott and others of being a "macho" writer for so long. But how difficult is it for you at this point to write women. Is it becoming any easier with *Dalva* and your experience with Clare?

JH: Well, she's a little ahead of the rest of them. [Laughs.] But then I'm not responsible for being anthologized, and I don't have anything to do with that. And no, I don't think it ever becomes easier. It's just a hell of a lot slower. I think it came from that Jungian concept that the culture has you lose the twin sister you had at birth. And then with me of course my younger sister Judith died when she was nineteen. Particularly in our culture, you're not supposed to deal with the whole spectrum of human behavior, men aren't supposed to comprehend women, but why wouldn't they be able to? In a family of strong women, I had to be able to pick up something. I got the idea for *Dalva* when my younger daughter, Anna, was having a lot of problems at fourteen. And one summer evening she just went out and sat on the picnic table and I could see her through the window, you know, looking at the setting sun. And also there's a strange Edward Hopper painting of a girl sitting on the bed looking out over the prairie out the window, you know, that kind of thing. The technique of writing in a woman's voice was treated as if it were something revolutionary, but there's a great basis for it in European literature, *Madame Bovary* and on and on and on. It lets me say things in a woman's voice I can't say myself. There's no reason we can't understand. When "The Woman Lit by Fireflies" appeared in the *New Yorker,* Joyce and I counted something like 120 favorable letters, which is an awful lot. I don't set any kind of limitations, except I don't like people trampling on another's private religion.

PS: In the *Los Angeles Times Book Review* Judith Freemen was very complimentary toward "The Woman Lit by Fireflies." And in a review of *Julip* in the *New York Times Book Review* Jonis Agee claimed that in the war of the sexes women are better able than men to negotiate the "dark waters of strife." So that's praise indeed, but do you see a certain evolution in your female characters? You have Catherine and Rosealee in *Farmer,* who seem to be opposed to each other, and then Clare who seems to be naive and sees a lot of things for the first time.

JH: Well. Clare, of course, came after Dalva. But the interesting thing about Clare is that she really did get liberated after crawling over that fence, like a conversion or a *satori,* that way that she starts seeing almost holographically. She gets such a jolt that she can see her life rather clearly. Whereas Dalva—and I think that's probably the attraction of a lot of women to Dalva—is already an inordinately strong woman, the kind you don't often see even in some women's fiction, or the novel of "nifty guys at loose ends," the contemporary white male middle-class novel. You know I don't like pushovers in fiction, so when people have asked me about Dalva's strength, I say, "Well, yes, I adored Dalva but I wouldn't want to know her particularity. I wouldn't want to be her lover." Who could deal with this kind of person? It would take all your time. [Laughs.] I think the evolution you ask about is not so much an incremental evolution as it is seeing the whole picture. Dalva, Clare, and Julip are distinctly different people but all are, I hope, fully realized in their own way.

PS: Now that you've written *The Road Home,* what is your perception of what Americans need to know? Has it changed at all since you began writing?

JH: Oh, I don't know. I don't know. It's what it is. That's why I take the whole novel to say it because I can't reduce it. *The Road Home* is as long as it is because I can't reduce it anywhere. In particular, I keep coming back to that idea of "otherness" that Paul Shepard talks about, our connection with the animals and so on like that. It represents a world that we've very largely abandoned. I'm not saying that it's a better world, but I think that novel might be better than some of my earlier work because it's not as overtly angry. It has a narrative perspective that carries the people convincingly. It gets at that character of longing for a life that would have been at peace with the landscape if we could have done things right from the start. But that isn't the way we treated Native Americans, so I like to think that *The Road Home* addresses the soul history of our country. I'm so eccentric in researching this that I thought a lot of these concerns are new to me. Then I went back and found the same thing in D. H. Lawrence's *Studies in Classic American Literature* and William Carlos Williams's *In the American Grain.* I had that perception—I used it in that essay "Poetry as Survival," too—that Michael has in *Dalva.* Once you really know the history of Native Americans, if you put a sheet over the American continent you can see all the places where the blood soaks through. And once you know that, once you start in on that, you can become buried in an instant thinking about what went on in terms of human suffering. We need to pay attention to what we have done to the land and native peoples before we strangle on our own detritus, which we of course already are doing. We've shit on our doorstep until we can't see the doorstep anymore. When I was asked in a interview about how Chief Seattle's curse haunts us, I said, "They got even with us by allowing us to invent television." Curses come in very ordinary ways. Television is their curse on us. We don't live anymore, we watch. The attention span in America now is very non-literary.

PS: The contradictory, paradoxical nature of existence is a central proposition in your fiction. You say in the Introduction to *Just Before Dark* that "negative capability" keeps "the work's heart pumping."

JH: You can limit your paradoxes by limiting your life. But the more you want to see of life, the more the contradictions are right there in front of you.

When I first read Keats, whom I loved very much even in high school, that quality was right there. The hairs on my neck rose when I read about negative capability because that's obviously what a novelist has to have more than anything else. It's still the best tool for a novel, the negative capability to just be willing to juggle ten thousand things at once and not arrive at any specious conclusion about them, I think. The best example of it is in Shakespeare and Dostoevsky. Nothing human is alien to them. There is nothing that can't be explored. And they don't ever limit themselves the way we see happening right now in some arenas.

RD: You mean in social and political arenas?

JH: It's that mono-ethic again. The danger is that America is becoming a fascist Disneyland. Whether it's animal rights people or vegans or regular vegetarians, everybody wants everybody to do the same thing. With all this diversity, they want some kind of unanimity. It's amazing. Our intoxications become proposterous. And that's sometimes short-lived. People that would only drink white-wine spritzers for years and wouldn't smoke are now drinking martinis and smoking cigars. You never know about these weird sociological pendulums. I don't know if anybody learns from anybody else, in that way—if it's even possible at all. But reading the right people can help. At nineteen I was being moralized to death and I got a hold of Rimbaud and Appolinaire and all of Henry Miller. I wanted to be James Joyce, but needed Miller for power, to keep going every day. Miller was a massive blood transfusion. If I had *Tropic of Capricorn* or *Tropic of Cancer,* then I could come out of my despondency pretty fast. There is a guy that knows what the fuck is going on, you know? Henry Miller still can have that effect on people.

RD: Well, your work can have that effect too. In *The Washington Post Book World* in 1990 Arthur Krystal said you have a narrative voice "that fairly defies the reader to ignore it." I take that to mean that you want to change the way people look at the world. Do you think it's fair to say that your essential subject is the dimensions, the shapes, of consciousness? Or maybe our individual and collective soul history?

JH: Sure, I think so. But that comes from the conscious decision that consciousness is all we've got, like Nelse says. [Laughs.] D. H. Lawrence said the only aristocracy is consciousness. So from reading so much literature, poetry, anthropology I realized that perception, consciousness, is essentially consensual. If you talk to your mother or talk to the guy at the gas station or even a colleague you quickly realize that often they see a totally different world than you do. Totally different. I don't want to get goofy on the subject, but this is verily true, so to me the nature of consciousness is just overwhelming. Gary Snyder says there's an extraordinary similarity in all our biographies, but what's different is our dreams and our visions. So what is it that informs our differences? We glance at essentially the same world every day and all that changes is our consciousness of that world. Consciousness is all we've got. And your consciousness is up to you, which is a terrifying idea, you know, if you think of Dosteovsky saying in *Notes from the Underground,* that to be too acutely conscious is to be diseased. Sometimes you wake up in the morning and your mind is whirling, but the world isn't whirling. It's the same place. Philosophically speaking, the principle I find most interesting for a novelist comes from the Zen master Dogen who said, "To study the self is to forget the self. To forget the self is to become one with ten thousand things." In other words, you do not become one with ten thousand things, but when you forget the self, ten thousand things become one with you. That's an enormous consequence, and opens you to a whole world out there, the world that's on both sides of me. It's holographic. [Laughs.] I think the novelists that interest me, like Faulkner and Marquez, are capable of entering that degree of consciousness, which is not always linear. That unbearable fragility of Caddy Compson. Faulkner was certainly an obsessive influence. I don't mean stylistically, but the way he looked at reality. I remember some newspaper hack tried attacking the way certain great novels started out, and she couldn't stand the way Faulkner started *The Sound and the Fury,* which I think is one of the three greatest opening paragraphs in American literature. Because his sense of reality is always cumulative, you know. That accretion and layering is what you hope for. When critics say you have to write realism, well, at any given moment we are all that has ever happened to us, so what are they talking about, when they say "real?"

PS: Pico Iyer, one of your most astute reviewers, has written that you are "driven by a quintessentially American openness of heart and innocence of spirit that enable you to glimpse and then to chase ideals." Do you think that's a fair assessment of your work? Do you think you've given to chase ideals in your fiction?

JH: Maybe. Yeah, a bit. I have to exhaust them for my own purposes before they go away. I don't know if it's therapeutic so much as I want to know the range of them.

RD: So you think of yourself as a philosophical novelist? You told Jim Fergus *Sundog* was a philosophical novel. Your novels are often fueled by the exploration of ideas.

JH: Maybe so. A French critic told me he considered *Sundog* a philosophical novel, and I can see what he means. I think probably basically, but I try to hide that, because ideas don't naturally attach morals to themselves very comfortably, and I like to avoid the decals and applique that some people paste over them. But ideas are there, like in "The Beige Dolorosa." What is happening in terms of a split Santayana called a religion behind a religion, which often gets to be quite totemistic. What happens to us when everything we had hoped for disappears? Philip Caulkins truly believed in his academic career. He didn't realize that you could still get railroaded as many people have. I suppose every novel has a set of concepts, but the philosophy that influenced me the most when I was in high school was Kierkegaard's *Either/Or*. I like that anecdotal range kind of philosophy. I don't like to read Wittgenstein, or Kant or anybody like that. I like someone where you see primary colors of some sort.

PS: All your fiction shows "primary colors." Do you have a favorite novel among all your works?

JH: I don't have any favorites. I don't have any feeling that way. It's really like having children. I don't have any sense that I prefer one to the other. And I don't know why. You know I'm not a very attentive reader of my own work, so once it's gone it's really gone. I should add that "The Man who Gave Up His Name" is poignant to me because of my mental condition when I wrote it. But I don't have any extensive feeling about what's good and what's bad. *Warlock* is the one novel I don't like at all. I wrote it during a crack-up and it was just a comic book to me. And over the years I have met some people who like it a lot, so there you are. I have favorites with everybody else's work, but I don't have much sense of that myself. Some novels actually have more range just because it's built into the subject matter, and so you have to expand your range in order to write the book, which creates a strong feeling of attachment, at least for a time. Like now, in "Westward Ho," Lone Martin pawns Brown Dog's bear skin. So now Brown Dog is broke, on the outskirts of L.A., and he can't go home to Michigan. On a metaphorical level, that's autobiographical—how am I going to get my nuts back from those movie people? [Laughs.]

PS: A number of years ago a critic claimed in *Great Lakes Review* that your characters are "not heroic or brave, but they are survivors." You think that's true? Are there heroic characters in your fiction?

JH: That's a tough one because I think there's such a history to that concept and the value of the word itself has disappeared. It's hard to have a true hero because I'm infected by the notion of the Shakespearean hero, and we don't have any high places you can fall from and recover. I certainly think on some minimal level that Clare would be heroic, Julip in her own way, Tristan more obviously with his passion for the ideal of taking care of his younger brother that he felt he had betrayed. In Tristan's case, you get what people call a "wild person." But I don't see him as that. It was Rilke who said there's a point at which the exposed heart can't recover. And Tristan was a classic case of that. His charge was Samuel, and protecting him didn't work. Not that anyone can protect anybody else anyway, you know? But after that, the die was cast. And I suppose certain writers who served as models for me are heroic—Henry Miller, Neruda, Loren Eiseley.

RD: Not to romanticize this, but in turn you've been "heroic" yourself to younger writers—Rick Bass comes immediately to mind—and also you've been extremely generous in touting younger writers, having supplied blurbs for many, many dust jackets and mentioned others frequently in interviews. Who are some of the writers you find compelling right now, either for personal pleasure reading or for your research?

JH: You know, I get hundreds of galleys and manuscripts a year. But unfortunately, I can't read fiction while I'm writing it. McGuane called in a fit of hysteria and told me to read an overwhelming book, *Independent People* by the Icelandic writer, Halldor Laxness. It just blows your ears off. You know, I can read some mystery, but that's about it. I can't read so-called serious fiction when I'm writing it, but mostly non-fictional stuff—natural history, biography, anthropology, history stuff. Mary Douglas, the English anthropologist who's so profound, so graceful. *Landscape and Memory* by the Englishman Simon Schama. The best book about environmentalism lately is Jack Turner's *The Abstract Wild*. He's a bear with very large brain. He does research for me. There's *The Wolves of Heaven*—a wonderful title— about the Cheyenne song ceremony by an anthropologist named Karl Schlesier. A couple of years ago I read Richard Slotkin, who is really extraordinary. And there's a historian named Richard White who's just unbelievable and gives a different view of America than Schlesinger's. Eric Torgeson at Central Michigan just came out with a really extraordinary book on Rilke, *Dear Friend,* about Rilke's early love life. Merrill Gilfallen's *Burnt House to Paw-Paw* is about a trip down in the Appalachians. Turns out his dad was a naturalist in your area down there. Remind me to give you both copies of that. He wrote a beautiful book of essays called *Magpie Rising,* and now this *Burnt House to Paw-Paw.* He writes such gorgeous prose, you know, and hardly anyone knows about it. Another instrumental book lately is Peter Nabokov's *Native American Testimony.* It's a tremendous book.

PS: You said in the "*Dalva* Notebooks" that it is easier to write a novel than survive it. When you finish a novel or a book of poems is there any sense of fulfillment at all, or is it just cathartic and you must decompress?

JH: Cathartic more than fulfillment. You're happy just to get shut of it and want to do something else. As we said this morning, that's what's difficult about proofing galleys, I mean, the copyedited galleys and the page proofs. Because by then, that's all behind you. That's the hard thing about a book tour, and interviews, too, because they take you back to where you were, not where you are now and you feel a little alien. People ask particular questions about what's in your books that never occurred to you on any conscious level. Also your explanations are curiously quite often not as interesting as somebody else's, so you feel a little alien about it, like you're already flying to a different planet. And there's always going to be misrepresentation. The whole culture is a very vulnerable, effervescent picture show, so your novel is its own gloss.

RD: On your life, you mean?
JH: On itself.
RD: Yes, I see.

Interview with Jim Harrison
Carrie Preston and Anthony Michel / 1999

From *Red Cedar Review,* 35 (Winter-Spring 2000), 24–44. Reprinted with permission of Carrie Preston and *Red Cedar Review.*

> "As a child, fresh out of the hospital
> with tape covering the left side
> of my face, I began to count birds.
> At age fifty the sum total is precise
> and astonishing, my only secret.
> Some men count women or the cars
> they've owned, their shirts—
> long sleeved and short sleeved—
> or shoes, but I have my birds. . ."
>
> from "Counting Birds" in
> *The Theory & Practice of Rivers and New Poems*

For a graduate student in American Studies just finishing his thesis and an English senior preparing to enter graduate school, traveling to Jim Harrison's home outside of Traverse City in Northern Michigan, was an unusual opportunity to go to an interesting area to speak with one of the more intriguing personalities in contemporary literature. Preparing to meet the novelist *(Sundog, Dalva),* screenwriter *(Legends of the Fall),* and poet *(Outlyer),* we were particularly intrigued by the implication in many articles that there is an ambivalent and, at times, tense relationship between Harrison and academics, journalists, or literary critics.

The day we spent with the Michigan State University graduate and recipient of last year's MSU Distinguished Alumnus Award, was starkly different from what we were led to expect by the increasing body of work devoted to explicating something like a "mythos" surrounding Jim Harrison's work and person. Meeting us at the door with a quip, "this one must be the girl," Harrison exuded a contagious sense of peace with his immediate surroundings. We found ourselves immediately drawn into conversation, and it wasn't until ten minutes after a tour of his home, when we had settled into an old granary, converted into Harrison's writing studio, that we realized the interview had already begun. With the exception of a quick changing of the tape, and an occasional formal question drawn from our seldom-used script, this interview is better characterized as a terribly interesting conversation with a man who speaks openly about writing as both a calling and the most preferable of the various types of labor he has done in his life.

The conversation that follows is permeated with a concern, found in Harrison's works, for rituals that mark the passage of time and the significant events in our lives: graduations, deaths, traveling, and returning home. The rituals appear with raw, coarse power in such acclaimed writing as Harrison's poem "Counting Birds," which uses images of nature and an Anasazi legend to represent birds as the messengers between temporal lives and transcendent spiritual existence. Asserting himself as an "outlyer," Harrison prefers the rivers and forests surrounding his secluded home to the more recognized reservoirs of culture including the academy, Hollywood, the East Coast publishing industry, and Paris. His works and life, however, belie a concern for how individuals move between the natural world and various communities. Following the day we spent with Harrison, including a tour of his farm, lunch at a local greasy spoon, and always, intriguing conversation, we understand this interview as less a commentary on Harrison's literary works than as a meditation on how each of us attempts to mediate the tensions between where we have been and where we may go.

Carrie Preston: How do you remember your experiences at Michigan State?

Jim Harrison: I had personality differences with some people. You know how you develop those with teachers (laughs). You simply don't like each other, and the people I didn't like in the English Department didn't like me either. But Herbert Weisinger[1] was in the position to facilitate things. He was the director of comparative literature. I don't even know if they have that anymore. It was very active then, and to me it was more interesting. I like to study world literature and, at the time, I was interested in French and Spanish literature. Weisinger, who died last year, was maybe the largest brain they

---

[1] Herbert Weisinger was a professor in the Department of English at Michigan State University from 1942 until 1966. In a personal remembrance written after Weisinger's death, Harrison describes the profound impact the teacher had on his life: "Herbert Weisinger was certainly the mentor of my life and for a while very early a stepfather." Harrison describes his forty-two year relationship as seminal in the development of his interest in good wine. Freud and Jung, mythology, iconography, anthropology, nature, and Mexican art.

ever had at MSU. He was at the Princeton Institute of Advanced Studies for a couple of years and the Warburg Institute in London, and he was one of these great European émigré scholars that didn't even have to read the book. He had a vast, vast library in Okemos you know, and a vast, vast wine collection. He was a different kind of teacher. As the head of the department he got to do whatever he wanted, and he got me the degree so that I could go up to Stony Brook with him. After three years of manual labor in northern Michigan, mixing mud and carrying sod in February, going to New York seemed more and more attractive.

Anthony Michel: So you went to Stony Brook to teach?

JH: Or as his assistant; I taught a course in modern poetics. I only lasted a year and a half. I sacrificed a whole truckload of student papers in a fire. So when they asked where their papers were, I said they're being kept for research. Already I was doomed, I mean, I flunked out of graduate school, and they finally facilitated my degree after I had my first book out with Norton. They never had a student that had a book out so they thought it would be nice.

AM: What would you have done if you didn't become a writer?

JH: I have never thought about it, but I can't come up with anything.

AM: Not teaching?

JH: No, the trouble with teaching, for me as a writer, is that colleges are always in the wrong place. I didn't mind teaching; I mean we're all proselytizers. For instance, I've got a children's book coming out this year called *The Boy Who Ran Through the Woods*. It's one of these recovery children's books that draws on my interest in the natural world as opposed to cities, where colleges are usually located. After I was seven years old when I lost my eye. I was more interested in rivers and forests and so on. While I like to go to Paris and New York occasionally, I can't live in a semi-urban atmosphere. Here we have one hundred and twenty acres, and I will never have to have any close neighbors. I'm claustrophobic, and when I got the MSU Distinguished Alumni Award this spring, I had to stay in a motel over in the southwest corner of the campus. Four times a day this driver would come pick me up to go do something I didn't want to do which was invariably nonsmoking (laughs). Anyway, we had to drive right past where I'd lived in married housing, thirty-five years ago. It was enough to puke a maggot. That sense of claustrophobia—I mean there's only one way to drive from married housing to Morrill Hall. After you've done it five hundred times there is an accumulation of emotions you have, which is called torpor or ennui. I have my cabin in the Upper Peninsula, and it's quite remote. And then our casita out on the border in the mountains where we don't have real neighbors for a couple of miles. Somebody said about Picasso once that he carried his environment wherever he went. As a writer, you have to create in your writing, and in where you live, your own sort of soul's habitat or else you can't function. I think the tough part for my writer friends who still teach, and the reason that I think they should get a lot more money than they do, is that they are never done.

AM: Do these friends of yours that are teachers work in universities?

JH: Yeah, but they have to be professors because the odds of making a living as a novelist are a hundred thousand to one, if that. I can't think of a more unpromising profession anyone could enter. That's what I think is sort of sad about all of the MFA programs. It's the same problem as the well-educated students in Africa. This is a bit of a jump, but it works. You have all these very educated Zambians and Nigerians and there's no place in the economy for them. There's no place in the U.S. economy where there's room for so many MFAs. It's what they call a revolution of rising expectations.

CP: Do you think higher education of that kind is worthwhile at all?

JH: No. Not for writing. I think a gorgeous model for universities is Italy in the 14th century where a scholar would take eight students and teach them everything he knew for a year. The contemporary university is a formalization of that process. You had certain teachers that you were sort of spellbound by. That's what makes it worthwhile.

CP: What do you think about literary theory? Do you think it adds anything of value to English education?

JH: Oh, sure. Oddly enough, I'm relatively intellectual for a novelist. I want to entertain all of the possibilities, and I think that the history of literature is important. I was fascinated by Northrop Frye, and Kenneth Burke, but I bypassed deconstruction because I thought it was an elaborate plot to make the instructors more important than what they were reading (laughs). But those things seem to fade. I mean they have their efflorescence for a while and then they dissipate.

AM: Do people send you their scholarly work?

JH: No, I don't cooperate in any way. But there is this guy, Bob DeMott, who is a big deal Steinbeck scholar and they're more interesting than ten thousand Eliot scholars. The big problem in America is that it is very difficult for critics to take a writer seriously who actually goes outside rather than stays inside. I tease Tom McGuane,[2] with whom I still correspond every week or two, that his problem is living in Montana. Larry McMurtry used to wear this wonderful shirt that said "minor regional novelist." It seems that every one that's not in New York City is a "regional novelist."

AM: Do you think that's changing at all?

JH: No, but I don't think it matters. One thing you learn is what to exclude in your life, and for me, a concern with that kind of thing would be something to exclude. Literary criticism is not my business or my calling. My business is to write the novels and the poetry. If you let what they say about you concern you, it could piss you off.

AM: So you exclude a concern over how you are being categorized.

JH: Oh sure. There's this Spanish critic, I forgot where I read this, but he said that I was doomed not to get certain prizes because I made fun of white men all the time (laughs). I don't know if I'm pro-feminist or not but they're on the money. The suits control the world, and in my mind that's comic.

CP: You've introduced feminism, and we found in *New York Times Magazines* where you talked about . . .

JH: Writing as a woman?

CP: Yes, using female narrators.

JH: Writers have always done that, and critics treat it like it's something new. Writers have been doing that for centuries, and Flaubert's *Madam Bovary* is just one example. If I can't write from a woman's perspective, then I'm cutting off half my world. I can't say whether I'm pro-feminist or anti-feminist. I let that kind of thing go by too. As with any form of politics, I can't seem to digest it all. I was an old laborite, and as a former member of half a dozen unions, I thought that when the Equal rights Amendment first started they ought to strike for equal wages for equal work. That's the one that counts. When I went to Stony Brook with Herbert Weisinger, the first thing he did was to pay female assistant professors the same as male assistant

---

[2] Tom McGuane, a founder of *Red Cedar Review,* is author of several acclaimed books and essays including *The Sporting Club* (1968), *The Bushwacked Piano* (1971), *Nobody's Angel* (1981). *Something to be Desired (1984), and Nothing but Blue Skies* (1992).

professors. Before we got there, the women were about twenty percent lower. Anybody who has an ounce of democratic sentiment knows that's just wrong. If you don't have equal pay for equal work, you're fucked from the beginning.

AM: Did you make any kind of conscious decision to start using women's voices in your writing?

JH: No, I was just tired of what I was doing. I wanted something new. When I wrote *Sundog,* that was an interesting, different kind of man. But—I first said it in *The Paris Review* years ago—I don't want to be limited to the main subject matter of white middle class novelists in America which is "nifty guys at loose ends."

CP: How is your character in *Sundog* different from one of these guys?

JH: Because he's not the usual kind of man. This is a more interesting person than a professor on summer vacation who has an affair with his babysitter. There are all sorts of permutations of that kind of thing.

AM: It seems that in *Sundog,* there is a recovery of the invisible workers.

JH: Oh, yeah. You know, there's a fascinating thing you should read in the new *Harpers* on that. In the front, where they gather work from other places, there is part of an essay by Hayden Carruth, a very good poet, where he identifies the real working class that nobody knows exists. These people don't even own farms, and they don't really have factory jobs. They sort of mill around and do odd jobs. A farmer is a different thing. A farmer is a landholder. On the border, and here to a certain extent, if you own some land you're a Mister. Down there, you're El Don. But I like the way Hayden Carruth identifies this whole class of people. I was one of them until I was forty. I could even finish roughing houses or big footings. You do everything just to make a living, in addition to your writing, which doesn't do it.

CP: I think that kind of work is different from what most writers engage in.

JH: Well that's true, but it's very bourgeoisie. I was reading a Dan Wakefield essay where he says that when he was in New York, his parents would visit him on a train. That was totally out of the question for somebody from my background. I moved to New York with twenty dollars, and I don't know if my parents had ever ridden a train. I think my father had been on a train. We didn't quite make middle class, well, I suppose we did when my dad was a county agent.

CP: My dad was a farmer and also a 4-H county agent. I'm curious, because our family backgrounds are somewhat similar, how your background informs your work.

JH: Well, it does because it links you to the natural world and as Nennius said, "We're a heap of all we have met." It's the foundation of how I look at the world; it's the way my brain is programmed. I know the names. Robert Graves advised poets to know the names of things. My dad could drive down the county road and name all of the weeds by the smells, all of the trees, all of the crops, natural watersheds, the way the earth is shaped. That's a different kind of knowledge. I don't mind mentioning the mind doctor I visit in New York at least once a year. He told me once, "Think of what it's like to treat people who never see the sun and the moon and the stars and the earth." You see, there's a whole set of problems there.

AM: I'm really interested in the contrast between the way you describe your orientation to the natural world and the way you describe driving through the campus area in East Lansing. Does that kind of orientation to the natural world seem more consistent with your sense of the way you're marking time?

JH: I'm sure that, just because your parents and grandparents did, you think in terms of specific seasons, and everybody is happy at the solstices and it's actually sort of primitive. It's just the way you look at the world. But even those midway points in Lansing . . . I remember a bunch of students and graduate students were growing pot in the big swamp behind Spartan Village. They were watching out, but I don't even think at that time, in the late fifties, that it was particularly against the law. It wasn't any good anyway; it was like the pot people used to get from Indiana where you'd have to smoke a cigar before you would get anything.

CP: This poem called "Counting Birds," that Anthony and I discussed for most of the drive up here, I heard you read at MSU two years ago and it really stuck with me. You use an Anasazi myth about birds, and it seems that the speaker in the poem is using the birds as a way of marking time in the way that Eliot's Prufrock marks out time with coffee spoons.

JH: Yeah, maybe so. I never thought of that connection, but that's obviously true. The Lakota and the Chippewa, had what they called winter counts. They had a cane and they'd draw little petroglyphs of the events of the winter. It's like time, a time passing, though they tend to be less swallowed by time. In other words, it's not the clock, but it's the event. I've never been good at time at all. For instance, I don't remember my career in terms of the books, but of what dog I owned at that time. That's how my mind works. I was at the Tucson airport and my watch had stopped. I was getting my boots shined and I asked five different passing Mexicans what time it was. Nobody had a watch and it was marvelous. It was the usual gringo question, and this old man told me, "What time is it? Who the fuck cares!" Sometimes they want to help you: "Uh, it's maybe noon" (laughs). That is a wonderful attitude compared to the way the White Anglo Saxon Protestant thinks about time.

CP: Do you think we have this necessity of marking time or counting time or accounting for your life in terms of something?

JH: Yeah, we all have these ways. The Romans used to mark time by how they were aging: "Oh I have a wrinkle," or something like that. What are the events in your life? How many divorces? We're always keeping track. With so many men, it's how much do I have in my 401K or my IRA. What's my salary now? What is the inflation compared to what it was, because we are always counting.

AM: Do you find yourself feeling a sense of counting time through the events of your publications?

JH: No not any more. I did for a while. Everybody in our culture teaches that if we even blink, we're going to fall behind. People aren't even taking all of their vacation time. Now they're working longer hours because there's always this fear of being outsourced. Even in our highest prosperity, people are more insecure than when they didn't have any money. I have a number of friends who are very wealthy and they seem to be more like victims than Joe Blow who spends his last five bucks down at the tavern. I was thinking of it in Biblical terms. When you're reading the Bible, which I did a lot as a young man, so and so rich man had nine cows and three horses and a granary full of wheat. That was a rich man then. Now what is it? I had three Land Cruisers in a row, because I'm out in the boonies. When I went to get another one, suddenly they're fifty eight thousand dollars. I got in it and I said that the inside of this car looks like Liberace's toilet (laughs). It's no longer a functional vehicle; it's being built now for soccer moms. It's amazing. You can get the one I want, but you can only get it in Africa. They're about thirty grand there and they're functional, but they don't have our emission standards. I looked at a farm, I certainly don't need another farm, but I was looking at a farm and this is what drove me crazy—in the UP there's eighty acres and this house for fifty eight thousand. That's why it squared with me.

So you could buy a whole fucking farm for the same price as you can buy a car, you know. Why would anyone do that? But that's just an older man reflecting on how things have changed.

CP: This is interesting. In one of the poems I was reading, "Drinking Songs" from *Outlyer,* you wrote, "I want to die in the saddle / an enemy of civilization / while I walk around in the woods and fish and drink." Do you think that the Jim Harrison of today differs from this portrayal?

JH: Not greatly. I did that this summer, although now I've pretty much given up hard liquor in favor of wine. I like really good wine. It's a little expensive compared to just a shot and a beer, but it's basically the same thing. I feel most at home at this one place up in the UP that's fifteen miles from everything. But I also like certain cafes and bistros in Paris very much, and I feel at home there. I feel much more at home in Paris than I do in New York City. I think they're more receptive. You know, my last book got up to number three in France.

CP: Why do you think the French are more receptive?

JH: Just because they're tired of only Parisian literature which is more like New York literature. The French are more fundamentally rural than we are. If they live in any of the big cities, they're always trying to get out. Except the upper class, of course, but they already have an estate.

AM: One of your interviews suggests that the mainstream is shaped by New York, and having grown up in Iowa, I found that everybody's sort of aspiring to that conception of cosmopolitan life.

JH: McGuane and I used to always try to get each other to say things that needed to be said so that we could blame it on the other person. But McGuane said, "Why don't you say that southern writers have always had their crotchless panties aimed at New York" (laughs). That's a real McGuane witticism. He did an interview once with a gay magazine, and everybody has a lot of friends that are gay. I told him to say that you can't make a philosophical system out of your weenie. So, he said that and he got viciously attacked for years on that comment (laughs). I thought that was funny. But I feel uncomfortable because the University Press of Mississippi, you know Old Miss? They are considering a collection of my interviews next year with DeMott, the Steinbeck scholar, and Patrick Smith as the editors. I'm doing a lot of French interviews too, and I have no monetary interest in this. I'm just wondering what they're going to come up with. The French are odd because there are about eighty newspapers in France that have full time literary critics, and here we only have one in Washington, one in Los Angeles, and some in New York. This old man said to me once, "How much has your poetry been affected by the early poetry of Robinson Jeffers?" I've never been asked that question in America. It is strange how much they have studied American literature.

CP: When I first started talking about wanting to interview you, I was told there was no way possible that I could get you to do an interview. Why did you agree to talk with us?

JH: I don't have any idea (laughs), because I turn most of them down. I think it was an odd image to me that you should publish this. When they started *Red Cedar Review,* with McGuane and Walter Lockwood and those guys, I was an aesthete then. I wouldn't have anything to do with something so tawdry (laughs). I remember going into this office in a corner room of Morrill Hall. I said once, "Where's Tom?" We didn't know each other that well, but we would stop and talk about literature, because we both wanted to be writers. It was either Walter Lockwood or somebody else that said, "He's in the closet with a bottle of whiskey and a secretary from Lansing." I admired Tom because he was so good looking. He was worldly and rather than putting up with coeds, he and a couple of his friends would go down to Lansing to these dances. They were secretaries' dances and they would just clean up. He had all these girls with beehive hairdos driving around with him. Just normal girls, not some difficult, neurotic student, but a living breathing girlfriend from Laingsburgh . . . Where did you grow up in Iowa, Tony?

AM: Ames.

JH: Oh yeah, that's a fascinating place. I finished a new novella a couple of months ago with an odd title: *The Beast God Forgot to Invent.* It is about a guy, a young man. The narrator's an old creep, but it's about a guy who has a head injury from running his motorcycle into a beech tree. I got hundreds and hundreds of books on the brain under the hubris that after a couple of months of reading I could understand the human brain. Well, forget it. Anyway, here's one of the great ones, one of the most difficult ones that I've almost made it through. I love this title: *Neural Darwinism.* Wow. Anyway, one of the great brain centers in the world is in Ames, Iowa.

AM: Did you spend a lot of time driving around the Midwest?

JH: Yeah, because that used to be one of my so-called therapies. The other trouble with teaching is that you don't have freedom just to go. My wife's secretary always could tell when I was getting weird, when I just needed to go on one of my car trips. I remember driving 12,000 miles in a big circle, down into Mexico. I rarely ever drive on freeways. I have a compass in the car and go on the county roads.

AM: So you have a sense of being able to do that at any time?

JH: Yeah, number one it's not expensive compared to anything else.

AM: What about that looming pressure for getting the next book out?

JH: I don't think about it. I might have at one time, but the biggest liberating point was when I quit writing screenplays essentially two and a half years ago. That's why I know a lot about the money trap, which is the big trap.

AM: How would you characterize your relationship with Hollywood now?

JH: I still have some friends out there. It's one of those places where you like one out of a hundred people you meet, which is about the same as academic life. I don't find it morally or ethically any different from book publishing. I don't find Hollywood types any lower on the squeeze box of life than the book publishers. Nine of our biggest publishers are owned by the Germans. Before that it was corporate America blah, blah, blah . . .

CP: Why did you stop writing screenplays?

JH: Just fatigue. What happened was that ten years ago, I hadn't saved any money and I had to go back to work out there to make some money. Because I'm in a free economy, and I don't work for anybody.

AM: I was really interested in your comments about teaching a while back. Do you think it is possible to teach writing in college or high school classrooms?

JH: I don't know, you know, it's an odd thing. There was a teacher at Michigan State who was quite extraordinary—and then he had some problems. But he was a big shot, and after Michigan State, he went to Berkeley as a full professor. He was a brilliant man who taught the only essay writing course I ever had in my life. Every week, our assignment was to imitate a great essay writer, and I just loved doing that. I thought that this was a way you could teach writing. Philip Caputo, who's a novelist friend of mine and wrote *A Rumor of War,* went broke as a novelist and taught up in Cedar Rapids, Iowa. He was supposed to be teaching a course on the modern novel but ended up teaching six course of composition. It really pissed him off. I bet they learned something, though, because he's a tyrant.

AM: What do you remember about learning how to write?

JH: Nothing except what I remember from that essay writing class. You can only learn how to write by writing, and I started in high school. You know, writing down thoughts—your pompous thoughts (laughs). And I read a lot because, oddly enough, for an agricultural family we read quite a bit—mostly modern fiction. It was my dad who gave me Sherwood Anderson and Faulkner and things like that.

AM: So, were you pretty clear that you wanted to be a writer from the beginning?

JH: Yeah, and I didn't really know if I needed college. I quit school five or six times to go to New York or San Francisco or Detroit to write, but when that didn't work out, Johnny Wilson who was the head of scholarships would always give me my scholarship back. And then I got married rather early, and the year after I got married, I took eighty-eight credits just to get the degree. I also worked practically full time, so it's no wonder I was a Wombat.

AM: This distinction between academic knowledge and experience reminds me of one of the major threads in *Dalva*. There is an interesting comparison between two conceptions of history embodied by the characters of Michael and Dalva. Michael seems to be unfavorably cast as the Western academic in comparison to Dalva's more nativist, circular, conception of history.

JH: Yeah, although I find academic history very interesting. That's one thing about Michigan State. I never took a course from him, but I knew Russell Nye very well. And you could walk down the hall and ask any question you had in your brain about American history and he'd know about it. Then you could go down the same hall and ask Weisinger anything you wanted to know about world literature. Both of them would start dictating these monstrous answers, and that's the real value of a university. It can promote a kind of contiguity with people.

In *Dalva*, Michael presents one possible view of history. It reminds me of a new historian—I wish I could remember her name—who was at Harvard. She said that she liked *Dalva*, except for Michael. But you have to have a character like Michael who serves as the clown, just like in Shakespeare. He's the buffoon outside comment. And Michael has a lot of very valid points. But he also represents conceptions of American history that we were taught in school that leave out women, Mexicans, Indians, and immigrants. It's a vision of American history that never existed in the first place.

AM: What is interesting about that is there's a line where Dalva says something about his writing and, I can't remember exactly the line, but his writing is a bit stiff.

JH: Yeah, there's a great saying—he's got the top screwed on too tight. Of course Michael's an obsessive-compulsive manic-depressive, and I often find that these kinds of people are the ones you want to listen to. Because any conception we have of normal is always an extrapolation of someone who's bored with his life.

AM: Do you think that academics do a kind of violence to history?

JH: Well, sometimes they do. But then without them, we don't have anything. For instance, in all of this stuff about the Columbine high school shooting, nobody has mentioned Richard Slotkin's absolutely epochal study, *Regeneration Through Violence*. I was going to write Noah Adams at NPR about it, but I keep forgetting. I mean, you have a lot of dimwitted pundits blaming the television, and no one considering how such events fit into the tradition of America. When I was in high school, if you had a difference you'd walk the distance down to the grain elevator and fistfight. That's how things were done. Even the coach would have us put on sixteen ounce boxing gloves. This sort of thing happens less now. I've been going down to Montana for thirty years and it's interesting that today the cowboys are the dope smokers and they don't fight anymore (laughs). I mean it's really amazing how things, like smoking dope, have made their way down the food chain. So it's interesting that in some places like bars, there isn't as much violence as there used to be.

CP: Do you think that is unfortunate?

JH: No it's a good thing. They banned arm wrestling at Dick's tavern a couple of years ago, because it was causing fights. One guy would get pissed off after he lost.

So, to answer your question, no I don't think academics necessarily do violence to history. Sometimes they do, but then what kind of history could we have without them? I used to complain about university presses a lot, but in a totally market driven economy, you have to have venues for academics to publish important studies.

AM: A related question: How do you feel about seeing your book, *Legends of the Fall*, go through the process of being mediated through Hollywood which is increasingly being viewed as the source for historical and literary information? That's unsettling for a lot of historians.

JH: Well it should be. It's just so funny. I mean there are mines of material in anything you read from some of these University Presses. Oklahoma and the University of Nebraska Press are just fabulous in contrast to Hollywood's views of history. Fortunately, the guy who directed *Legends* is a Harvard graduate. We talked on the phone a lot and there was no way he was going to sacrifice important historical information. Unfortunately, that has been done over the years in Hollywood. The Indian nations are represented by Jeff Chandler and that kind of garbage. But, I do think they're trying to be a little more accurate as the years pass.

AM: Were you pleased with the way that film went?

JH: I'm never pleased by anything, because I saw it differently. I think the main thing that went wrong with *Legends,* which wasn't a bad movie, is what Jack Nicholson said about it: It wasn't gritty enough, whereas the book is gritty. The art director got a little out of hand, you know, and everyone looked too pretty. But they essentially told the story. I went to a couple of early versions of the screenplay, but then I gave it up. The guy that did the best work was the screenwriter who also wrote *Lonesome Dove,* Bill Wittliff. *Lonesome Dove* was the best thing on TV that dealt with the Western movie. It was really on the money. But Wittliff was a Texan with a background in that area and *Lonesome Dove* was totally accurate. So anyway, he had done the basic version of *Legends*. It is the only reason it was as acceptable as it was.

CP: What is the fascination for you with the American West?

JH: Oh, I don't even think there is one. I hitchhiked out there a lot when I was young, when I was sixteen, seventeen, eighteen to look it over. I suppose it is just the natural extension of the American East: Greed goes West. Fucks it up. Hits L.A. Then it filters back across the country drowning everything in its lint. The West is misunderstood. Demographically, the L.A. area has a much higher concentration of readers than the New York area. Isn't that amazing? But if you think of New York, people often mistake Manhattan for New York and that is only a hundred thousand people on the uppity side.

AM: Jim McClintock gave the Russell Nye lecture last year and it was about your writing and the relationship of your writing to Carl Jung and James Hillman.

JH: That Hillman thing was interesting. I don't know how directly apropos it is, but my brother is quite a book collector and, for a brief period, we owned together the collected works of Carl Jung. All twelve volumes. I really liked the pictures, you know, the pictures of a tiger eating the sun and all those primitive images. So, I read a lot of Jung and it seemed like Hillman was his best explicator. And Jungian theory isn't as dreary and sodden as Freudianism.

CP: How have you used Jung and Hillman in your writing?

JH: I've been influenced by some of their ideas, especially in regards to conceptions of masculinity and femininity. I think it was Hillman quoting Jung who asked, "What have we done with our twin sister that the culture has forced us to abandon at birth?" So many Middle Eastern poets and Spanish poets were virtually androgynous in the way that a shaman is androgynous and can move between sexes, at least philosophically. I think poets are mostly shamans without portfolios, and very bad ones at that. Failed shamans. Take Robert Graves's *White Goddess,* about Celtic folklore and the emergence of poets in ancient Ireland. Graves writes that if you wanted to be a poet, you traveled around with a woman who taught you the names of everything. The woman was thought to be more related to the moon, hence more related to poetry.

CP: What kind of spiritual orientation, if any, informs your work?

JH: I don't know if any does. I suppose I am essentially Christian because that is my mythos. I said once in my food column in *Esquire* that I found it was easier to believe in the Resurrection than the Republican Party. For me anyway, it still is. I've studied Zen for twenty-five years but that is more of an additive than an attention to detail. Most of our lives are dissipated on garbage and nonsense, and Zen philosophy keeps you attentive. There is this old Japanese guy who taught that you must concentrate yourself wholly to each day as though a fire were raging in your hair. You know, there is a high level of attention there, which is good for me because I don't have any discipline, I never did. I'm only writing because that is what my calling is.

AM: Do you have to instill any structure or sense of discipline in your practice?

JH: Not when I'm working on a novel or a novella or poetry. When I wrote screenplays, I had to tell myself, "Go do three pages and then you can go bird hunting or fishing." I had to write by quota every day.

AM: Conversely, do you have to stop yourself?

JH: Yeah, that's my main problem. When I finished *Dalva,* both my eardrums were broken and I didn't even know it. I mean, I had the flu, and it was just insane. The same thing happened when I wrote *Legends,* which I wrote in nine days. I was clearly deranged by the time I got done. It is what Walker Percy calls the *re-entry problem.* that is why writers are generally drinkers. Alcohol is a way to get back to the world from your daily voyage in your fiction. It is an interesting point of view. And some people like to stay in that world all of the time which is problematical. Even though I was gentler with myself on *The Road Home,* it still caused a lot of problems. The back and forth between these parallel universes is hard on yourself physically and mentally.

CP: I read an interesting piece in *Smart Magazine* called "Mid-range Roadkill." You tell the story of how a friend illegally shot a turkey and brought it to you. I'm wondering if cooking is another way . . .

JH: Oh, I'm sure. See, when I was ruining my brain by going to the bar directly after work roughly twenty years ago, I got more and more interested in cooking as a great way to return to earth. An illegal wild turkey is a great gift. There is nothing that tastes any better than a not totally adult wild turkey. And this guy was real coy because he said, "I hit it with my car," and there was a neat little .22 hole in it. I said, "Do you have a .22 mounted on your bumper?" If you are depressed, gifts like that change the nature of your thinking. Once when I entered in a depression, I went to Costa Rica and I was fine. That was where I met the man who gave me the idea for *Sundog.* This brings up another trap with academic life, at least for me. Just about all of the novels I wrote after *Wolf* depended on me being free and easy in my travels. I don't know if I would have gotten any of those ideas if I had been limited to the classroom. I can't think of any of the novellas that didn't depend on knowledge of the Mexican border, or Canada, or Europe, or parts of the United States. I mean academics can have quite a free schedule, but it is still a schedule.

AM: So, you met this guy in Costa Rica and then some idea started to germinate . . .

JH: Yeah, it starts to germinate. Sometimes it takes several years. Right now I'm working on a novella, a comic, in the Jacobean style. Not a farce or anything but I'm trying to write something about success and it is called, *I Forgot to Go to Spain.* Because that was true in my own life. When I was nineteen I was obsessed with Spain and Spanish poets: Lorca, Neruda, Hernandez. I just had to get to Spain. I never got around to it, and then when I made a lot of dough, I just wanted to go to Michigan's Upper Peninsula and get away from the accoutrements. So, when I was in France in May, I finally thought, "Hah, Why don't I fucking go to Spain?" I was busy in Paris, and I just thought, "Hah, I'll go to Barcelona for the night." It's only a couple of grand, you know. I'll stay in a simple hotel. This guy reserved my room and when I got in this hotel, it was just a bathroom with a balcony. This woman came in and spread a linen cloth by my bed so my feet didn't have to touch the rug. And I thought, "This is the real Spain that I thought about when I was nineteen." That kind of crap. And then it got very hot. It hadn't occurred to me that it would be hot because I like to walk, and I could only walk at night. I stayed two nights. It was sunny and this French *Vogue* magazine gave me some money, in cash, for something I had written for them. I got an air-conditioned Mercedes and a guide who spoke perfect English, an architectural graduate student or something like that. So I went to see a bunch of art work without getting out of the car. You know, it is what happens to successful people—so-called successful people. What happens is that you become utterly removed from any kind of life you value—unless you are very careful.

CP: Do you feel like you have avoided those kinds of problems in your life?

JH: Somewhat, but not totally.

AM: What about the threat of having a mystique built around you—if you lived in New York for example.

JH: I couldn't do it. It is harder for me in public in Paris than it is in New York. A lot of people recognize me in Paris. New York somewhat, but what I do is just avoid everything now. I didn't for a while. You can avoid a lot of problems associated with success with sufficient alertness. Only there are some situations where you are trapped. I did a nineteen-stop book tour last fall, and it took me three months to recover. I got over it by writing last winter. I correspond with Louise Erdrich who is a writer that I greatly value, and she was making the same complaints. She was sitting with a bunch of Bostonian ladies at a book luncheon and she told me that she had this really strong urge to say, "Wouldn't you old bitches just like to sit down and have a bunch of martinis? Wouldn't that be better?" But she also said, "Just remember back when nobody wanted you to go on a book tour." It's just something that you have to do, that I find really difficult. But, of course, it is even tougher *not* to have a successful book tour. Like when you make a stop and nobody shows up. That's something you have to keep in mind. But, if you have a situation like I did in Mississippi last year, where I signed seven hundred books in four and a half hours, you're not really very happy about it.

AM: Do you feel like you are expected to maintain a specific persona at such events?

JH: Yeah, you do a little reading and then go to dinner. But writers are never famous. I mean someone like Hemingway was, but writers are usually well enough known to get irritable but never famous. I spend a lot of time around people like Jack Nicholson, Harrison Ford, and Sean Connery and those are really the people who can't go anywhere without people being insane.

CP: Do you ever desire that kind of recognition?

JH: No, no, Christ no, nobody would in their right mind. Nicholson was a master because he always wore dark glasses. That means no eye contact, so people will feel nervous. Even being blind in one eye, like I am, it's harder for them. I can always get away with it because they don't know if I'm returning their look. So they can't say, "Hi, I'm dirt. Maybe you would like to read the manuscript of my novel."

CP: How do you think you are perceived here in Michigan?

JH: Oh, I've always gotten along OK because I started out here. I did a lot of manual labor, so I feel no resentment. Rich people who move in here don't know that if you aren't nice to the plumber, he doesn't come to your house. If I call the plumber, he's here in five minutes. If they call the plumber, he'll let them wait four or five days—which is appropriate, if you ask me.

AM: Another interesting thread that seems to be coming out of this conversation and also out of a book like *A Good Day to Die* is this notion of the outlaw. In some ways, there is a suggestion that the outlaw, or the people who define themselves as being outside of mainstream society, are the sane ones.

JH: Well, possibly, but this is odd. I remember once when we were broke and it was just before I had gotten successful with *Legends*. They called me from this university, because even then I had a small cache, three books of poems and a couple of novels out. They had a creative writing program and they offered me seventy-five or eighty thousand dollars—and this was over twenty years ago. I said, "You're kidding, that's a lot." But I said, "No," to the discouragement of my in-laws. "I can't do that," I said. Somebody's got to stay outside. That is what *Outlyer* means. I can't say that they are the sane ones because they are transparently not. But it gives you a way of looking at your own culture if you are on the outside.

AM: What would you say is the state of our culture, U.S. society, now—especially in contrast to when you wrote *A Good Day to Die*.

JH: Sometimes, the places I choose to live in don't give you as good a view of the entire culture as even television does. Living in the U.P. and on the Mexican Border where it is really remote offers a view of a different kind of sub-subculture. For example, I was asking this guy, a sort of hippy, half Mexican, and half gringo, "Why isn't there any crime around here?" And this hippy said, "I don't allow no fucking crime." This is definitely a subculture.

But I've seen over the last thirty years that we are as completely submerged and drowned in outright banality, where greed and apathy are the ultimate virtues as we were in the twenties. It's hard on university people too because they say that they and their families have bypassed that. They are really getting paid miserably compared to what they probably should be, as far as I'm concerned. I noticed that in France, the reason teachers are so respected in each community is because they are usually the highest paid people in the community, outside of the banker and the doctor. And if you don't value your teachers, the culture snubs them. By making fun of the government, Reagan did a great deal of damage to the country because to infer that the populace is collectively more intelligent than the civil service is a big mistake.

There is another myth: these small businessmen feel that if it wasn't for the constraints of government, they would be wildly successful. I ought to ask them about Bill Gates. I mean, give me a break. Obviously, even here in my so-called retirement, I would deeply enjoy a fifty percent drop in the stock market. Anything to slow down this craze.

CP: You mentioned the affect of this craze on professors and their families. Have your decisions made it easier for your family to have a different perspective on work?

JH: My youngest daughter hated college. She's too excessively attractive, which, Carrie, you probably know about. Anyway, she just likes to work in bookstores. But my older daughter graduated from a little podunk high school. Her counselor, they are usually lamos, told her to try to go to a small college but she went to U of M and graduated Summa Cum Laude. I mean, she was her high school's first National Merit Scholar, and that didn't merit a sentence in the newspaper because they've never had one before. But, I never could understand where she got her study habits. I certainly didn't have them. I started out a term and took perfect notes the first day. The second day it's tits and ass, and the third day I cut class and I'm at Mac's Bar playing pool. I mean it was just hopeless. It was a good thing that I was sort of smart because back then, they let you comp the basics. You could take the test and not take the class.

AM: How was high school?

JH: I was reading James Joyce when I was sixteen. I had a couple of good teachers, one even subscribed to the *Nation* magazine, which caused a little talk because he was a left winger. I had another high school teacher who was a POW from WWII who had been in a German prison. That kind of experience gives you a view of the world. But, I naturally liked to get out of there. I hitchhiked to New York when I was sixteen. I knew that was where I wanted to go. I wanted to be a bohemian instead of hauling corn.

AM: What did you think about the whole Bohemian movement then?

JH: Oh, it just seemed like more freedom. When you're that age, all you want is freedom. I don't even know how young people survive these days because back then we had so much less scrutiny from the world. We were people with our own culture, and now right from the cradle these kids are under such incredible scrutiny from parents, PTA, and everything. They are being told never to talk to a stranger, you know . . .

Index

Abbey, Edward, 152, 157
Algren, Nelson, 213
Altman, Robert, 21
Anderson, Sherwood, 13, 24
Appollinaire, 47, 216
Aristophanes, 178
Auden, W. H., 25, 60

Banks, Russell, *Continental Drift*, 85
Barth, John: *Giles Goat-Boy*, 22; *End of the Road*, 22
Bass, Rick, 219
Batchelor, John Calvin, 85
Baxter, Charles, 85
Bellow, Saul, 13, 14, 52, 69, 104
Berger, Thomas, 14, 171
Bergman, Ingmar, 123–4
Bergson, Henri Louis, 80
Blake, William, 180; *The Marriage of Heaven and Hell*, 58
Bukowski, Charles, 213

Campbell, Joseph, *The Hero with a Thousand Faces*, 53
Camus, Albert, 21
Caputo, Philip, *A Rumor of War*, 231
Carruth, Hayden, 226
Chandler, Raymond, 16–7, 70
Chatham, Russell, 59–60, 107
Chatwin, Bruce, *Songlines*, 138
Chekhov, Anton, 206
Cobb, Edith, *The Ecology of Imagination in Childhood*, 160
Coleridge, Samuel Taylor, 76
Crane, Hart, 119
Crumley, James, 110
Curtis, Edward, 125–6

DeMott, Bob, 225–6
Dinesen, Isak, 29, 84, 108, 202–3
Doctorow, E. L., *Ragtime*, 14
Dogen, 152, 159, 180, 217
Dorris, Michael, 107
Dos Passos, John, 13
Dostoevsky, Fyodor, 21, 47, 108, 158, 216; *Notes from Underground*, 68, 217

Douglas, Mary, 177, 219
Duncan, Robert, 42
Durrell, Lawrence: *Alexandria Quartet*, 205; *Mountolive*, 205

Eisley, Loren, 151, 219
Erdrich, Louise, 107, 237
Erikson, Erik, 161, 170

Faulkner, William, 13, 16, 21, 22, 39, 50, 53, 69, 74, 76, 84, 130, 158, 170, 217; *The Sound and the Fury*, 68
Fellini, Federico, 21, 124
Fitzgerald, F. Scott, 13, 86
Flaubert, Gustave, *Madam Bovary*, 225
Ford, John, 125

Gardner, John, 22
Gerber, Dan, 107, 121, 135
Gilfallen, Merrill: *Burnt House to Paw-Paw*, 220; *Magpie Rising*, 220
Grass, Gunter, 41, 104; *Tin Drum*, 14, 22
Graves, Robert, *White Goddess*, 235

Hadley, Drummond, 136–7
Hamsun, Knut, 29, 84, 203
Harrison, Jim: on academic writers, 71–2; advice for younger writers, 85–6; on animals in his work, 36; on audience, 51, 134; on book reviewers and critics, 10, 110; on conservation of nature, 27–8; contemporary novels and novelists, 13; on creating characters, 42, 108–9; on criticism, 39–40; on dancing, 79; early interest in writing, 11, 24, 35; on editing of his work, 60, 78–9, 103, 110; on euthanasia, 20; favorite motion pictures and directors, 20–1, 123–4; favorite writers, 107; on literacy, 25; on literary theory, 224; on lycanthropy attack, 91, 129, 135, 146–7, 181–2; M.A., on receiving, 24, 36; on memory, 65; on nature, 179; on nature writing, 151; on philosophy, 80; on poetry, 11, 24, 99, 170; on portrayal of women in his work, 26–7, 42; on psychotherapy, 159; on publicity, 55; on readers, 57; on regionalism in literature, 70; on rural background, 66–7; on sense of place, 40; on storytelling tradition, 23–4; on suicide, 73;

on teaching, 38, 47, 223; women novelists, 76; on women's liberation, 19; on writing process, 11–2, 27, 48, 60, 77–8, 170, 209; on writing screenplays, 26, 38–9, 58–9, 130, 131; on Zen, 235
—**Works:** "Beige Dolorosa, The," 161, 179–80, 206; *Boy Who Ran to the Woods, The*, 160, 223; "Brown Dog," 168; *Dalva*, 69, 76, 109, 110, 187, 203, 210, 214; "Dream as a Metaphor of Survival," 191, 206; *Farmer*, 13, 18, 20, 72, 79; "Going Places," 138; *Good Day to Die, A*, 72, 126; *Julip*, 134, 168; *Legends of the Fall*, 26, 42, 77, 80, 149, 170–1; *Letters to Yesenin*, 73, 99; *Locations*, 40; "Man Who Gave Up His Name, The," 30, 48, 77, 79, 171; *Plain Song*, 34, 53; "Revenge," 30, 77, 171; *Road Home, The*, 178, 190, 203, 204, 206–8, 215; "Sitting Around," 139; *Sundog*, 31–4, 35, 37, 48, 58, 65, 80; *Sunset Limited*, 107; *Theory and Practice of Rivers, The*, 65; *Wolf*, 17, 29, 53–4, 68, 72, 79, 124, 146–7; *Woman Lit By Fireflies*, 107, 184–5

Hemingway, Ernest, 13, 15–6, 17, 21, 22, 24, 78, 86, 170
Hemingway, Mary, 17
Hesse, Hermann, *Magister Ludi*, 11
Hillman, James, 47–8, 234–5
Hoagland, Edward, 13
Hofmannstahl, Hugo, 202
Hogan, Linda, 107
Hughes, Ted, *Crow*, 46
Hugo, Richard, 36
Huston, John, 26
Huxley, Aldous, 119

James, Henry, 24, 38
Jesus, 180
Jones, James, 84, 213
Joyce, James, 53; *Finnegans Wake*, 17, 41, 68, 84; *Portrait of the Artist as a Young Man*, 21
Jung, Karl, 235

Kafka, Franz, 22, 108
Kant, Immanuel, *Critique of Pure Reason*, 80
Keats, John, 35, 47, 84, 108, 216
Kerouac, Jack, 119
Kesey, Ken, 47
Kierkegaard, Søren, 80, 82; *Either/Or*, 218
Kubler-Ross, Elisabeth, 20
Kubrick, Stanley, 21
Kundera, Milan, 85, 104

Lawrence, D. H., 158–9, 183, 216; *Studies in Classic American Literature*, 215
Laxness, Halldor, *Independent People*, 219

Least Heat Moon, William, 52; *Blue Highways*, 51
Levertov, Denise, 29, 53, 101
Lewis, Sinclair, *Main Street*, 15
Lopez, Barry, 85
Lorca, Federico García, 20, 47, 85, 155, 162, 188
Lowell, Robert: *Imitations*, 103–4; *Life Studies*, 104
Lowry, Malcolm, 186

MacDonald, John D., 17, 70
Mailer, Norman, 14, 37, 52–3, 69, 104; "The Steps of the Pentagon," 81; *Why Are We in Vietnam?*, 81
Malamud, Bernard, 51
Mann, Thomas, 203
Márquez, Gabriel García, 30, 41, 104, 162, 217; *Chronicle of a Death Foretold*, 85; *One Hundred Years of Solitude*, 14, 66
Martin, David, *The Crying Heart Tattoo*, 85
Matthiessen, Peter, 14, 54, 88, 107, 182; *Snow Leopard*, 109
McGuane, Thomas, 13, 37, 47, 85, 104, 107, 200
Melville, Herman, 103
Miller, Henry, 16, 86, 216, 219
Mitchell, Stephen, *The Gospel According to Jesus*, 139
Moreau, Jeanne, 126

Nabokov, Peter, *Native American Testimony*, 220
Nabokov, Vladimir, 32, 104
Nelson, Richard: *Make Prayers to the Raven*, 152; *The Island Within*, 152
Neruda, Pablo, 87, 213, 219
Nichols, Mike, 129, 208
Nicholson, Jack, 75, 107, 124, 127, 148
Nietzsche, Friedrich, 80, 158
Nye, Russell, 232

O'Neill, Eugene, *The Iceman Cometh*, 26
Ortega y Gassett, José, 69

Peacock, Douglas, 107, 211
Picasso, Pablo, 224
Pollack, Sidney, 127
Porter, Katherine Anne, 108, 202
Pound, Ezra, 43, 44, 162, 190
Pynchon, Thomas: *Gravity's Rainbow*, 22; *V*, 22

Quammen, David, *The Song of the Dodo*, 153

Rabelais, François, 16
Rafelson, Bob, 127

Index

243

Rilke, Rainer Maria, 40, 65, 84, 87, 88, 89, 172, 186, 219
Rimbaud, Arthur, 47, 66, 87, 108, 119, 216; *Illuminations*, 68
Roth, Philip, 14, 51, 99

Schama, Simon, *Landscape and Memory*, 219
Schlesier, Karl, *The Wolves of Heaven*, 219
Sexton, Anne, 159
Shakespeare, William, 162, 216
Slotkin, Rick, 1, 219, 233
Snyder, Gary, 88, 217; *The Practice of the Wild*, 139
Stegner, Wallace, 47, 50
Steinbeck, John: *The Grapes of Wrath*, 84, 212; *Travels with Charley*, 168
Stevens, Wallace, 35, 38, 66, 124, 209
Stone, Robert, 47
Styron, William, 80, 130

Takahashi (Japanese poet), 51
Thompson, Hunter, *Fear and Loathing in Las Vegas*, 22
Thoreau, Henry David, 180
Torgersen, Eric, *Dear Friend*, 219
Truffaut, François, 21

Turner, Fred, *Spirit of Place*, 109
Turner, Jack, *The Abstract Wild*, 219
Twain, Mark, 203–4

Updike, John, 14, 51

Van Gogh, Vincent, 35
Vizenor, Gerald, 140
Vonnegut, Kurt, 13, 50

Wakefield, Dan, 226
Wakoski, Diane, 19
Weisinger, Herbert, 222–3, 225, 232
Welch, James, 85, 107
Welles, Orson, 26, 124, 127–8
West, Rebecca, 203
White, Richard, 219
Whitman, Walt, 60
Williams, William Carlos, 68; *In the American Grain*, 215
Witliff, Bill, *Lonesome Dove*, 234
Wolfe, Thomas, 84
Woody, Elizabeth, 140

Yeats, W. B., 85, 108

Zwinger, Ann, 151